This book belongs to

....

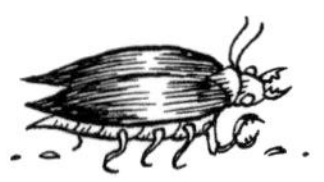

GUILLAUME BIANCO

BILLY FOG ™

AND THE GIFT OF TROUBLE SIGHT

ARCHAIA ENTERTAINMENT LLC
WWW.ARCHAIA.COM

"This book is dedicated to my little sister Anne."

BILLY FOG

~ and ~

THE GIFT OF TROUBLE SIGHT

original story, poems, and anarchic bestiaries

by

GUILLAUME BIANCO

Pages Laid Out and Subtly Arranged by Monsieur J.L. Deglin

Translated by Edward Gauvin

English lettering by Deron Bennett

CONTENTS

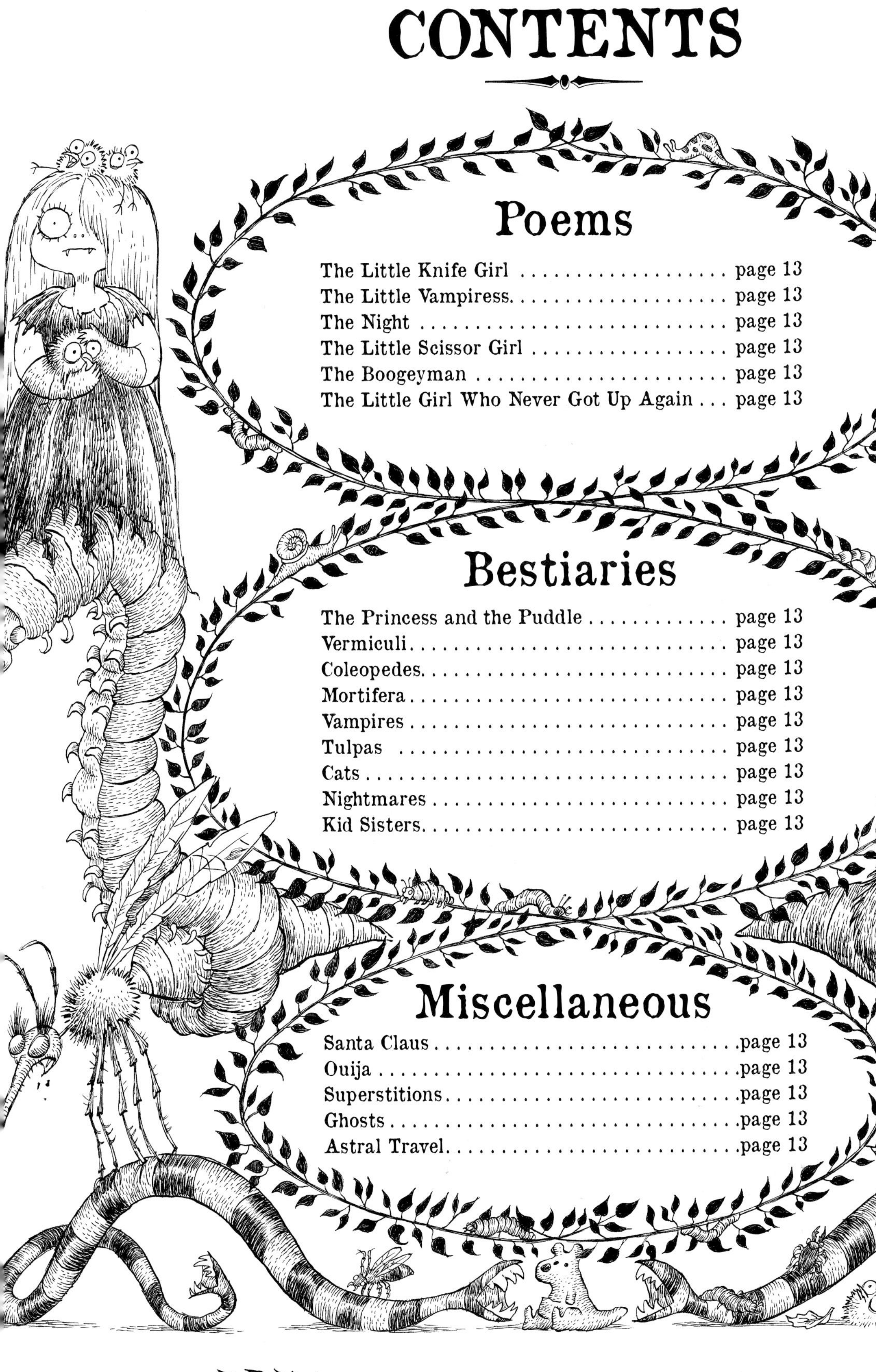

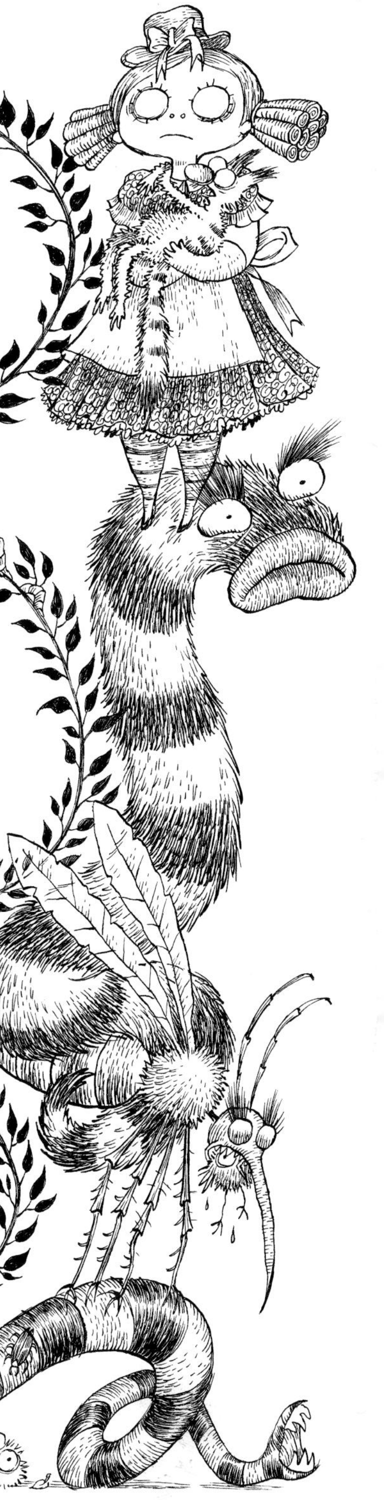

Poems

Bestiaries

Miscellaneous

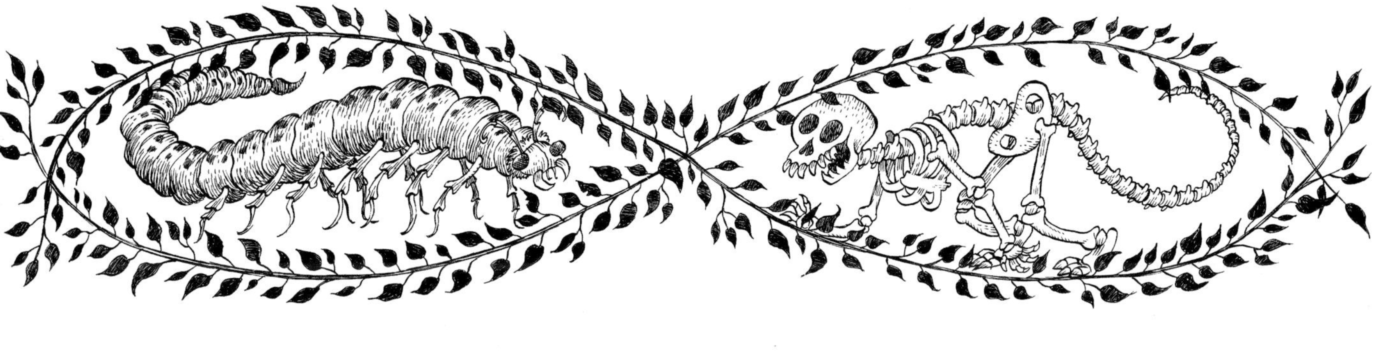

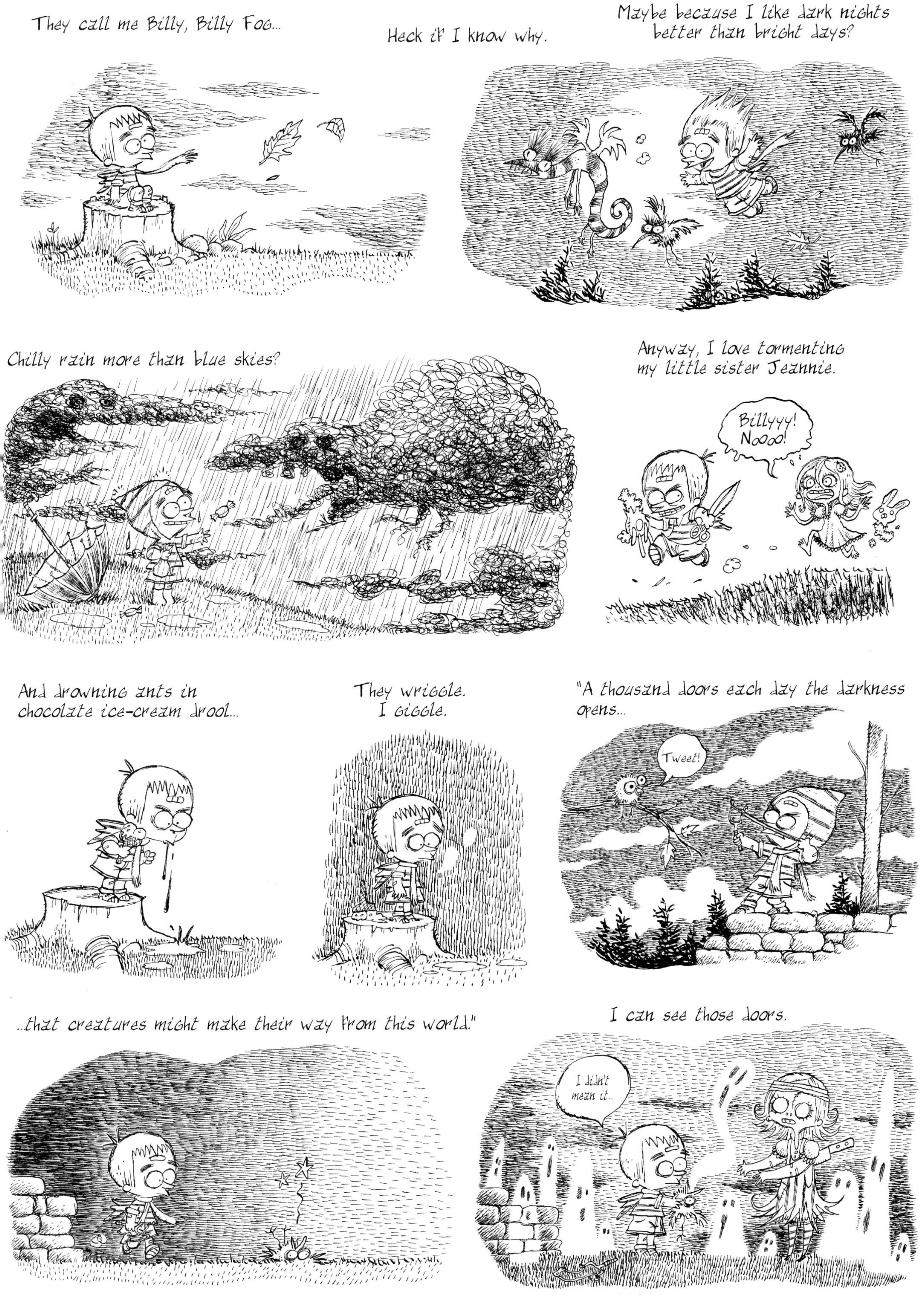
They call me Billy, Billy Fog...
Heck if I know why.
Maybe because I like dark nights better than bright days?
Chilly rain more than blue skies?
Anyway, I love tormenting my little sister Jeannie.
Billyyy! Noooo!
And drowning ants in chocolate ice-cream drool...
They wriggle. I giggle.
"A thousand doors each day the darkness opens...
Tweet!
...that creatures might make their way from this world."
I can see those doors.
I didn't mean it...

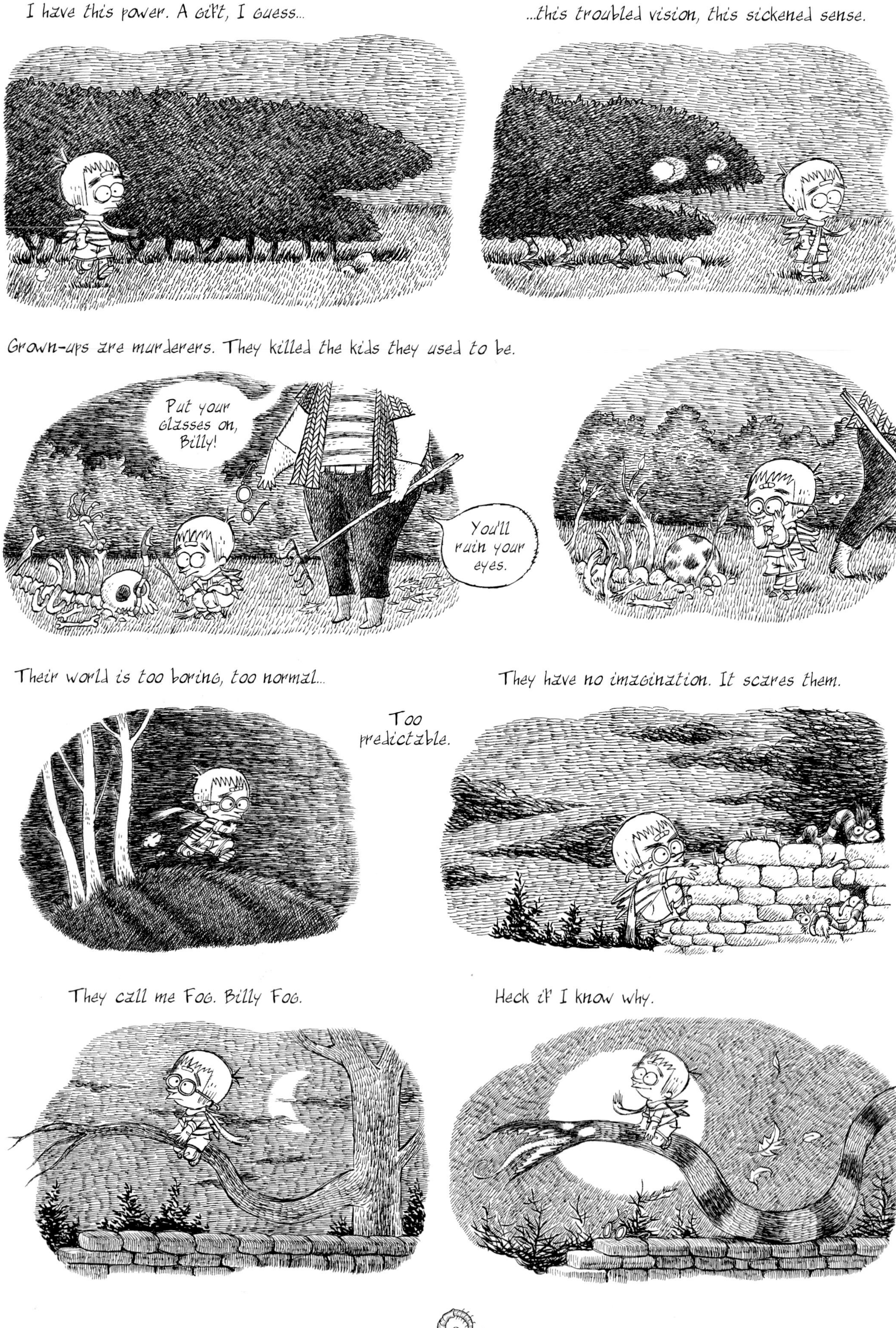
I have this power. A gift, I guess...
...this troubled vision, this sickened sense.
Grown-ups are murderers. They killed the kids they used to be.
Put your glasses on, Billy!
You'll ruin your eyes.
Their world is too boring, too normal...
Too predictable.
They have no imagination. It scares them.
They call me Fog. Billy Fog.
Heck if I know why.

Tarzan's dead.

It happened last Fall.

A Wednesday, I think.

At first, I thought he was pretending.

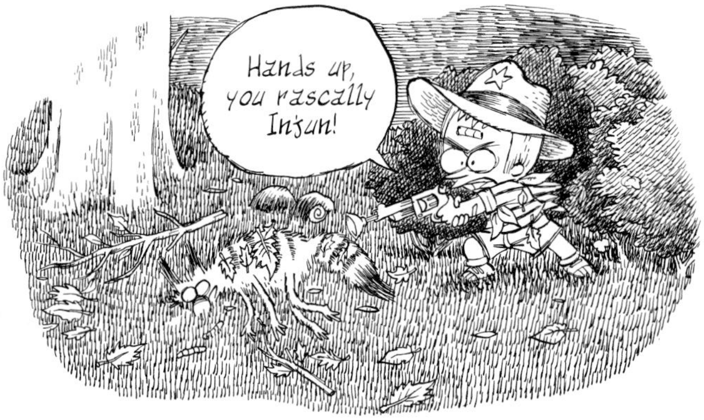
Hands up, you rascally Injun!

That it was some Comanche ruse. An old Apache trick.

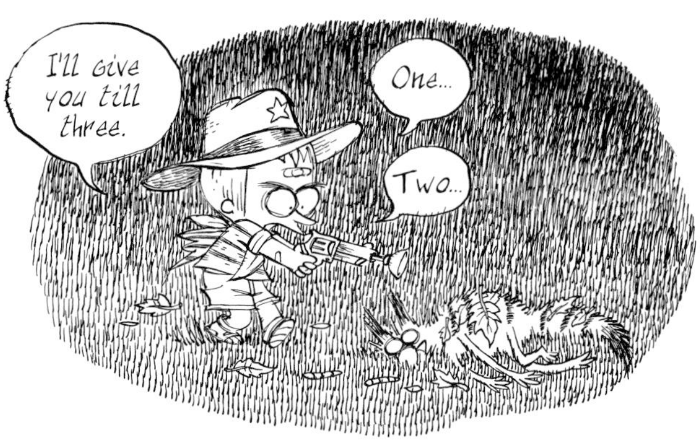
I'll give you till three.
One...
Two...

I wanted him to get up.

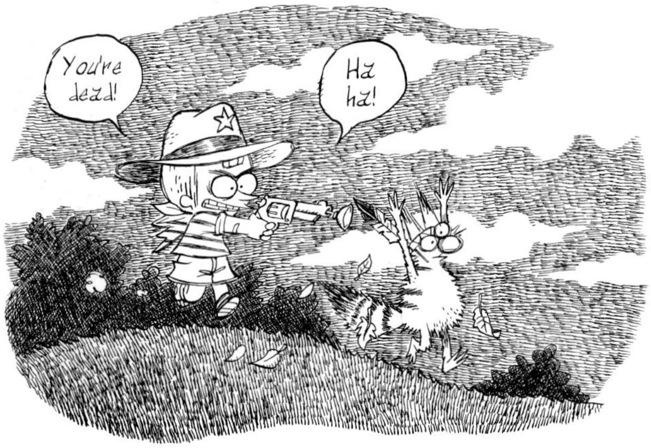
You're dead!
Ha ha!

So we could bury the hatchet.

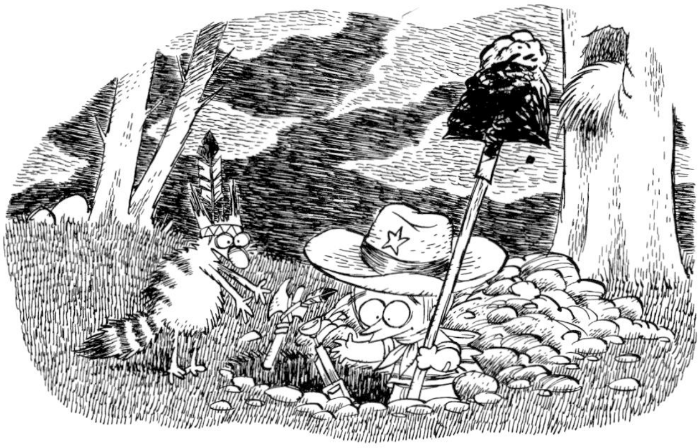

And then race back home.

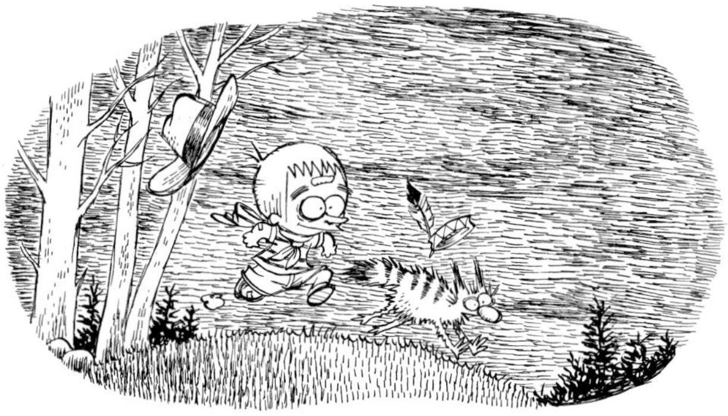

Mom would make us a snack on the old stone wall.

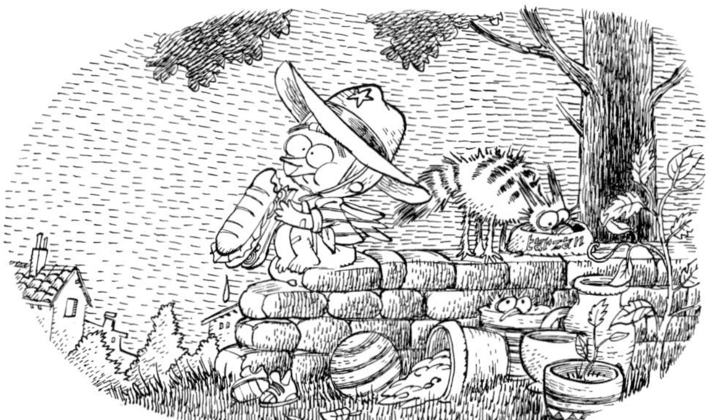

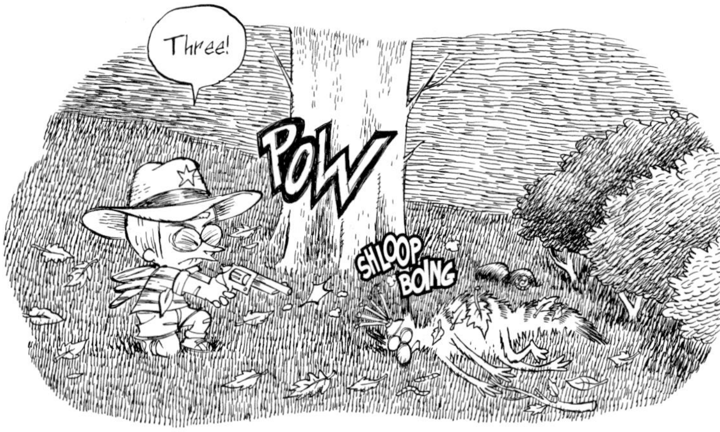
Three!
POW
SHLOOP
BOING

But Tarzan didn't get up.

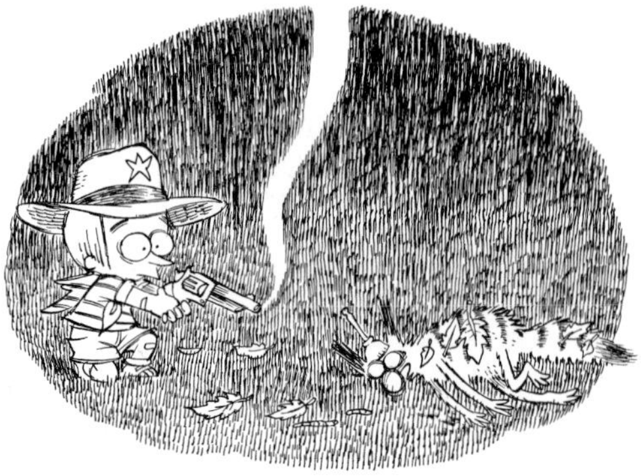

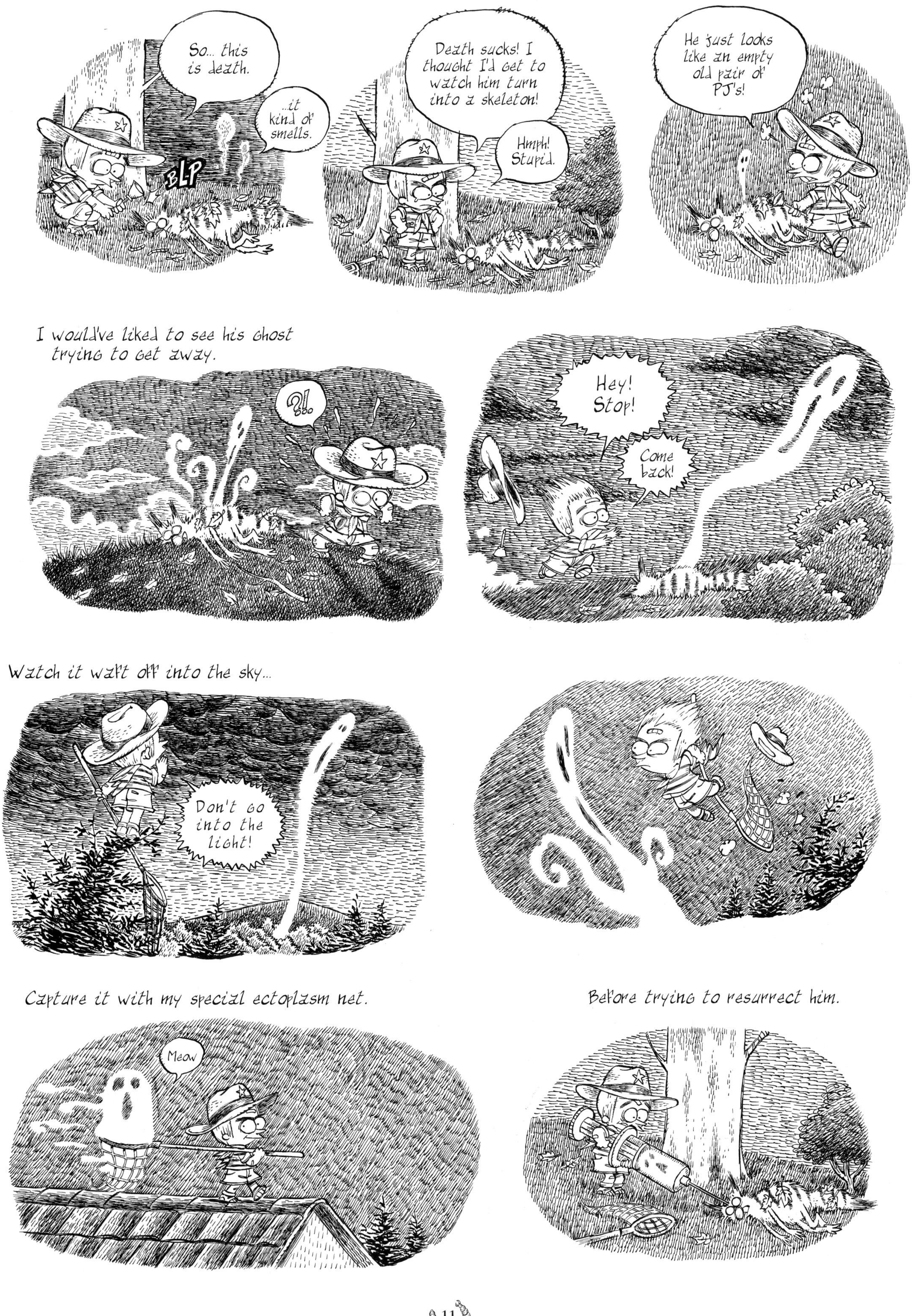
So... this is death.
BLP
...it kind of smells.
Death sucks! I thought I'd get to watch him turn into a skeleton!
Hmph! Stupid.
He just looks like an empty old pair of PJ's!
I would've liked to see his ghost trying to get away.
?!
Hey! Stop!
Come back!
Watch it waft off into the sky...
Don't go into the light!
Capture it with my special ectoplasm net.
Meow
Before trying to resurrect him.

But God works in mysterious ways.

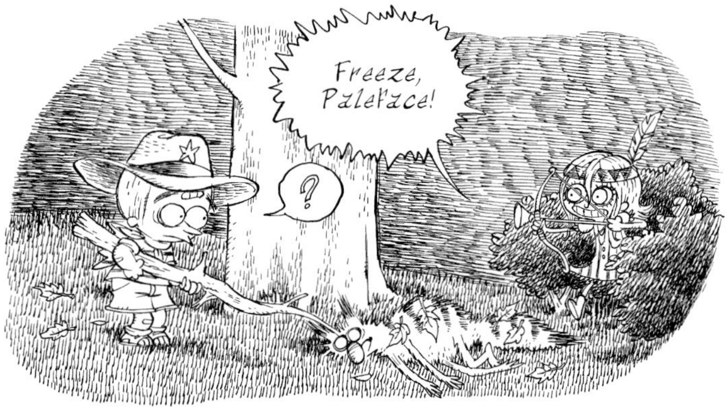
Freeze, Paleface!
?

I looked all over, but there was nothing, not a soul around. His must've flown away.

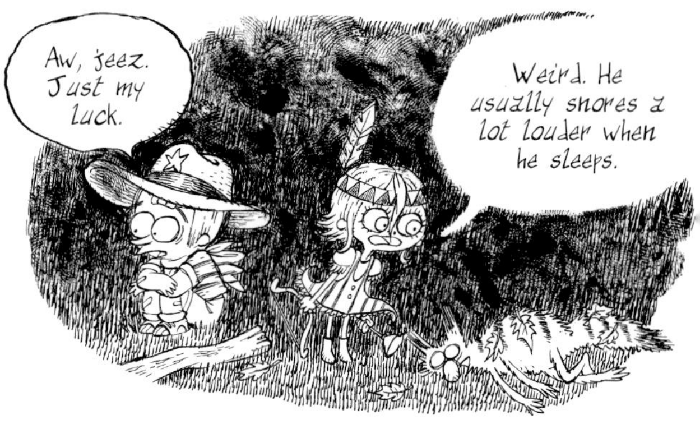
Aw, jeez. Just my luck.
Weird. He usually snores a lot louder when he sleeps.

All that was left was his body, stiff as a board, the bottom all flat.

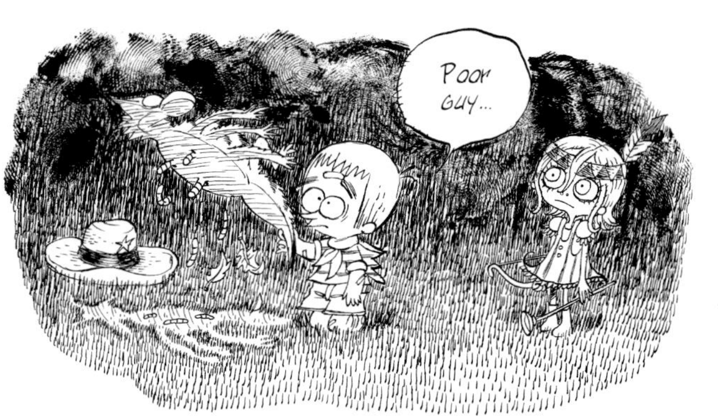
Poor guy...

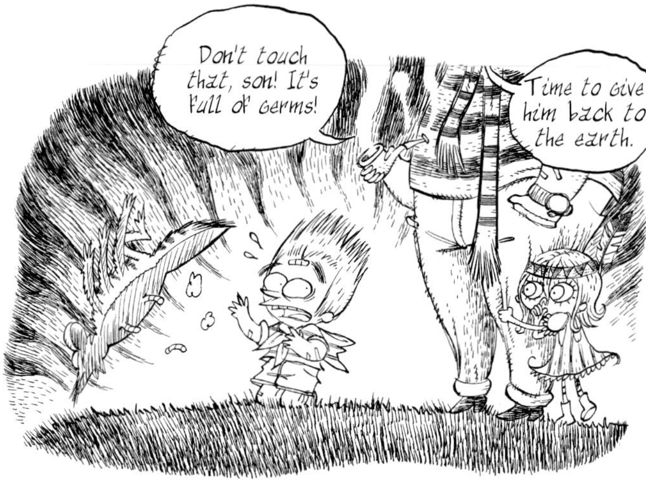
Don't touch that, son! It's full of germs!
Time to give him back to the earth.

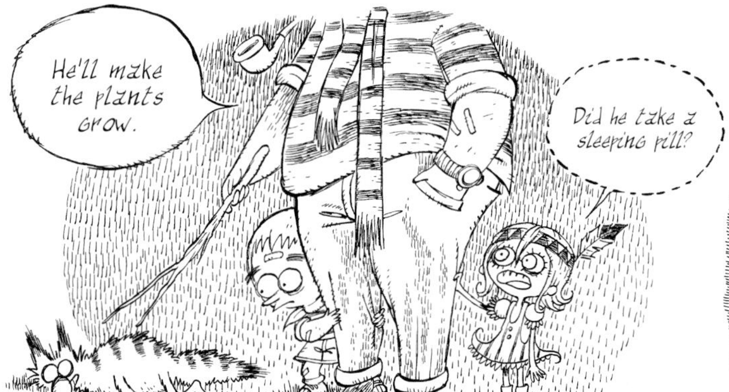
He'll make the plants grow.
Did he take a sleeping pill?

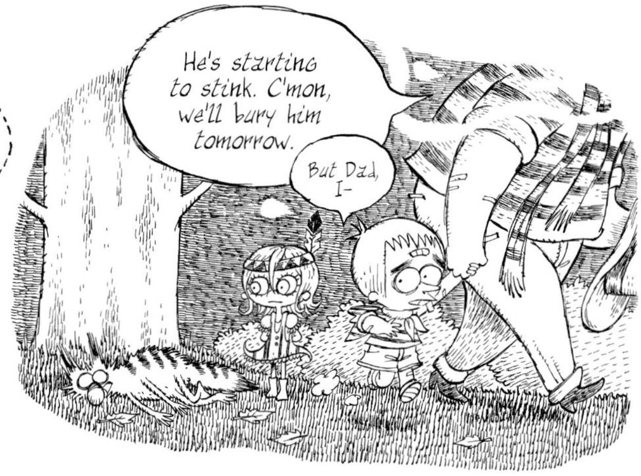
He's starting to stink. C'mon, we'll bury him tomorrow.
But Dad, I-

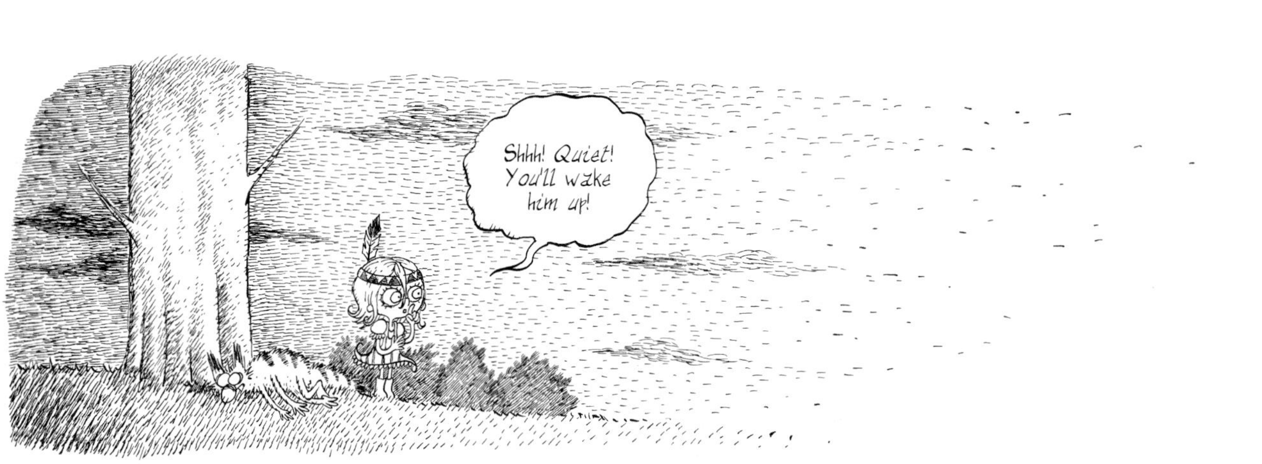
Shhh! Quiet! You'll wake him up!

"There are mysteries that sleep in cloudy waters..."
And death must be a mystery buried deep...
I found some interesting leads in an old trunk in the attic...

HOT OFF THE PRESS

Our editors are on a hot streak: solving today's mysteries for you, so you won't be surprised tomorrow!

EDITOR IN CHIEF
GARY RODWEED

"WE SAW HIM!"

CAPE COD
8 STRAWBERRY LANE
YARMOUTHPORT, MA 02675

Last Christmas Eve, around 12:15 AM, five little orphans had a surprising encounter.

Santa Claus no longer a myth, now a reality!

He was caught red-handed **DELIVERING "GIFTS"** by a band of children on the top floor of the St. Joseph Orphanage.

――― •••• ―――

Will we finally know the truth ?

――― •••• ―――

6-year-old Colette, eyewitness, reports:

"We didn't think he'd come. We were getting sleepy. Suddenly, there he was!"

– *"You might say our little a̶ bush really surprised him! ̶ told us that we should be ̶ bed at this hour, that childr̶ should be obedient and goo̶* **I managed to snap this pho̶ before he flew out the windo̶** *Our room was filled with gif̶ No way were we going back ̶ sleep! We played with our n̶ toys until dawn."*

HOT OFF THE PRESS

Dozens of experts, editors, journalists, and typists on the front lines to deliver what every honest man should know!

ACTUAL
ıtentions and motivations

etective Chief Inspector **Allan** **cCornick** didn't find any **gifts** hen he woke up that morning:

"I've never believed in him. We ill use every means to unmask is ***impostor!*** *Passing out gifts a winter's night—I find that ıspect! Such altruism can only a front for* ***shady dealings!*** *t the police do their work!"*

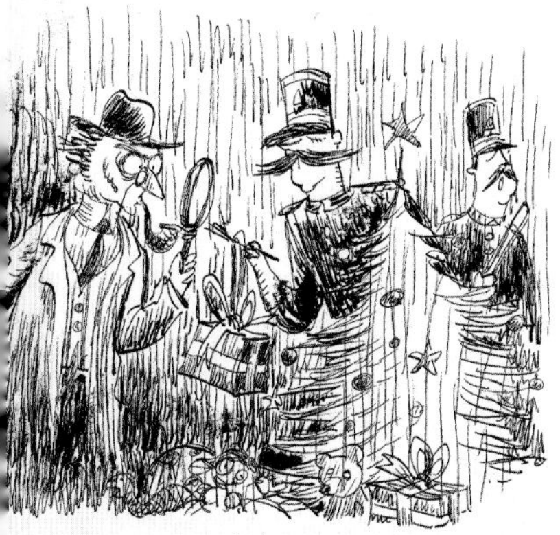

THE INVESTIGATION CONTINUES

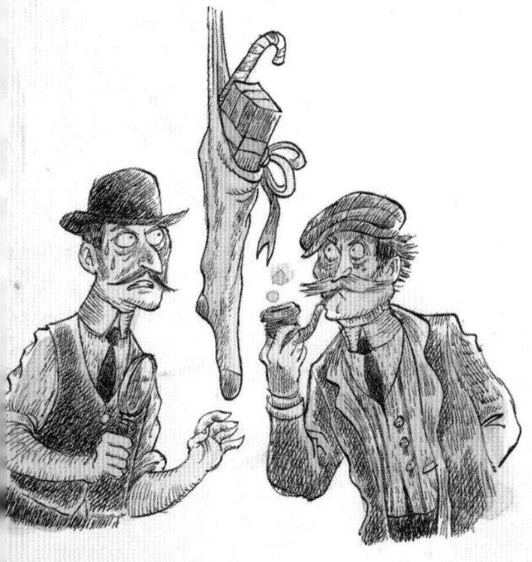

The police searched the location for several hours. Investigators eft no stone unturned, and offered no comment.

GOOD SAMARITAN OR NOTORIOUS CROOK?

LET each man think as he will. However, we must admit that **joy and good humor** brightened many a heart the morning of December 25, 1912.

Children still remain the best at describing Santa Claus:

– *"With his seven league boots, he can leap onto rooftops in a single bound!*

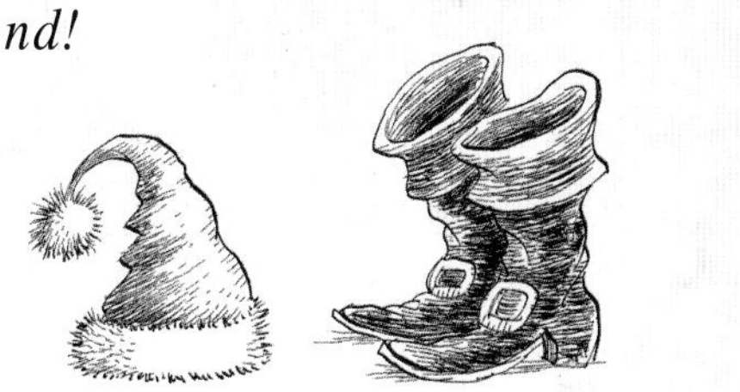

And the pompom on his hat is actually a kind of telepathic antenna so he can tell from far away if we're good or not!

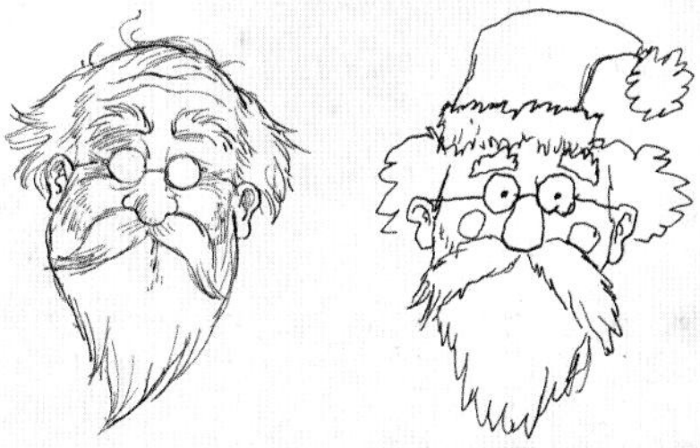

Our physiognomists are looking for the man behind this mask!

And the gifts we want just appear in his magic basket, which is never empty!"

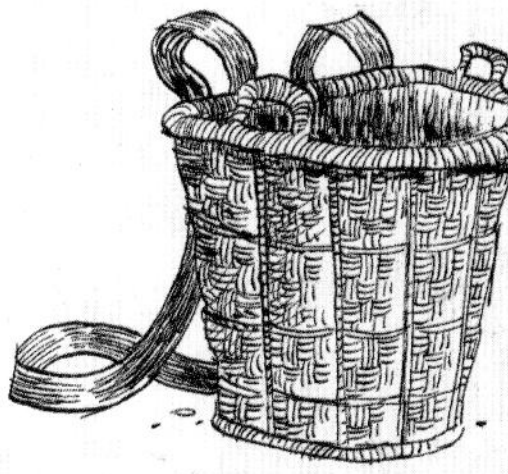

Judith, 7 ½ years old

FIVE HUNDRED YEARS OLD!

Even today, the "man in red" remains a mystery...

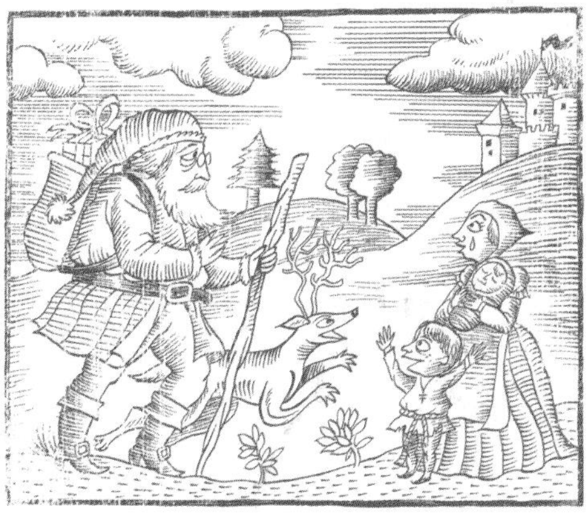

This 14th century engraving of him was found in London's National Gallery.

WHY
does he give out **gifts?**

WHY
does he insist on announcing himself with **"Ho Ho Ho"?**

HOW THE DEVIL
does he pull off his Paris-Canberra world tour **in just one night?**

What is the secret of his incredible longevity?
Has Santa Claus found a way to bend the rules of time?
Does he know the secrets of death?

G. Duroy

They say Santa Claus is more than 500 years old.

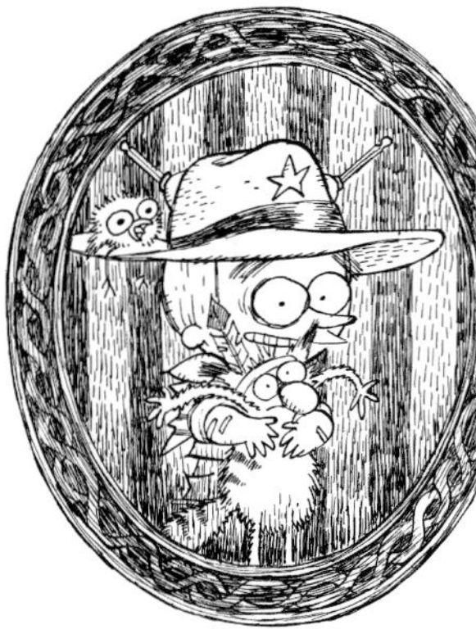

He must know all about foiling Death's plans.

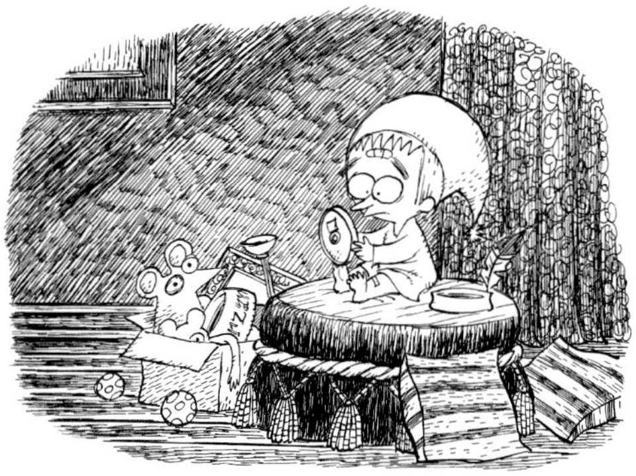

If only I could get him to help Tarzan...

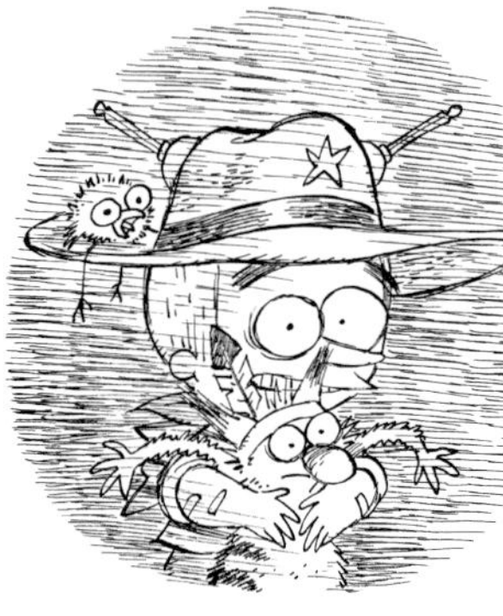

Mom put him in a brand new plastic bag.

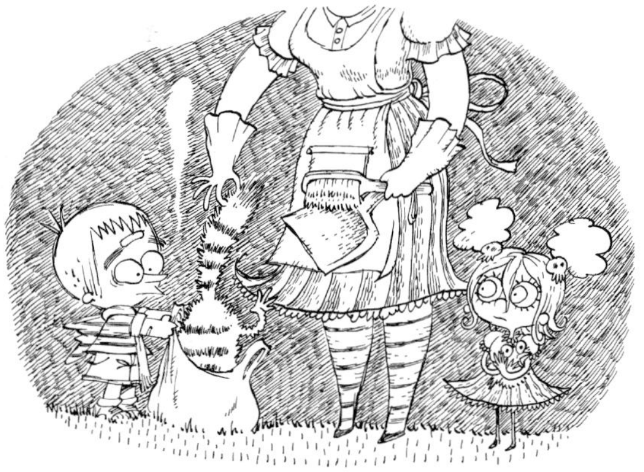

And Dad buried him in the backyard.

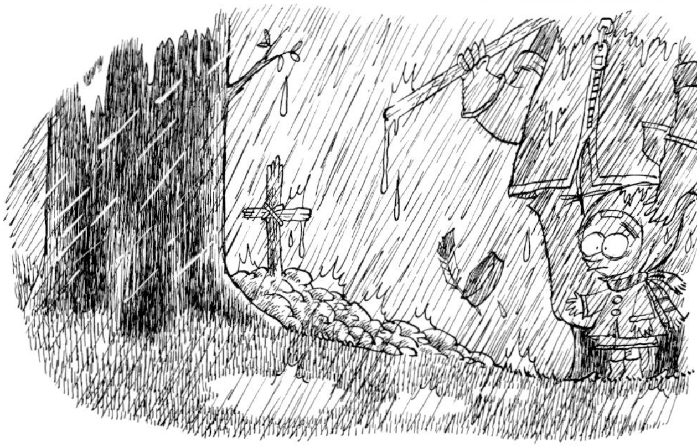

Under the big cherry tree.

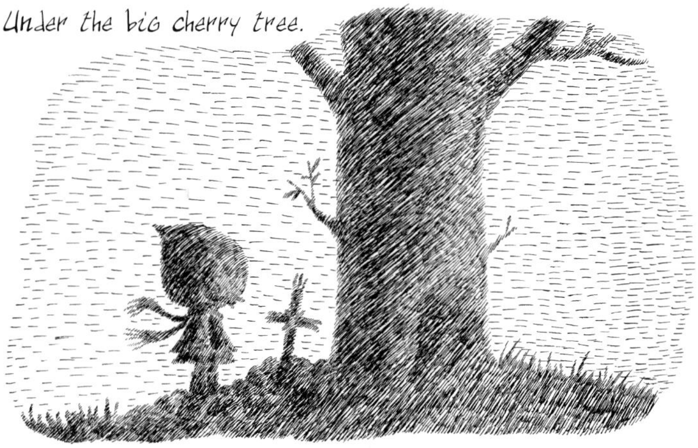

Tarzan was my best friend... my truest.

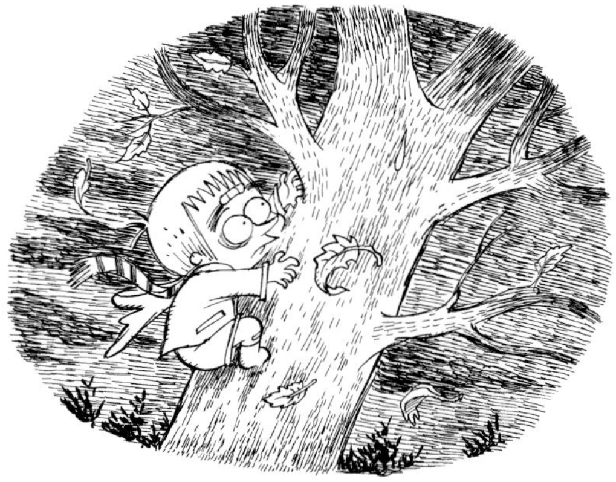

I'm going to write Santa a nice long letter.

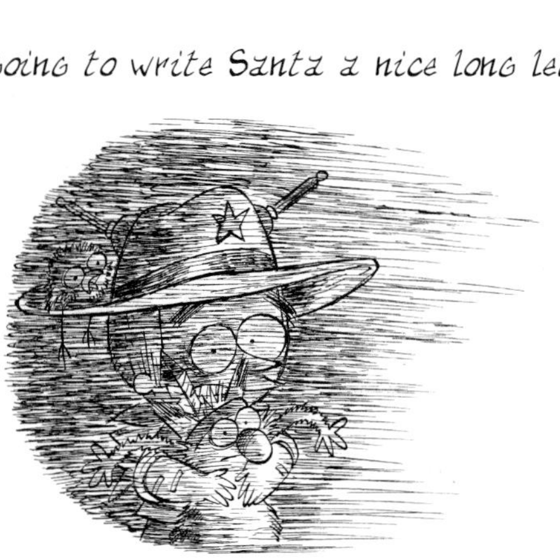

Here's hoping he reads all his mail...

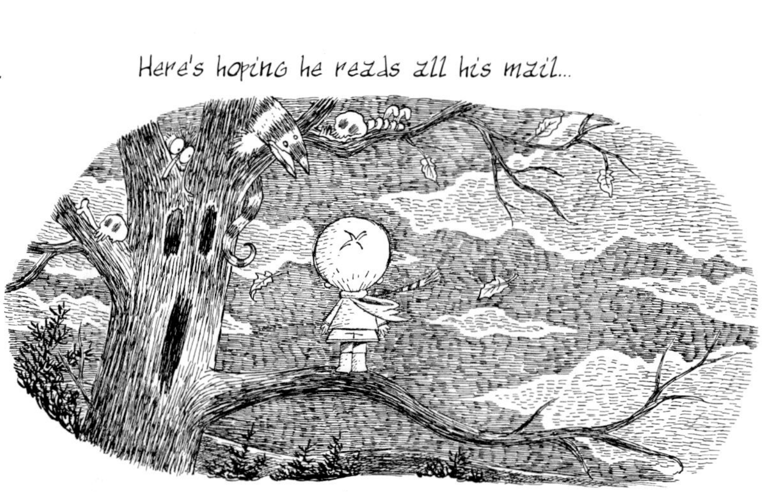

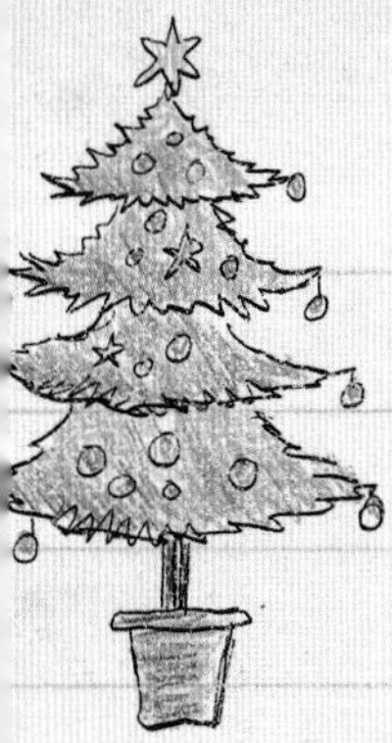

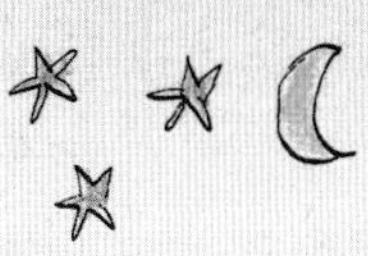

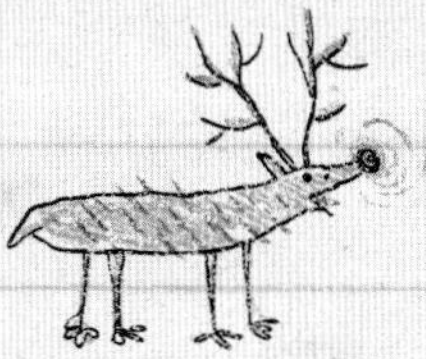

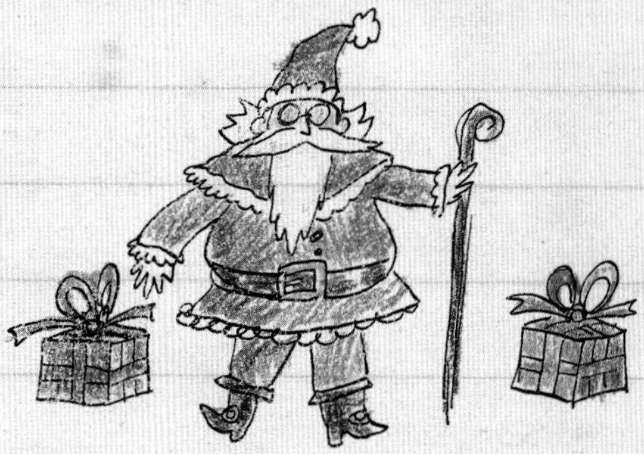

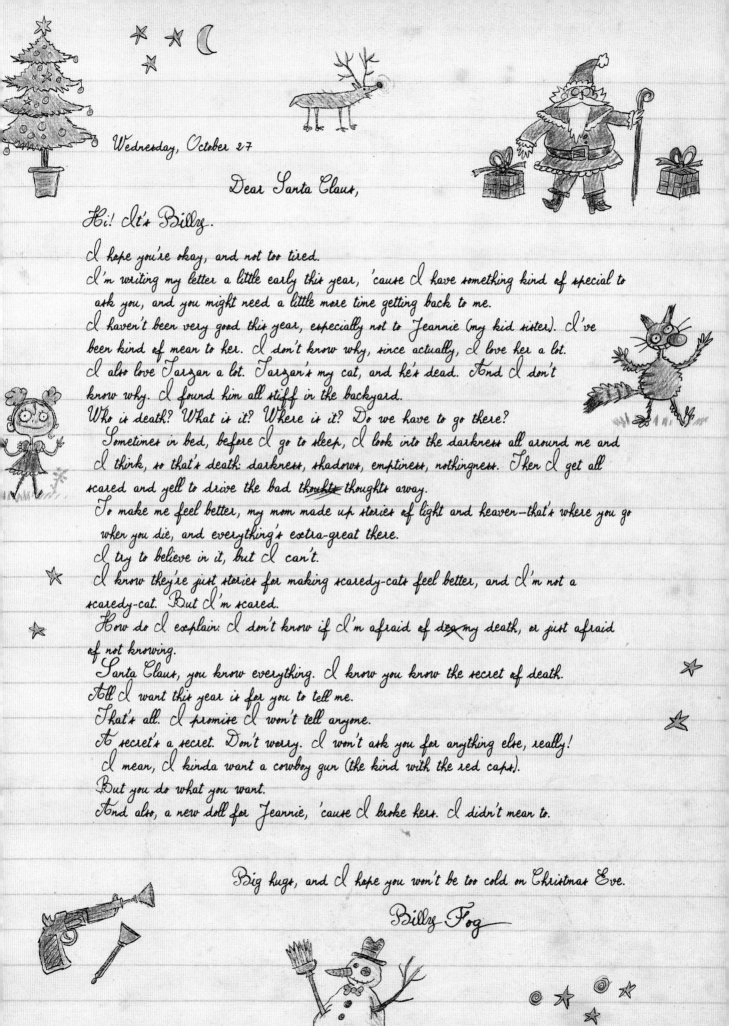

Wednesday, October 27

Dear Santa Claus,

Hi! It's Billy.

I hope you're okay, and not too tired.

I'm writing my letter a little early this year, 'cause I have something kind of special to ask you, and you might need a little more time getting back to me.

I haven't been very good this year, especially not to Jeannie (my kid sister). I've been kind of mean to her. I don't know why, since actually, I love her a lot.

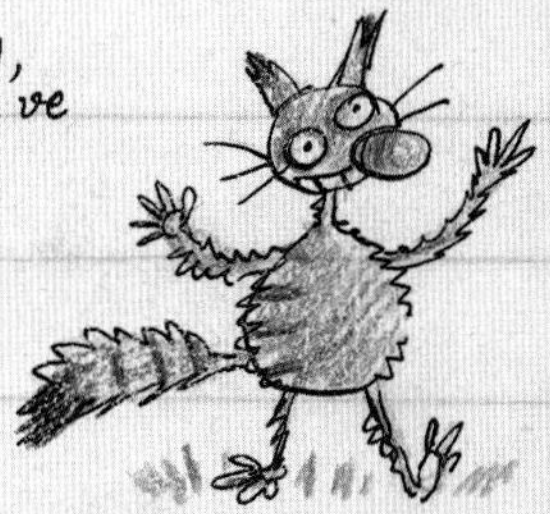

I also love Tarzan a lot. Tarzan's my cat, and he's dead. And I don't know why. I found him all stiff in the backyard.

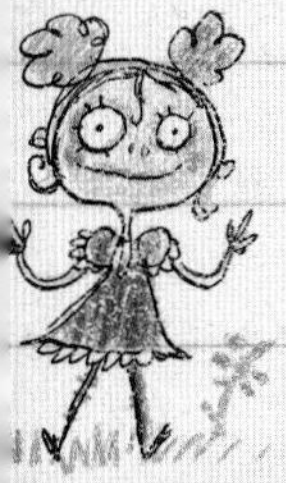

Who is death? What is it? Where is it? Do we have to go there?

Sometimes in bed, before I go to sleep, I look into the darkness all around me and I think, so that's death: darkness, shadows, emptiness, nothingness. Then I get all scared and yell to drive the bad ~~thouhts~~ thoughts away.

To make me feel better, my mom made up stories of light and heaven—that's where you go when you die, and everything's extra-great there.

I try to believe in it, but I can't.

I know they're just stories for making scaredy-cats feel better, and I'm not a scaredy-cat. But I'm scared.

How do I explain: I don't know if I'm afraid of ~~dea~~ my death, or just afraid of not knowing.

Santa Claus, you know everything. I know you know the secret of death.

All I want this year is for you to tell me.

That's all. I promise I won't tell anyone.

A secret's a secret. Don't worry. I won't ask you for anything else, really!

I mean, I kinda want a cowboy gun (the kind with the red caps).

But you do what you want.

And also, a new doll for Jeannie, 'cause I broke hers. I didn't mean to.

Big hugs, and I hope you won't be too cold on Christmas Eve.

Billy Fog

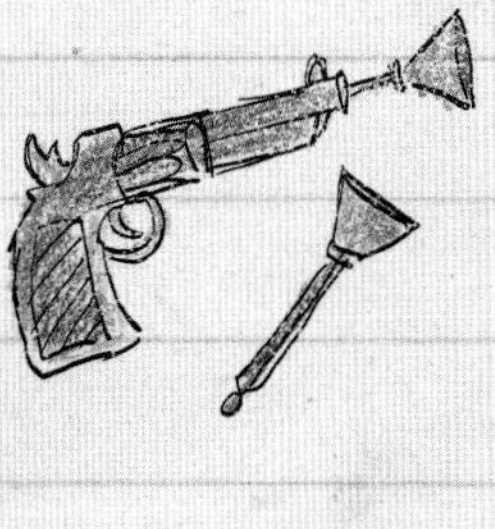

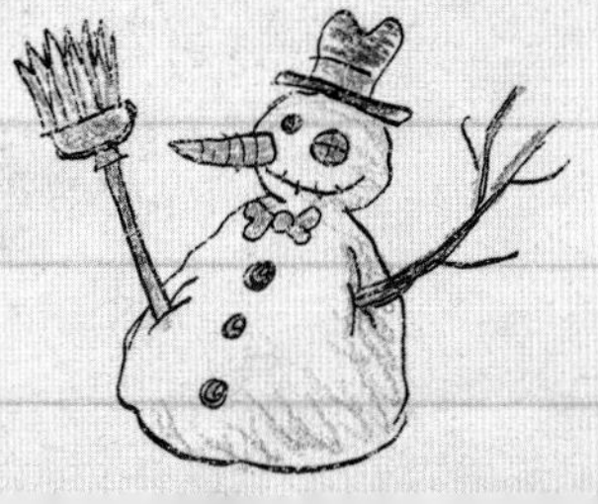

By now, Tarzan's probably already far away …

At least I hope so, for his sake.

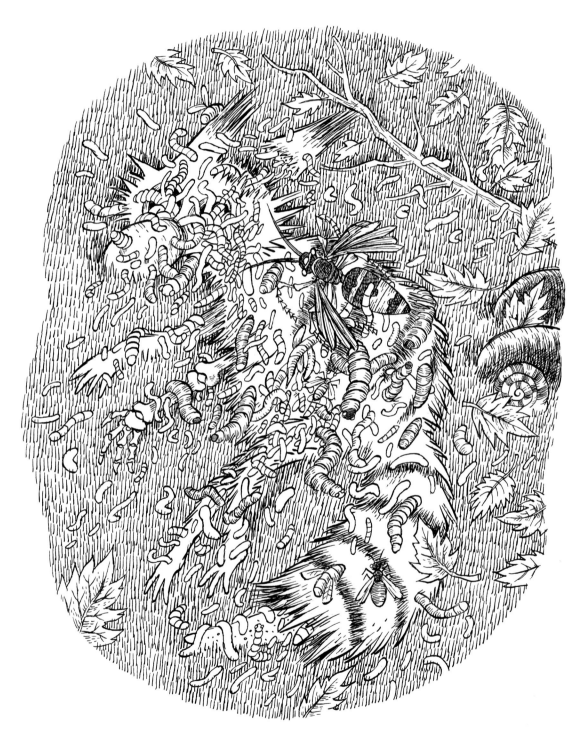

THE PRINCESS AND THE PUDDLE

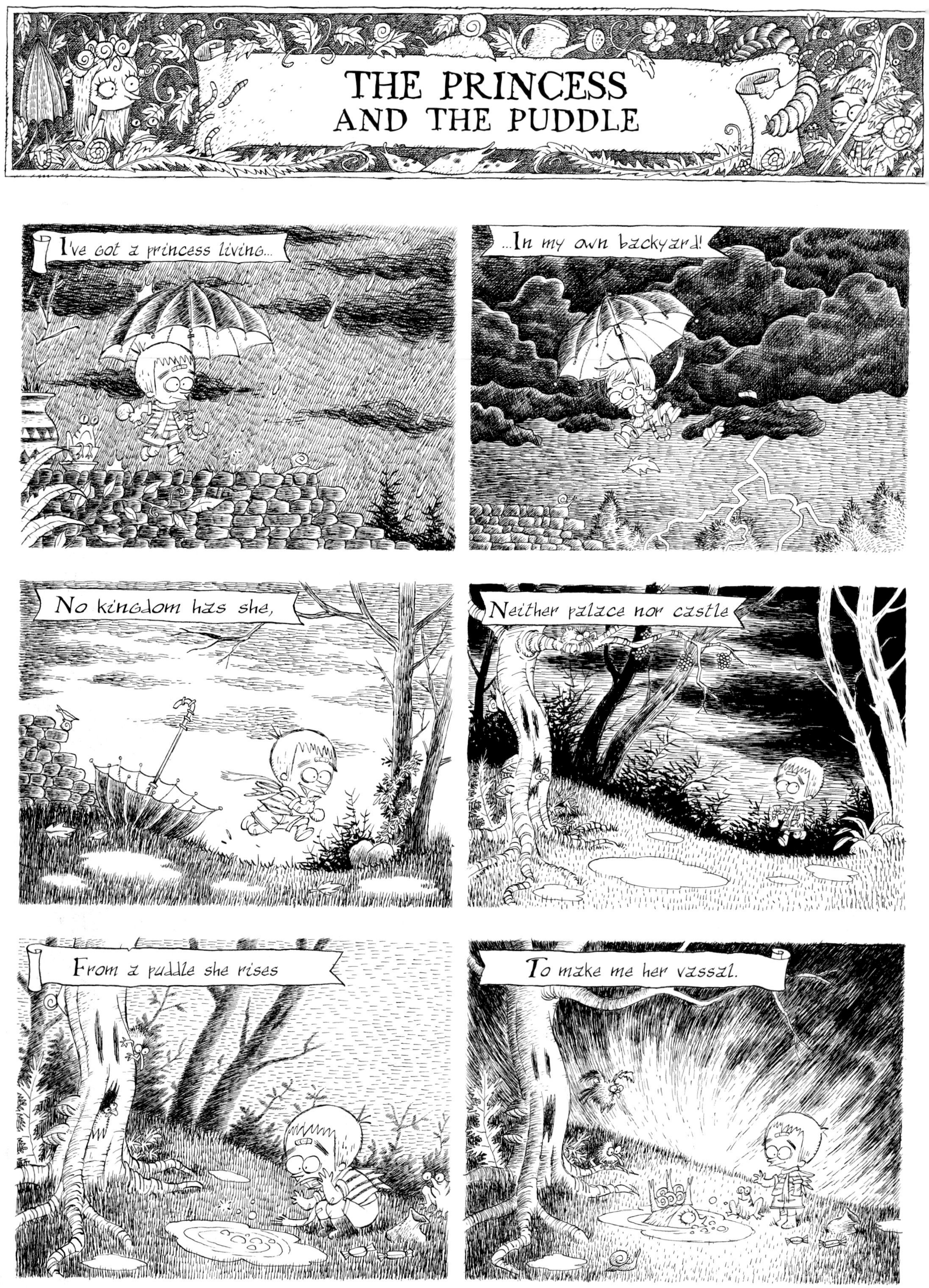
I've got a princess living...
...In my own backyard!
No kingdom has she,
Neither palace nor castle
From a puddle she rises
To make me her vassal.

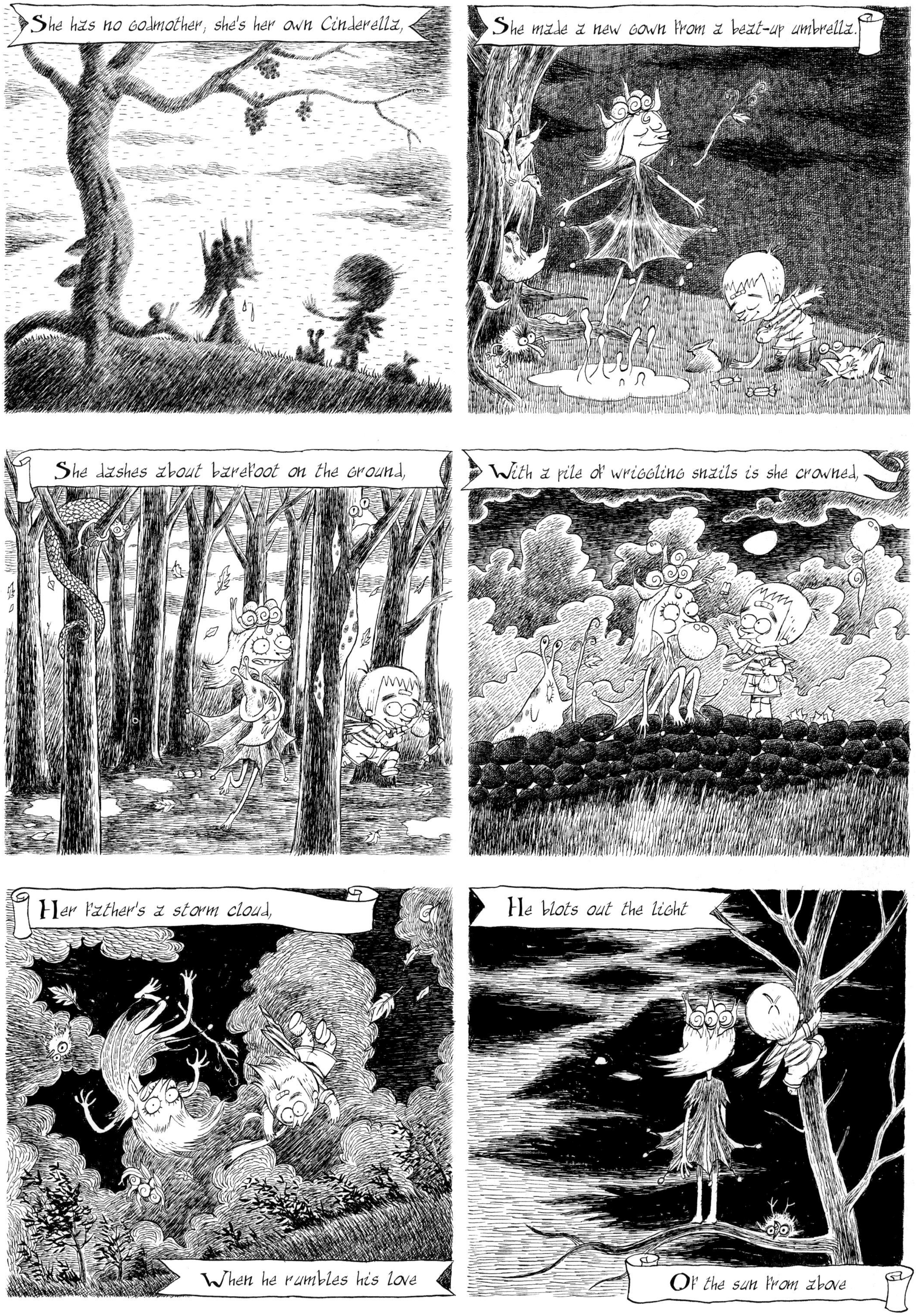
She has no godmother; she's her own Cinderella,
She made a new gown from a beat-up umbrella.
She dashes about barefoot on the ground,
With a pile of wriggling snails is she crowned,
Her father's a storm cloud,
When he rumbles his love
He blots out the light
Of the sun from above

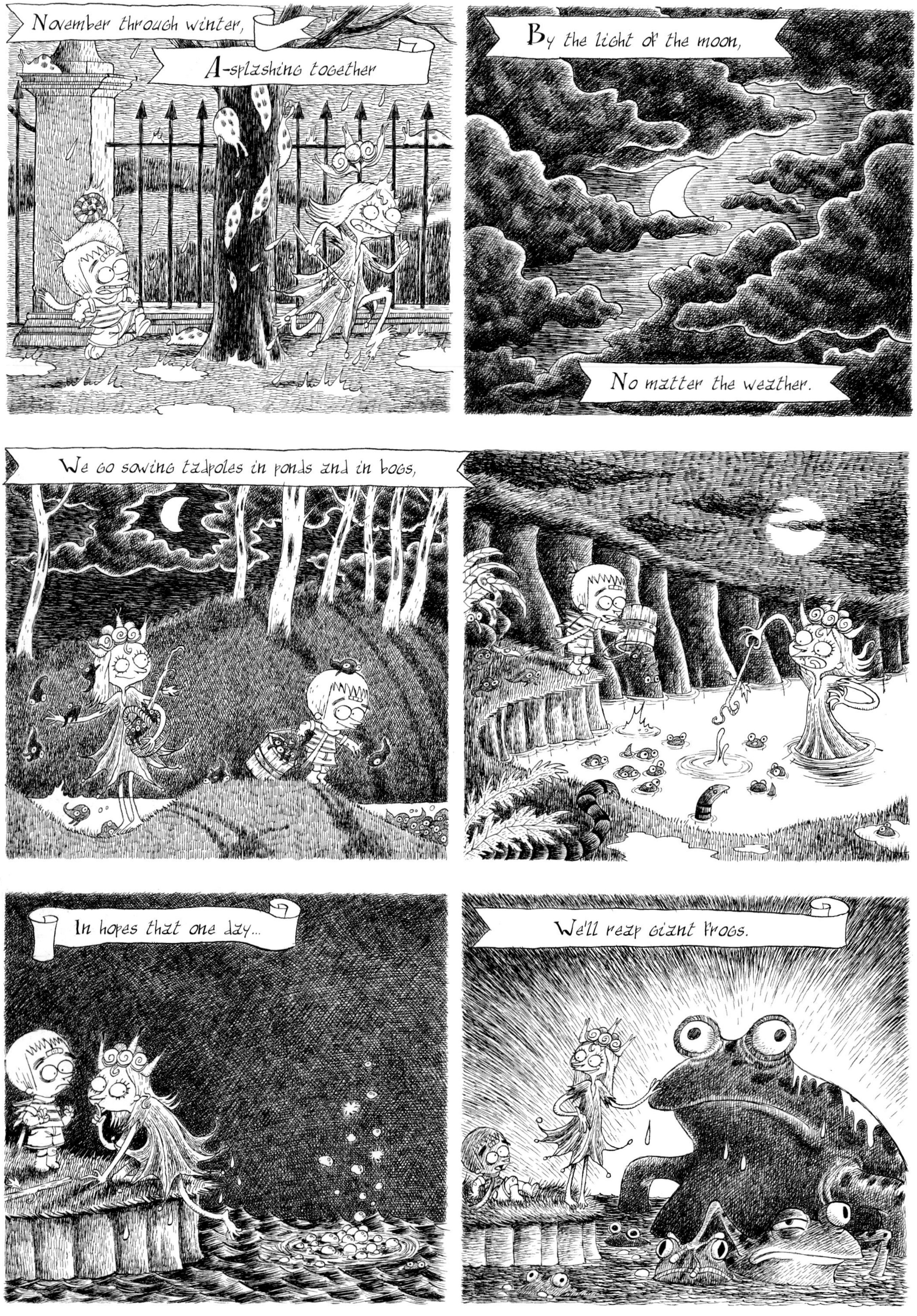
November through winter,
A-splashing together
By the light of the moon,
No matter the weather.
We go sowing tadpoles in ponds and in bogs,
In hopes that one day...
We'll reap giant frogs.

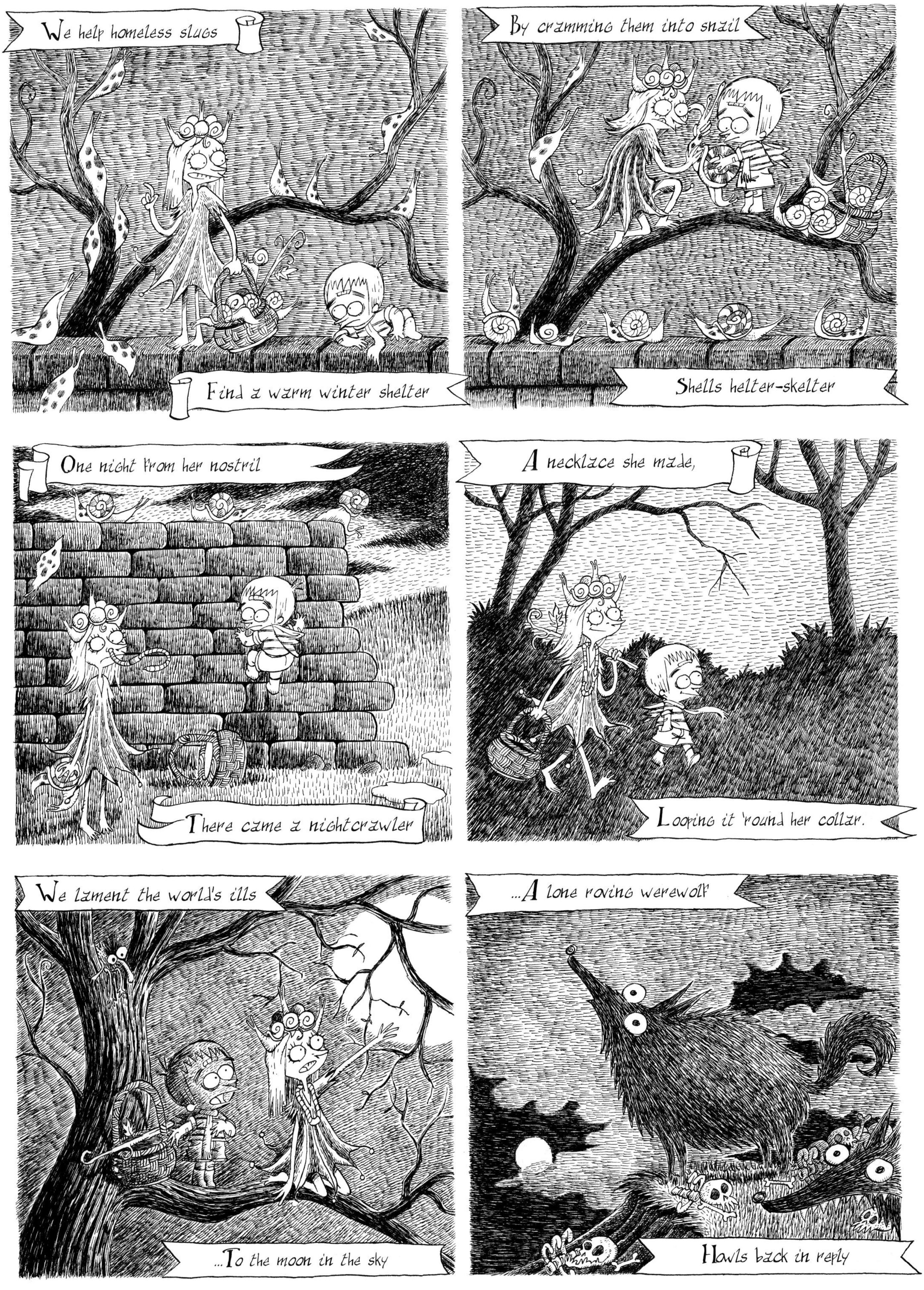
We help homeless slugs
Find a warm winter shelter
By cramming them into snail
Shells helter-skelter
One night from her nostril
There came a nightcrawler
A necklace she made,
Looping it 'round her collar.
We lament the world's ills
...To the moon in the sky
...A lone roving werewolf
Howls back in reply

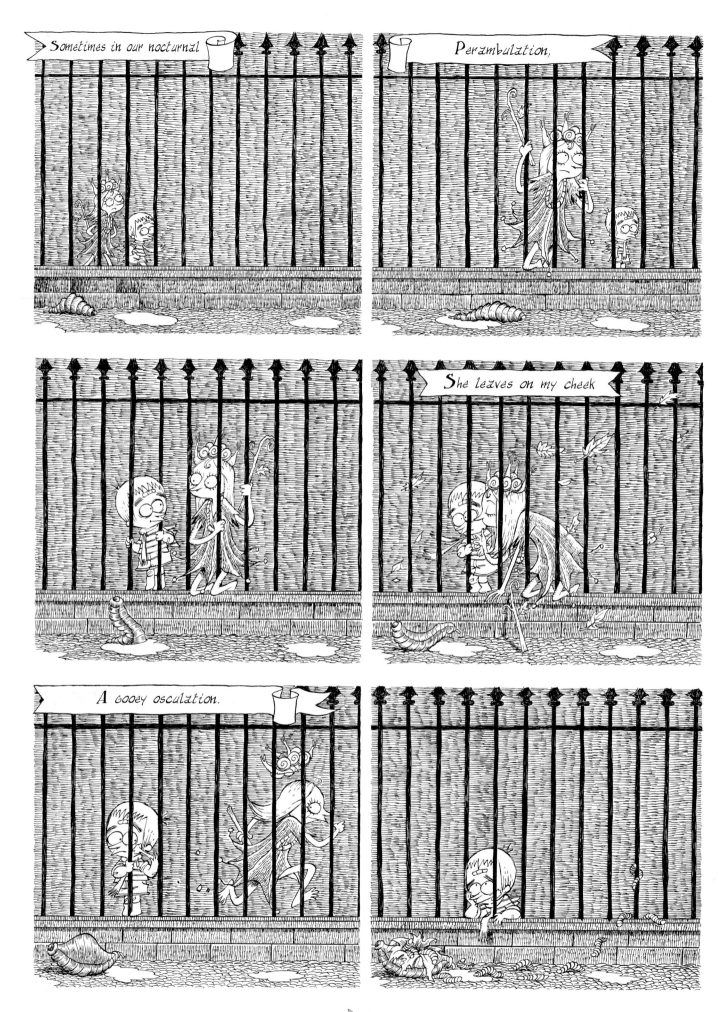

Sometimes in our nocturnal

Perambulation,

She leaves on my cheek

A gooey osculation.

13

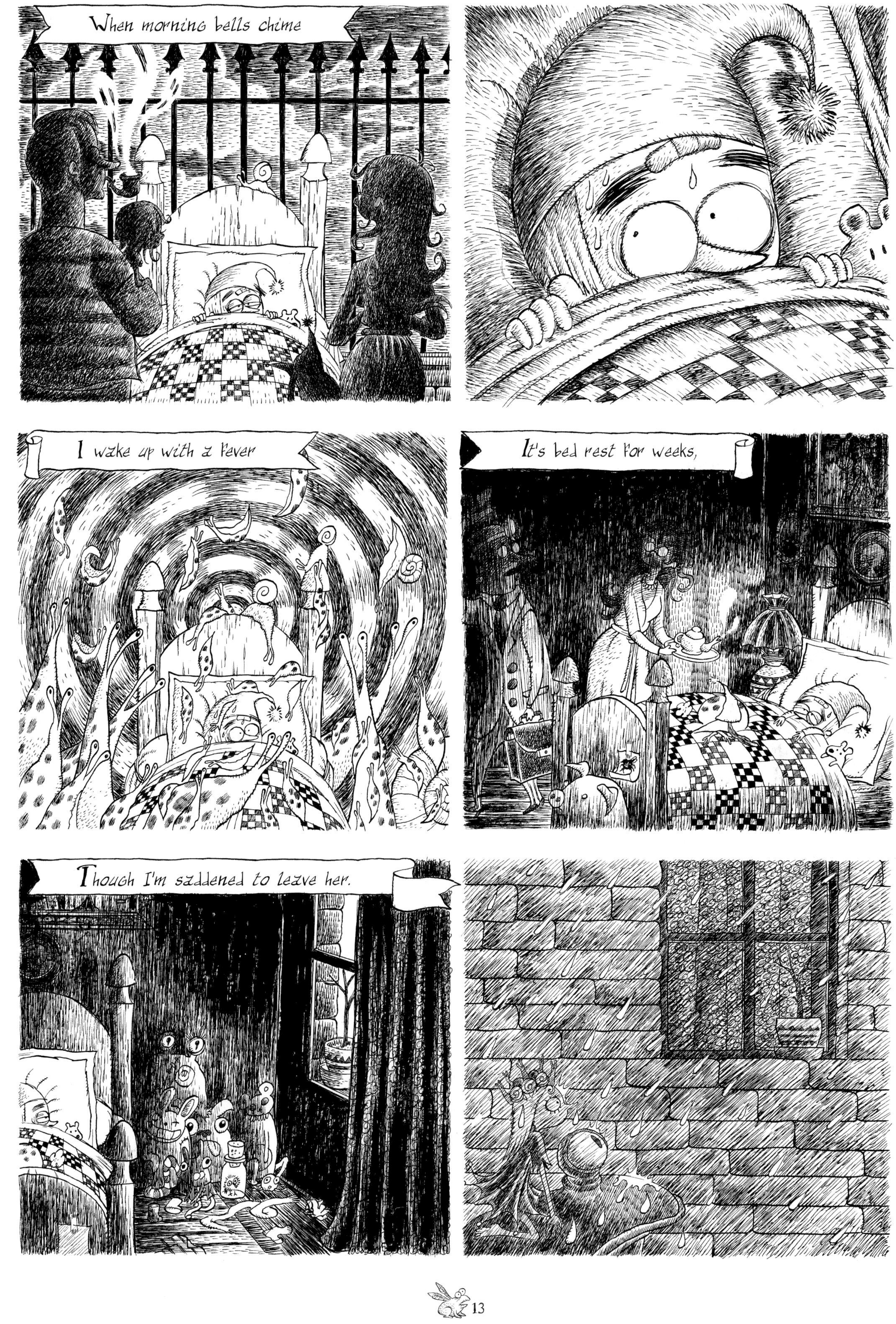

When morning bells chime
I wake up with a fever
It's bed rest for weeks,
Though I'm saddened to leave her.

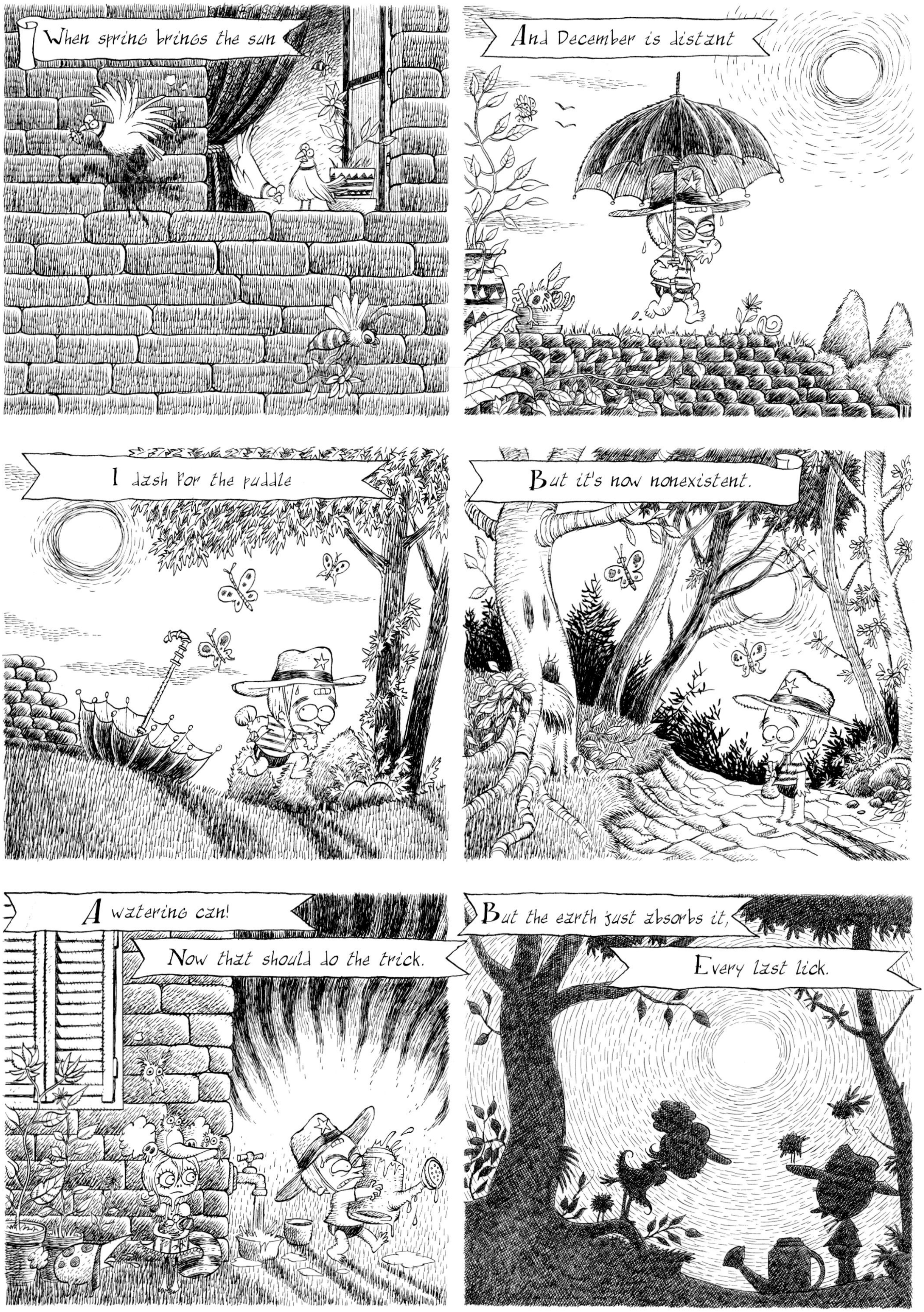
When spring brings the sun
And December is distant
I dash for the puddle
But it's now nonexistent.
A watering can!
Now that should do the trick.
But the earth just absorbs it,
Every last lick.

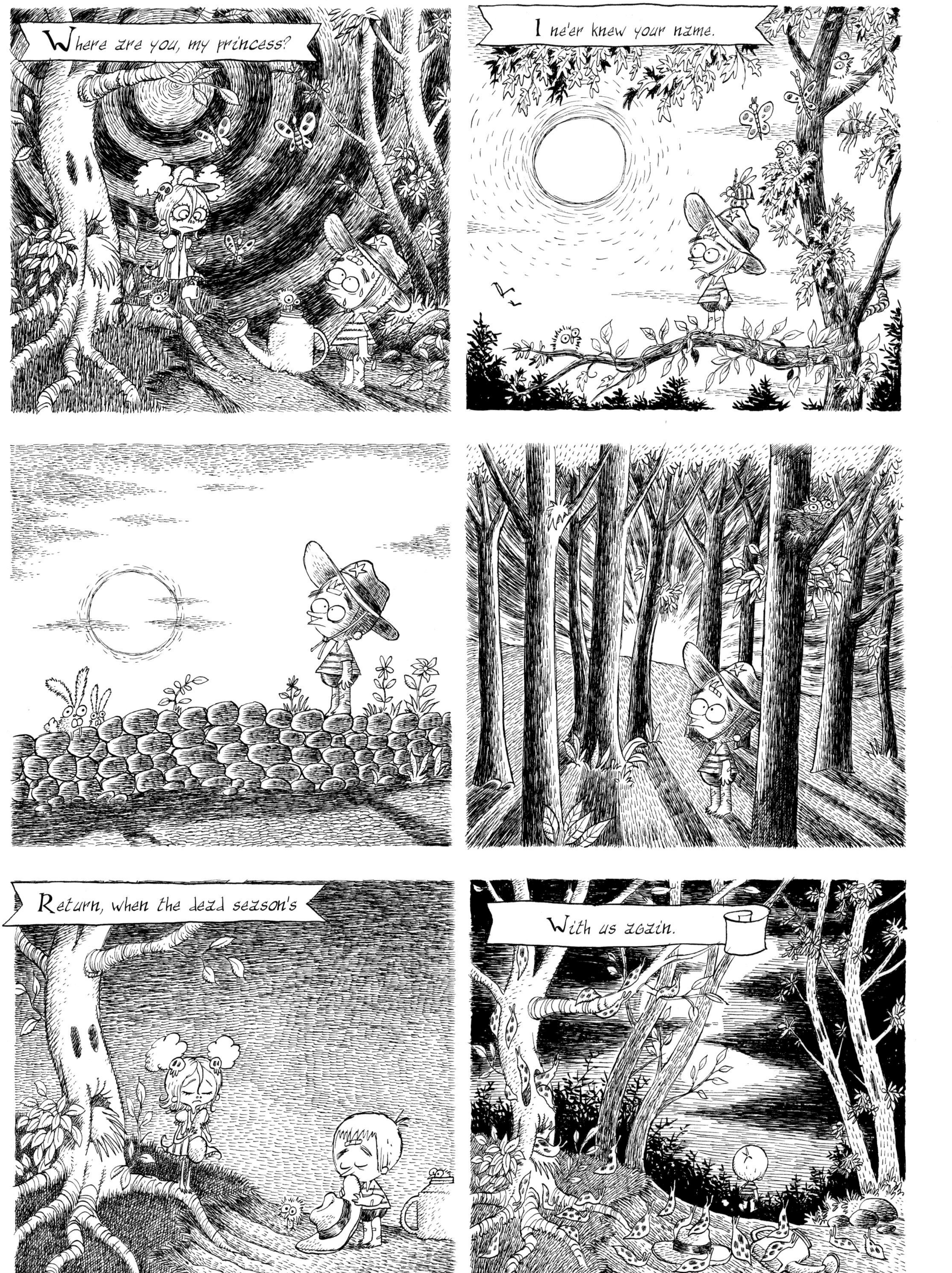
Where are you, my princess?
I ne'er knew your name.
Return, when the dead season's
With us again.

The Puddle Princess

Daughter of earth, rain, and winds,
she is nature's protectress.
She watches over all that grows,
crawls, and wriggles.

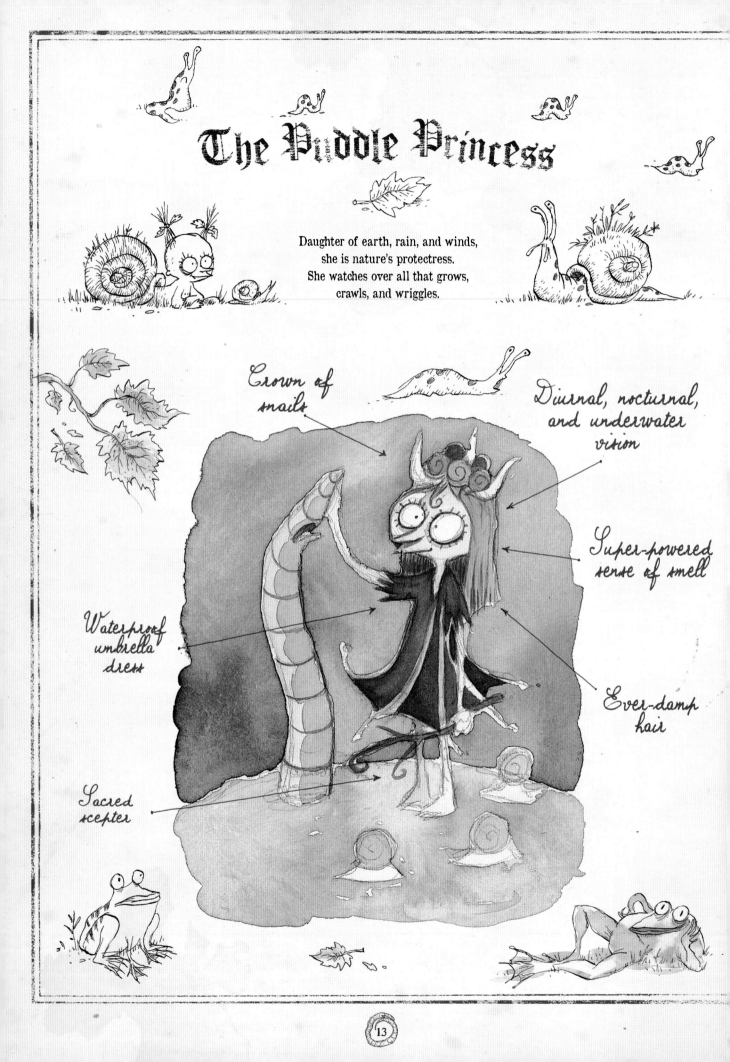

Crown of snails

Diurnal, nocturnal, and underwater vision

Super-powered sense of smell

Waterproof umbrella dress

Ever-damp hair

Sacred scepter

Birth Process

Fig. 1

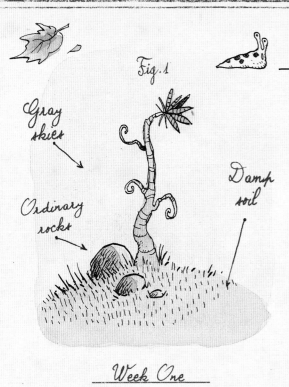

Gray skies

Ordinary rocks

Damp soil

Fig. 2

Dried petals smelling of mimosa

Scratchy leaf known as "Hades' Tongue"

Flexible but unbreakable stem

Week One

In a cool, damp,
often muddy spot,
a small bulb will give birth
to a long, fibrous, tentacular
plant with a single reddish-orange
flower at the end.

(Cucurbita Anguilae)

Week Five

Soon the flower will
wither, giving way to a giant
pumpkin-like fruit:
the squmkin, or Marsh Apple.

Fig. 3

Week Seven

No sooner is she hatched from the
pumpkin than the puddle
princess will consume it entirely
(save for the tip of the stem,
which will serve as her scepter).

This will be the only meal
she eats in her entire life.

Snails will teach her to drool,
and frogs to hop.
Slugs will teach her to crawl.

As for walking, she'll have to
figure that out on her own.

Ornaments and Adornments

Born at the end of October, the young princess will undergo her apprenticeship to nature during the November rains.

Mid-November:
She acquires her first snail.
She will have to acquire four more to form her crown and officially become a princess.

Impromptu "tadpole-sitting" session

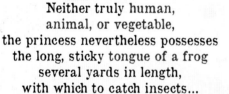

Neither truly human, animal, or vegetable, the princess nevertheless possesses the long, sticky tongue of a frog several yards in length, with which to catch insects...

 # Beware

Avoid jumping
feet first
into puddles!
The puddle princess spends
most of her time
hidden at the bottom,
feeding tadpoles
and teaching them to swim.

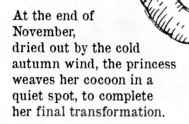

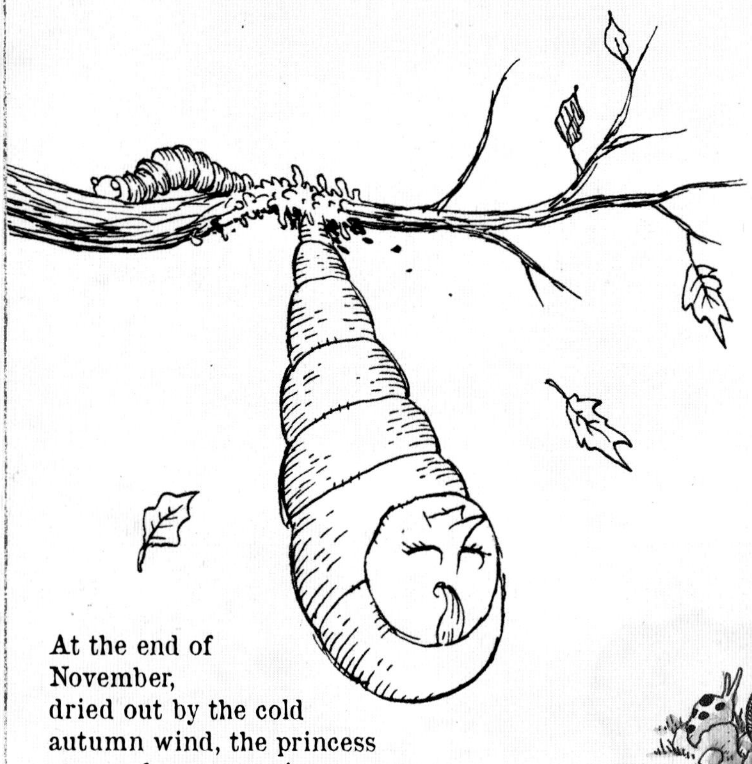

At the end of November, dried out by the cold autumn wind, the princess weaves her cocoon in a quiet spot, to complete her final transformation.

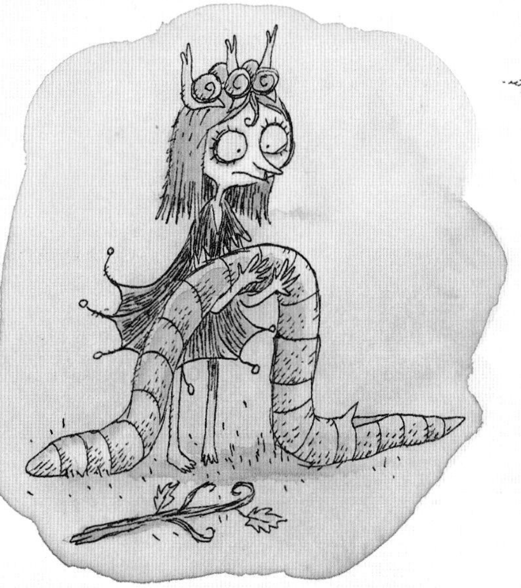

Period of Activity

(from the seventh week of autumn to the first days of winter)

Soon after emerging from her cocoon,
the princess immediately sets to work.

There is much to do in this final period:
nature falls ill more and more often.

In olden days, men helped her stand watch.

These days, they don't really care.

The earth is in pain... The worms are poisoned by chemical products.

So much work so little time!

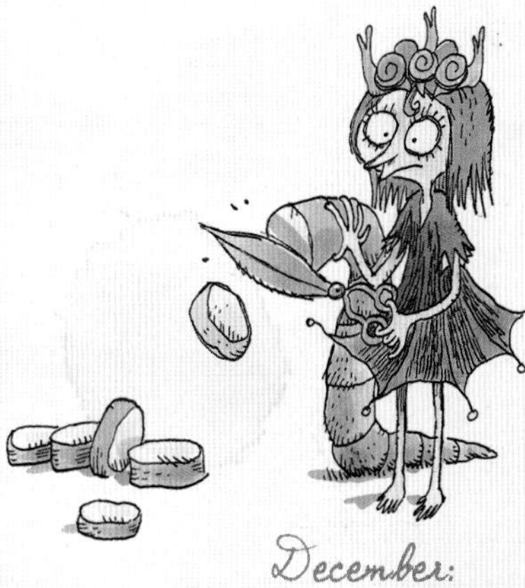

December: Worm-cutting season.

How Can You Help the Princess?

- *If you find a dead earthworm, cut it into ten equal pieces, along the rings.*
- *Dig 10 holes each about 20 inches deep, about 15 inches apart, in dry ground.*
- *Plant each piece and water copiously.*
- *Leave it for one whole month, and then dig up the worms... they'll have regenerated!*

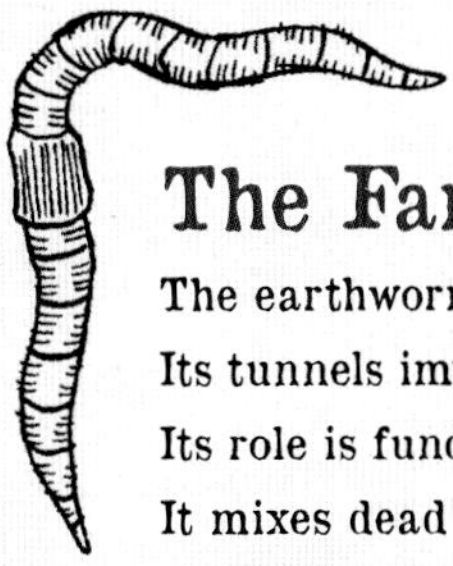

The Family Lumbricidae

The earthworm is a hard worker.
Its tunnels improve root growth and the circulation of water.
Its role is fundamental to the earth.
It mixes dead vegetable matter into the soil.
Plus, its poop contains bacteria helpful to the earth.

They are friends to all gardeners.

Protect them!

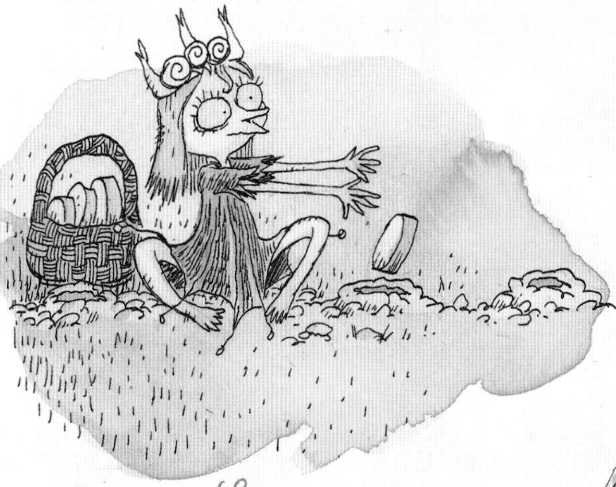

January: Sowing season.

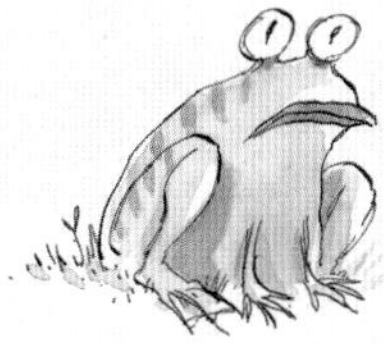

The Rings

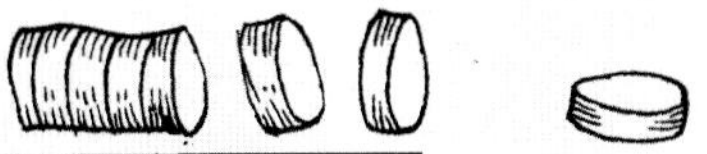

An earthworm's rings are band-aids that form where they've been cut.

Cut an earthworm into 10 pieces, and he'll come alive again in a month with 10 rings!

(Well, duh...)

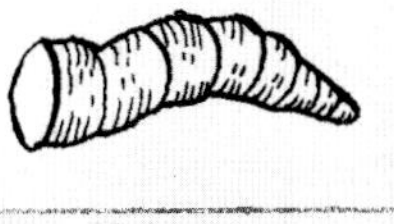

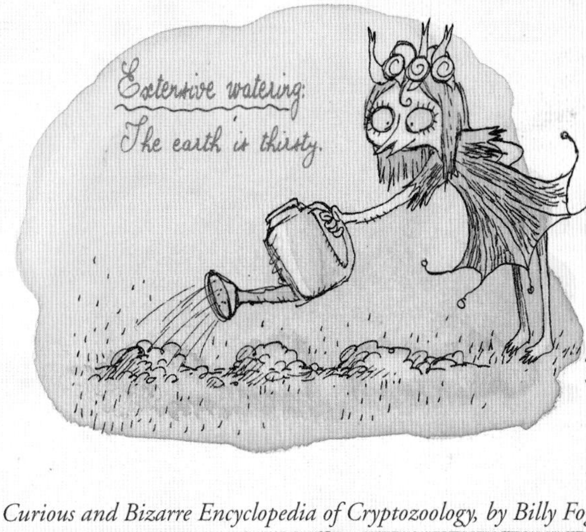
Extensive watering:
The earth is thirsty.

From the Curious and Bizarre Encyclopedia of Cryptozoology, by Billy Fog

"Billy? Yoo-hoo! Billy? Are you sleeping?"

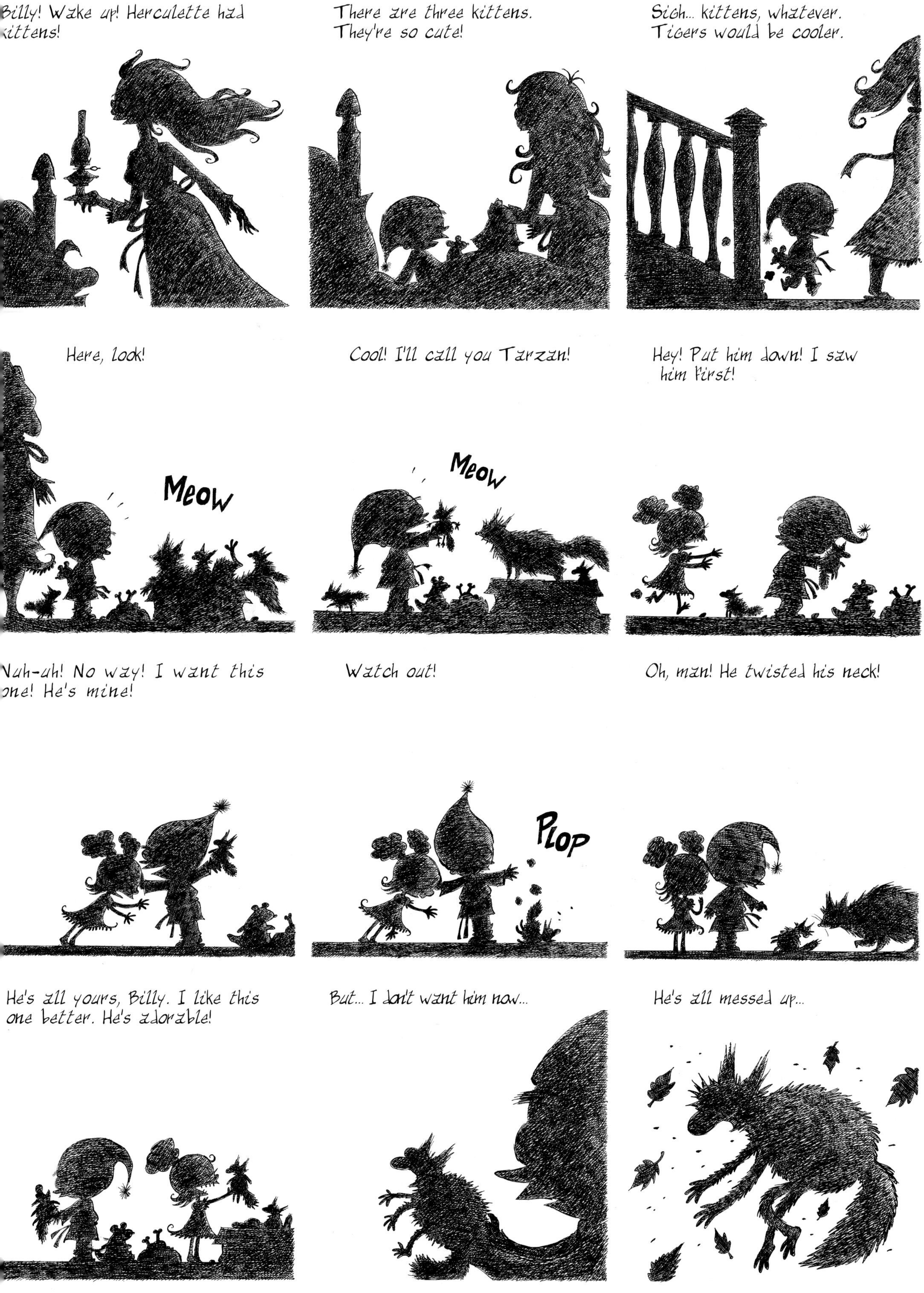
Billy! Wake up! Herculette had kittens!
There are three kittens. They're so cute!
Sigh... kittens, whatever. Tigers would be cooler.
Here, look!
MEOW
Cool! I'll call you Tarzan!
MEOW
Hey! Put him down! I saw him first!
Nuh-uh! No way! I want this one! He's mine!
Watch out!
PLOP
Oh, man! He twisted his neck!
He's all yours, Billy. I like this one better. He's adorable!
But... I don't want him now...
He's all messed up...

Still, he kept me warm when he'd sit on my belly and purr.

I liked peeing on him, just for fun.

And *throwing* him in water, to see if he'd float.

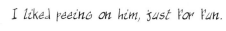

Tarzan was terrific at games on endless Sundays when I was bored.

I was never very nice to him...

I couldn't have known he'd go so quickly. Without even a warning.

They always say cats have nine lives.

Tarzan must already have been on his last.

Outside, the wind is howling. Shadows dance across the walls of my room...

...trying to make me feel guilty.

Billy...

?

Billy, are you asleep?

AAAAh!

13

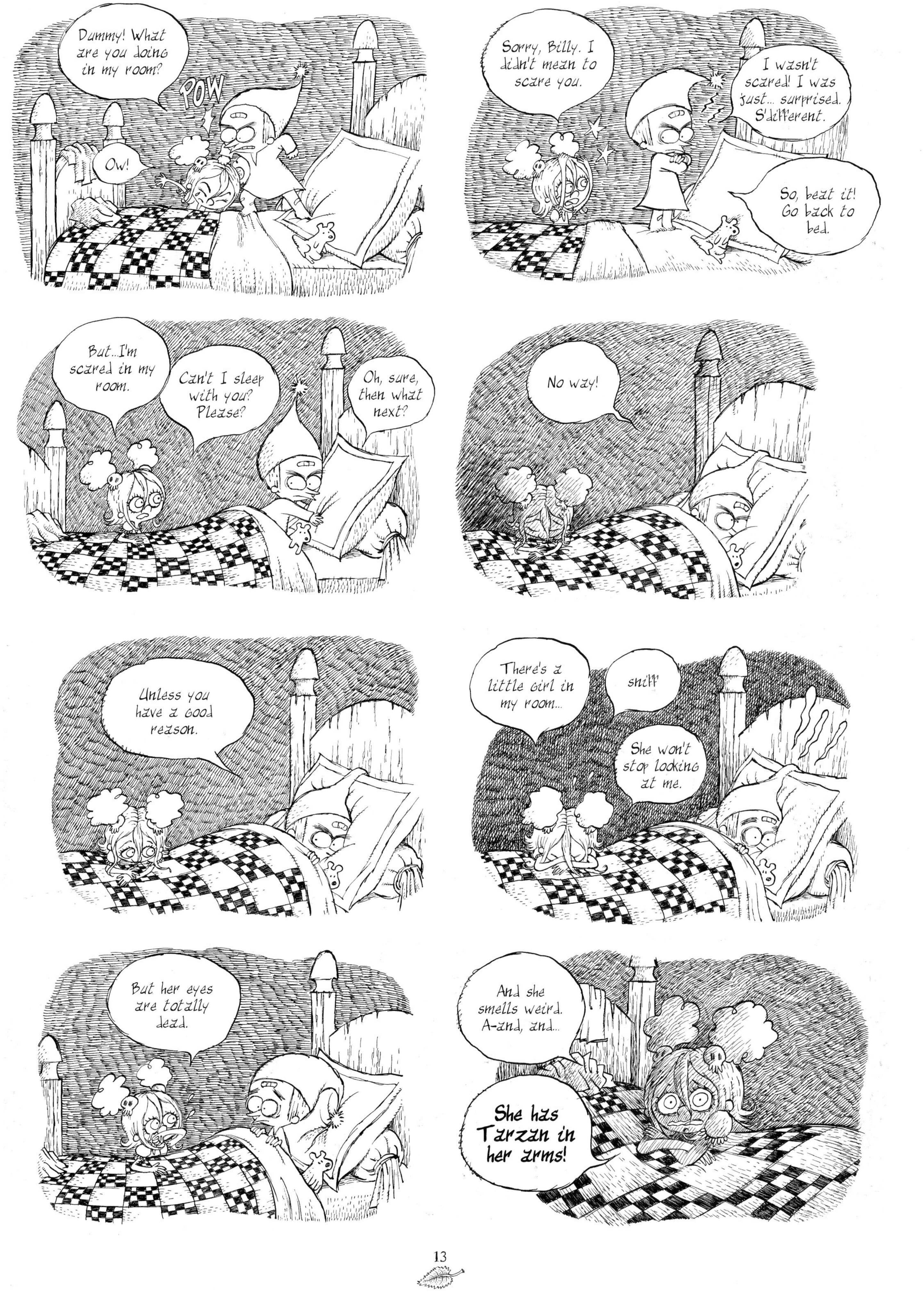

Dummy! What are you doing in my room?
POW
Ow!
Sorry, Billy. I didn't mean to scare you.
I wasn't scared! I was just... surprised. S'different.
So, beat it! Go back to bed.
But...I'm scared in my room.
Can't I sleep with you? Please?
Oh, sure, then what next?
No way!
Unless you have a good reason.
There's a little girl in my room...
sniff
She won't stop looking at me.
But her eyes are totally dead.
And she smells weird. A-and, and...
She has Tarzan in her arms!

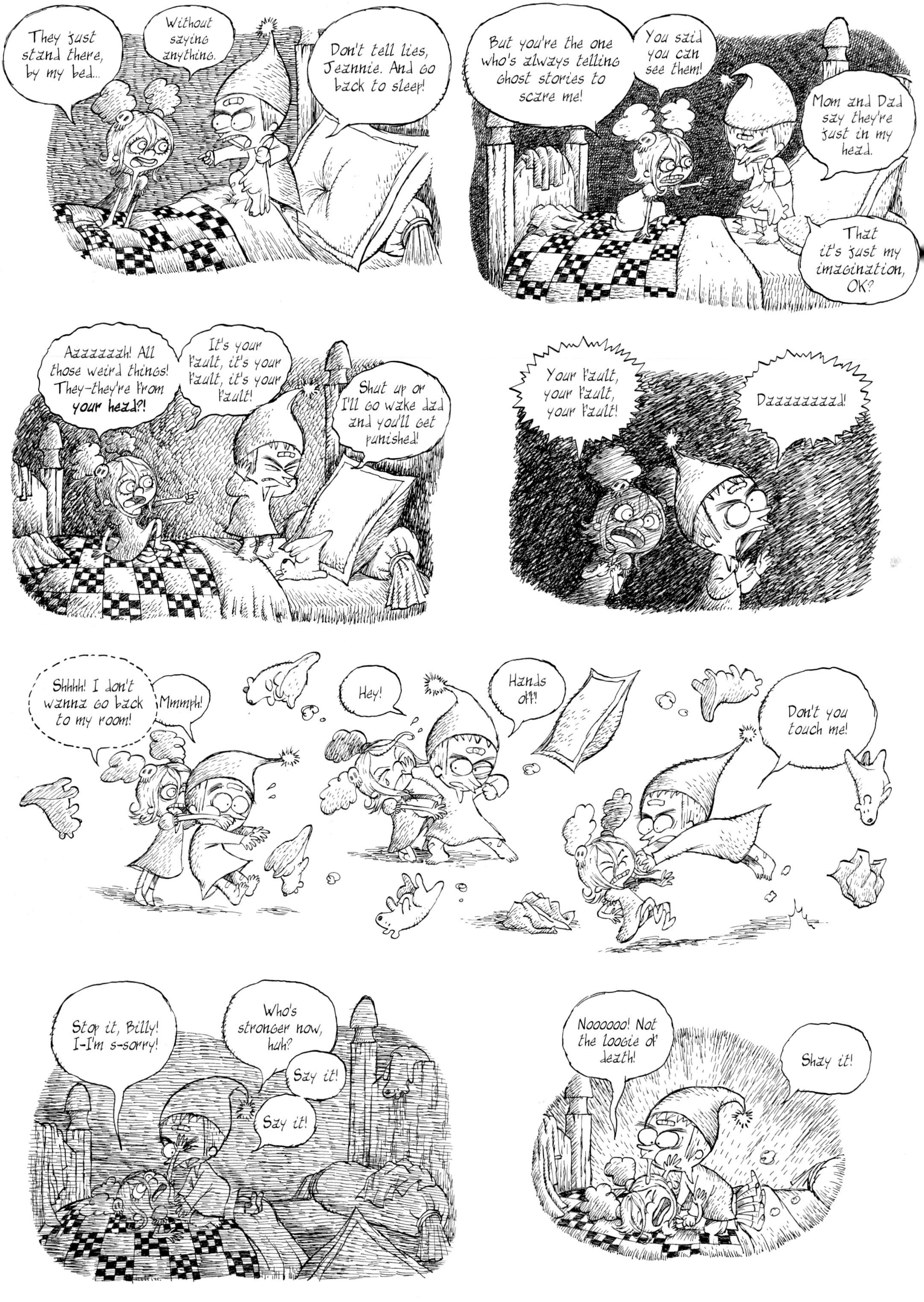

They just stand there, by my bed...
Without saying anything.
Don't tell lies, Jeannie. And go back to sleep!
But you're the one who's always telling ghost stories to scare me!
You said you can see them!
Mom and Dad say they're just in my head.
That it's just my imagination, OK?
Azzzzzzh! All those weird things! They-they're from your head?!
It's your fault, it's your fault, it's your fault!
Shut up or I'll go wake dad and you'll get punished!
Your fault, your fault, your fault!
Dazzzzzzzzd!
Shhhh! I don't wanna go back to my room!
Mmmmph!
Hey!
Hands off!
Don't you touch me!
Stop it, Billy! I-I'm s-sorry!
Who's stronger now, huh?
Say it!
Say it!
Nooooooo! Not the loogie of death!
Shay it!

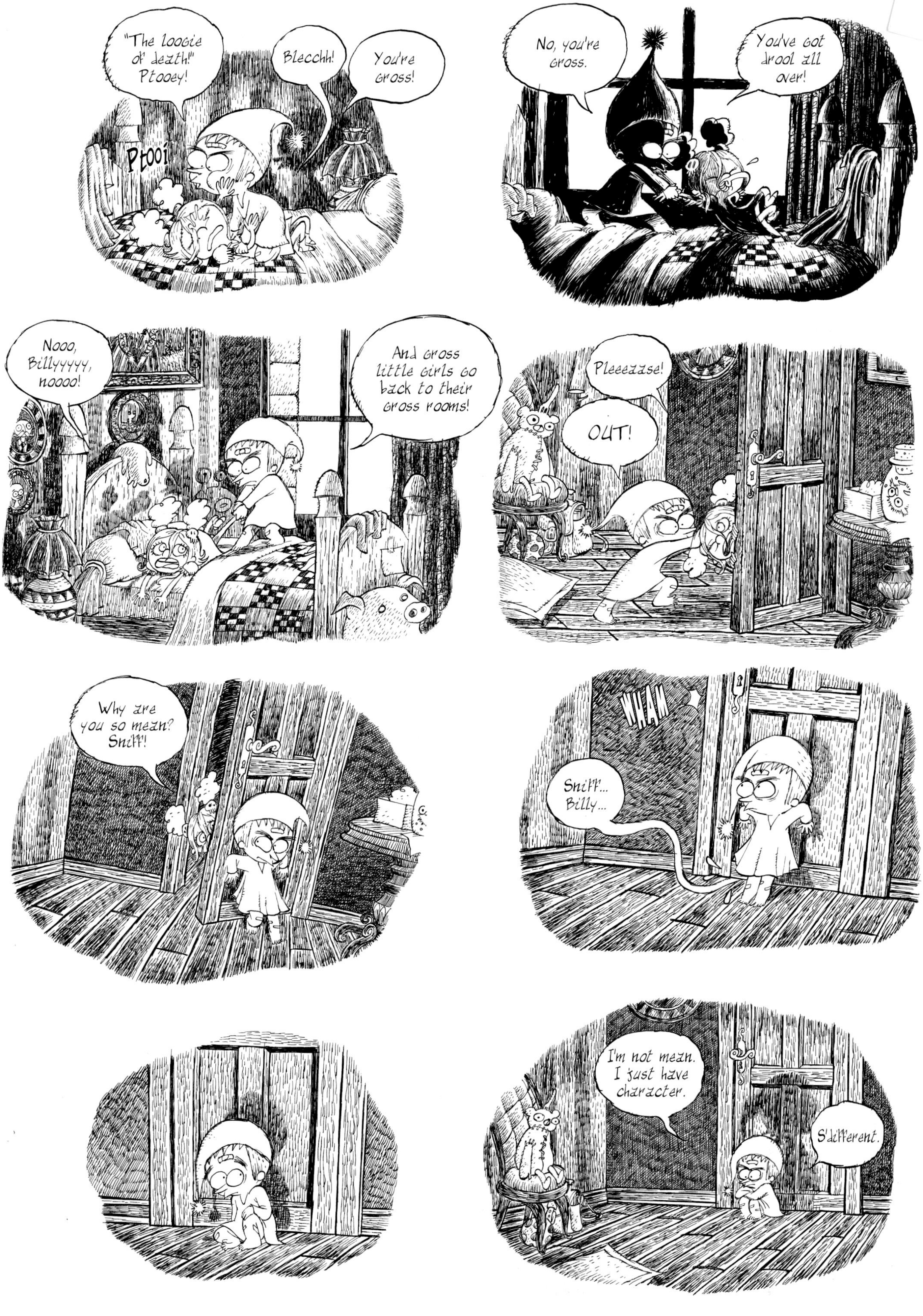
"The loogie of death!" Ptooey!
Ptooi
Blecchh!
You're gross!
No, you're gross.
You've got drool all over!
Nooo, Billyyyyy, noooo!
And gross little girls go back to their gross rooms!
Pleeeease!
OUT!
Why are you so mean? Sniff!
WHAM
Sniff... Billy...
I'm not mean. I just have character.
S'different.

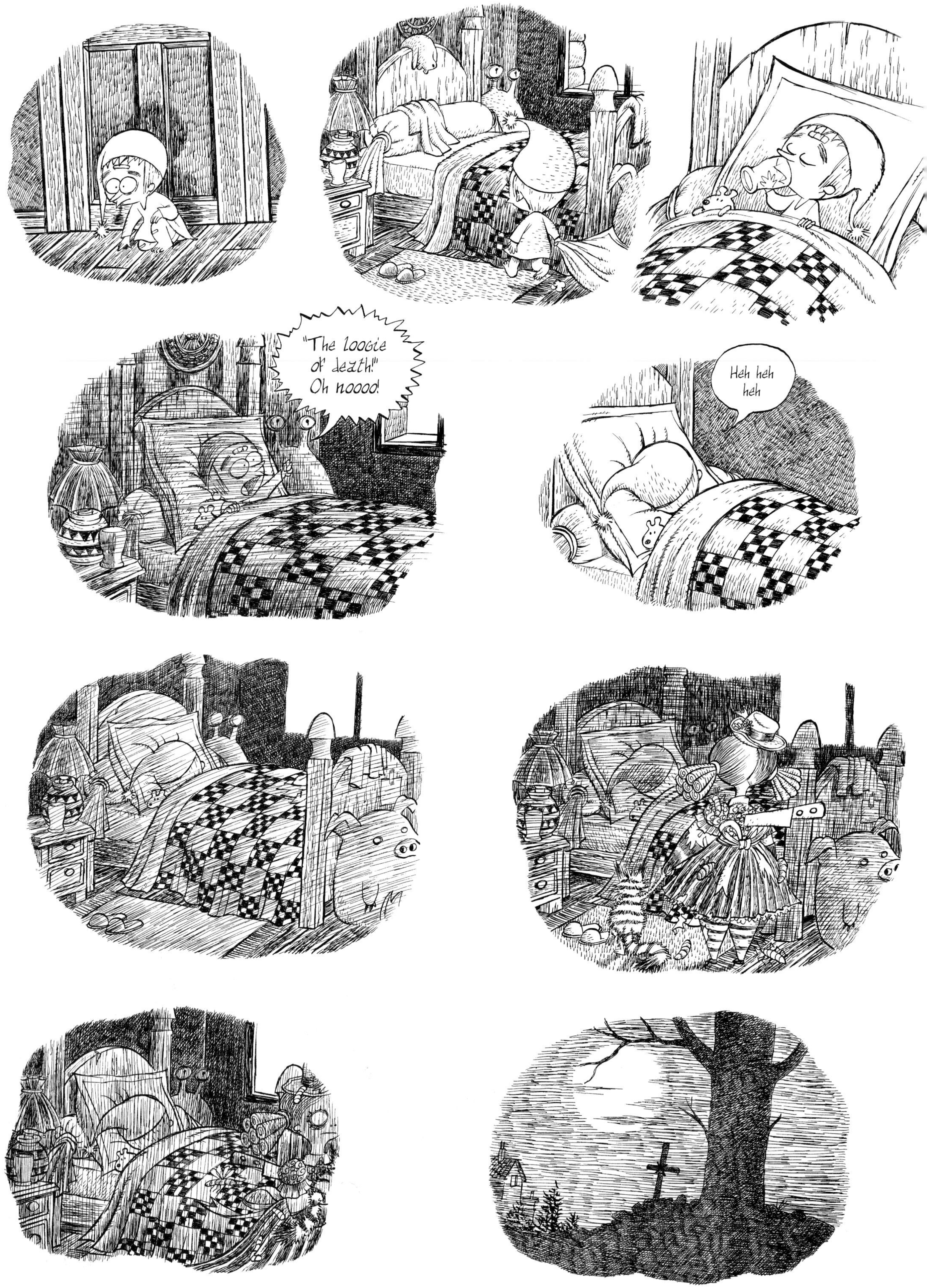
"The loogie of death!" Oh noooo!
Heh heh heh

 # Vermiculi

With a bit of luck, a dash of accident, and a good dose of foolhardiness, you can easily flush out a few on nights with a crescent moon, when the wind is in the East.

They are strange
two-headed snakes
(one head at each end).
One is male, the other female,
and it's impossible to tell them apart.

They live in holes in the mud,
in muddy streambeds,
well-hidden under rocks.

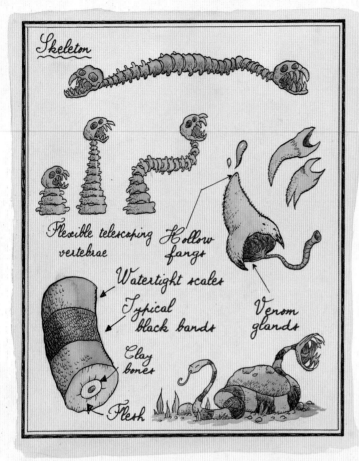

Skeleton

Flexible telescoping vertebrae

Hollow fangs

Watertight scales

Typical black bands

Venom glands

Clay bones

Flesh

But not just any rocks:
usually under big smooth ones,
which you will easily recognize
(they are covered in thick,
sickening greenish moss).

Fishing Equipment

Vermiculi eggs are hard to identify:
they look like tiny grayish pebbles,
and are bean-shaped,
a rough crescent with rounded ends.

Sickening moss

Bean-shaped egg

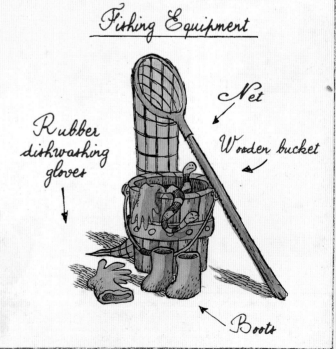

Rubber dishwashing gloves

Net

Wooden bucket

Boots

*When brewed in tea, they cure migraines,
soothe toothaches, and drive nightmares away.*

Smart Tips

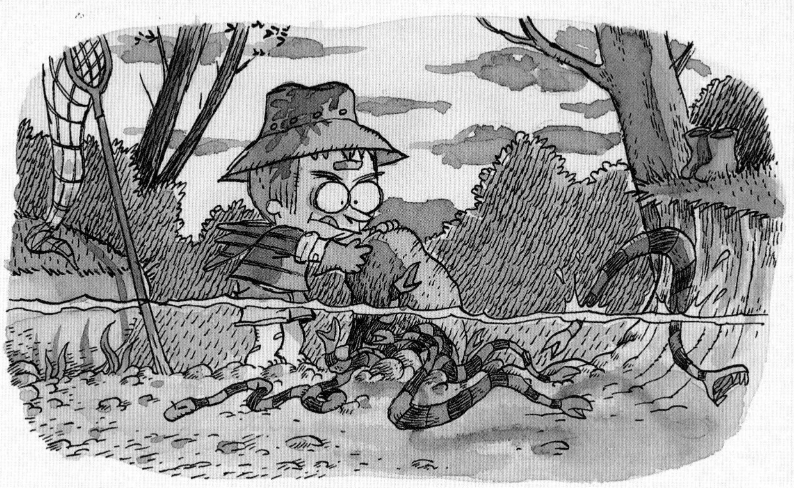

- Coat a Barbie® doll leg with extra-strong glue.

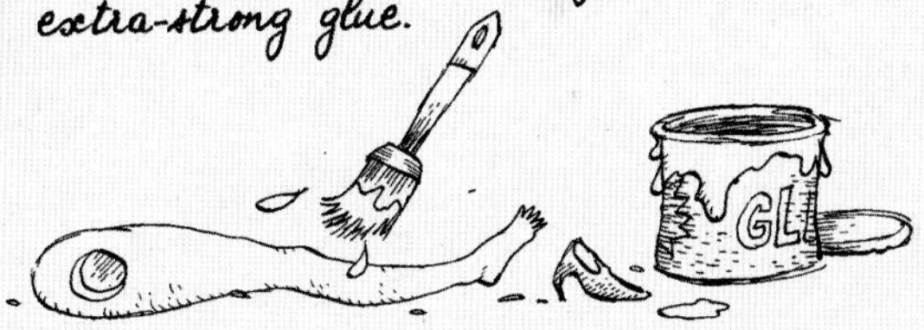

- Tie one end of it to your line.

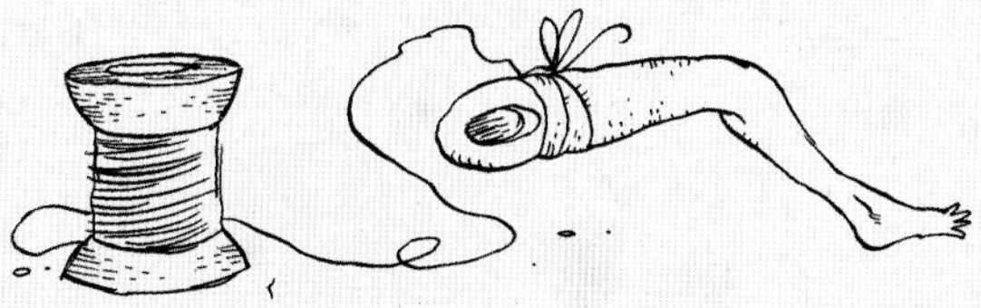

- Now you have formidably effective bait.

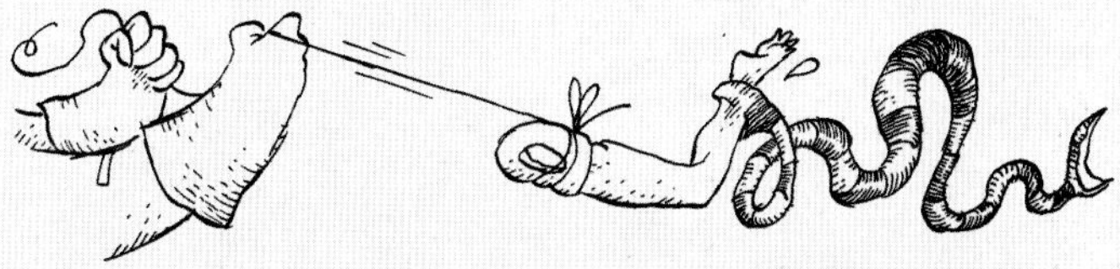

Special Recommendations

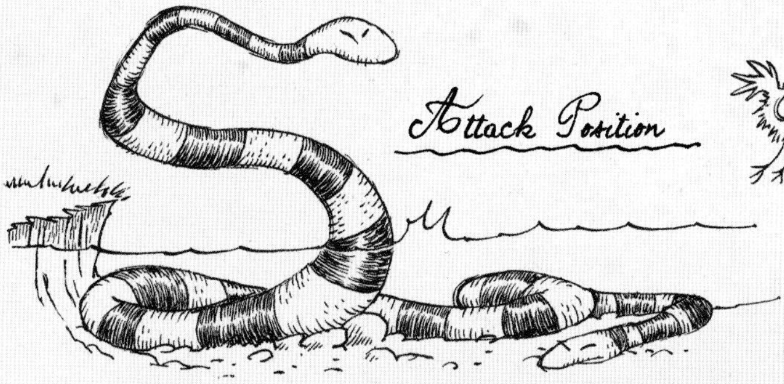
Attack Position

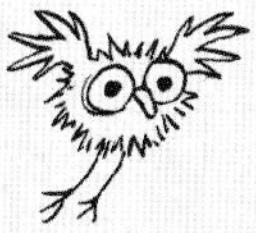

a) - Above all, don't forget your rubber boots! Vermiculi are ferocious and aggressive when defending their eggs!

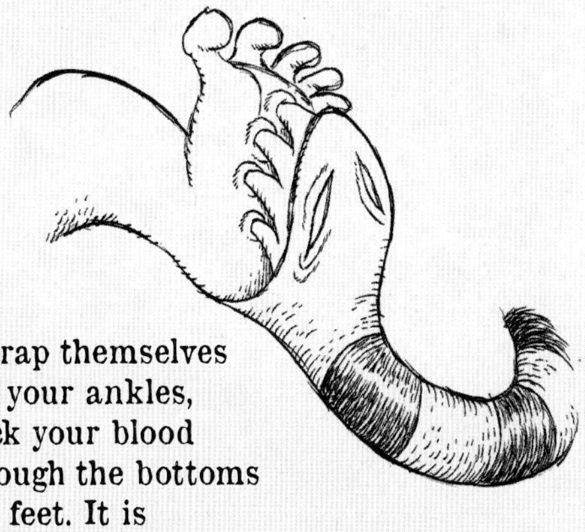

b) - They wrap themselves around your ankles, and suck your blood out through the bottoms of your feet. It is impossible to get them off with your bare hands.

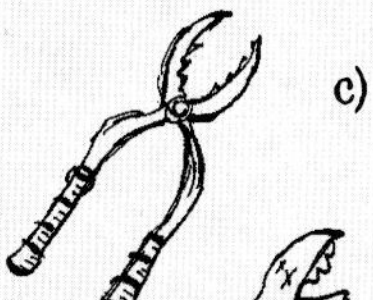

c) - Use large rusty pliers to cut off their heads. Their jaws will fall open.

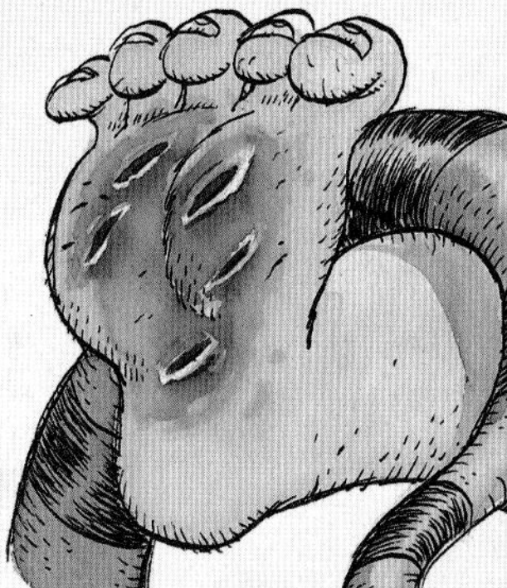

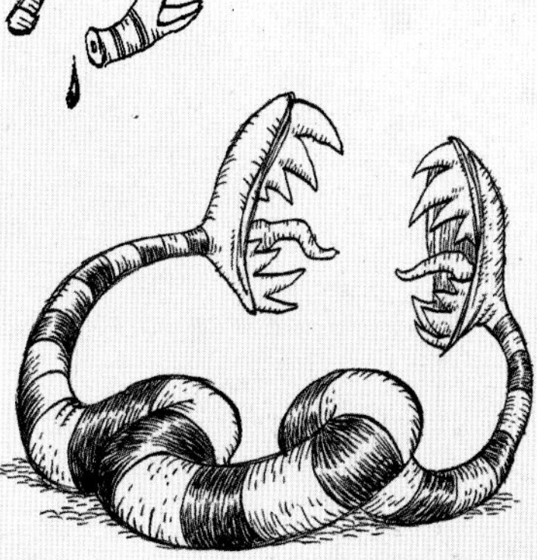

You will only have two hours to get them off. Otherwise, you will be doomed to walk around with weird wriggly shoes on for the rest of your life.

From the Curious and Bizarre Encyclopedia of Cryptozoology, by Billy Fog

Coleopedes

Insects of the family Culicidae, order Diptera, sub-order Nemacoptera, coleopedes are close cousins of the mosquito. Seemingly identical, they are different in every way!!!

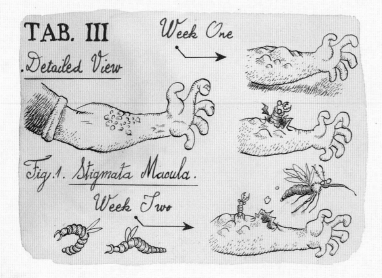

TAB. III
Detailed View

Week One

Fig. 1. Stigmata Macula.

Week Two

Though it too possesses membranous wings, its long snout (proboscis) is of the "sting-n'-lay" variety.

Nocturnal Insect

On summer nights, males lurk about our houses, looking to lay their eggs in a safe, warm spot: epidermis humanae!

- 1 -
Division of Labor

To help the females, males also lay eggs. This insect is a staunch supporter of equal rights between genders.

- 2 -
Parasites

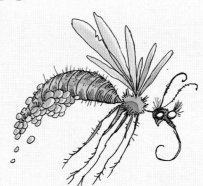

Once comfortably settled in under our skin, the little vampire-larva slakes their thirst on our venules. Thus we become wet nurses and carriers.

- 3 -
Egg-laying

Papa Coleopede ingurgitates his own eggs, and then, with his proboscis, injects them forcefully under the skin.

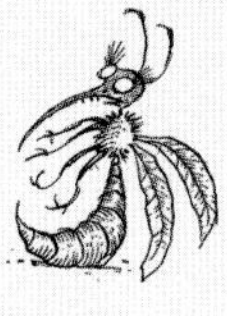

Feeding time for these little parasites may result in severe itching.

But have no fear! Although monstrous in appearance, Coleopede offspring are harmless.

Still, "extracutaneous" hatching can be a bit painful, and very disturbing (risk of high fever).

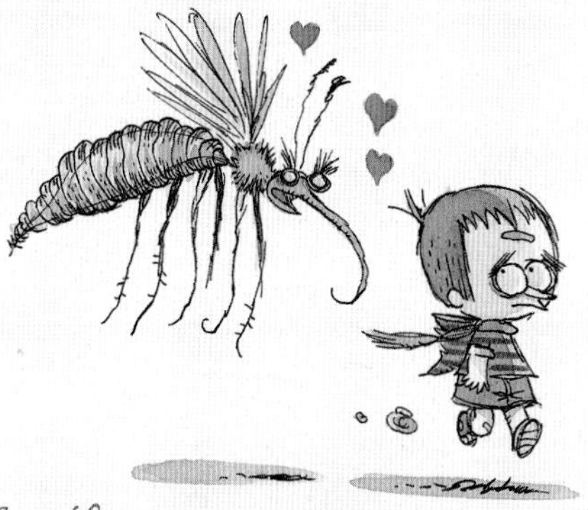

Fig 1. Somewhat embarrassed wetnurse-carriers.

Even after the eggs hatch, coleopedes remain true to their wet-nurse carriers for the remainder of their lives (1 to 2 months).

Deeply grateful, coleopedes will follow them absolutely everywhere!

Beware! Going to school followed by an enormous coleopede may prove a hindrance... especially in the bathroom!

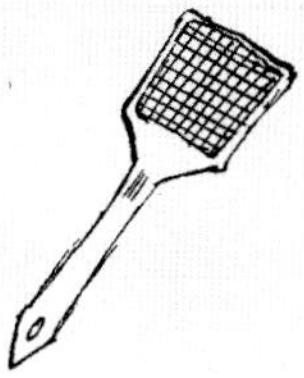

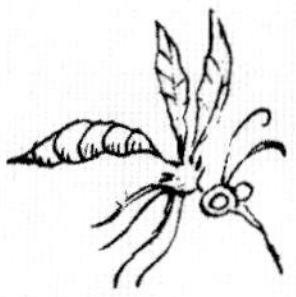

- How to Avoid This Inconvenience -

If you haven't the slightest maternal instinct, prevent bites by generously slathering your entire body in onion juice during the first weeks of June.

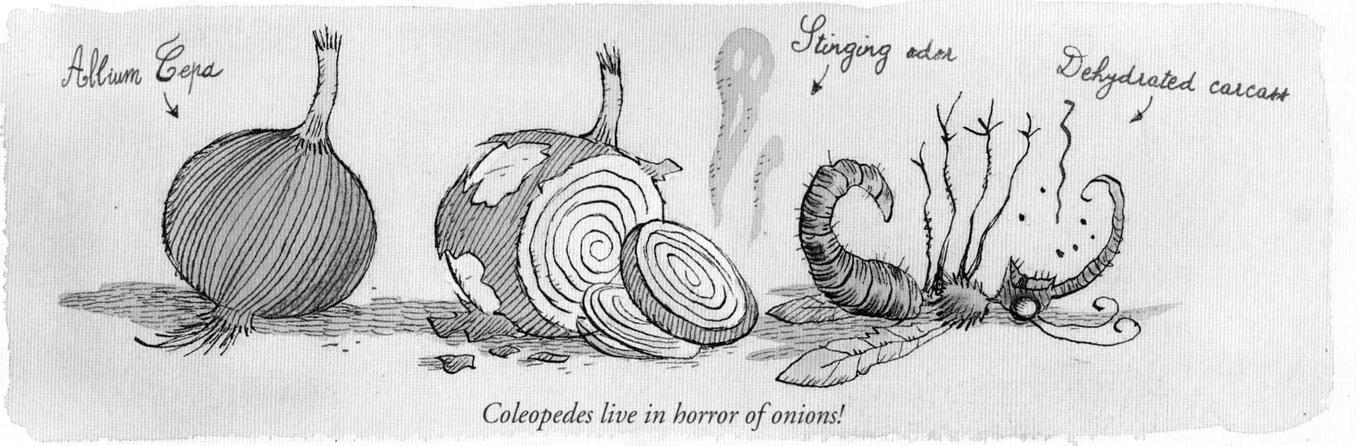
Allium Cepa
Stinging odor
Dehydrated carcass

Coleopedes live in horror of onions!

The onion's strong odor is an irritant that causes them to weep unconsolably for hours, thus draining them of all the water in their tiny bodies. Completely dehydrated, they pass away...

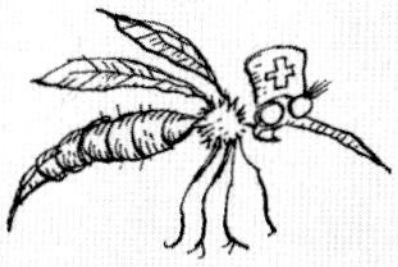

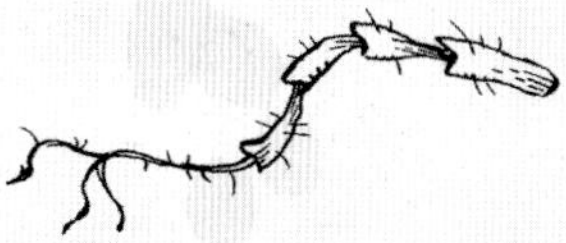

An Ounce of Prevention

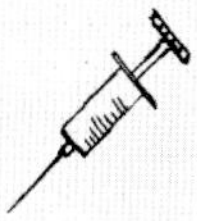

You are strongly advised against wearing red— it attracts them.

To protect yourself, place approximately twenty ripe tomatoes in a circle around your bed. This plant barrier will protect you from bites.

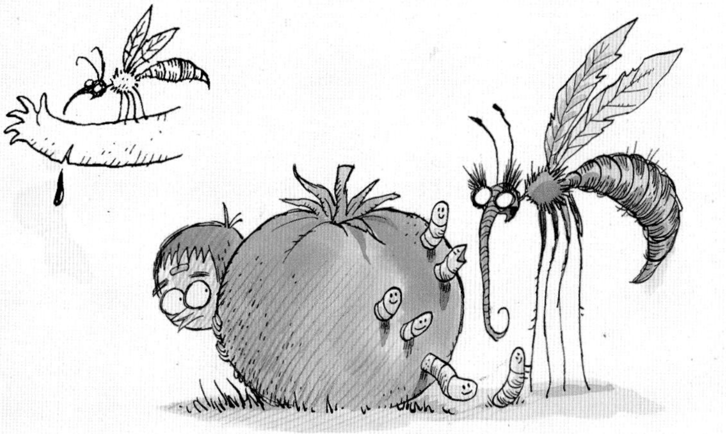

From the Curious and Bizarre Encyclopedia of Cryptozoology, by Billy Fog

Mortifera

Also known as "the devil's horns,"
the mortiferus (*Gastricum insectus mandibulae*)
is a polymorphic insect. Tiny but fearsome,
it proliferates in our vegetable gardens.

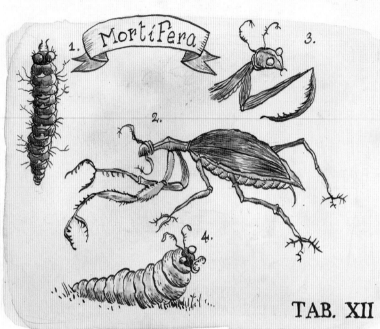

TAB. XII

1 - Microscopic pre-mutation state.
2 - Mature mortiferum with claws.
3 - Mortiferum with raptorial forelegs.
4 - Mortiferum larva.

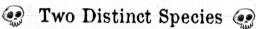

💀 Two Distinct Species 💀

- Mortifera with Claws

Their forelegs are terrifying weapons.
They can hack their victims into
tiny pieces in a few seconds,
for easier ingestion.
In fact, they have no jaws.

- Mortifera with Forelegs

They scythe away at their prey, cutting
the legs out from under them.
Their oral stingers are like sucking proboscises;
they drain their victims of gastric juices.

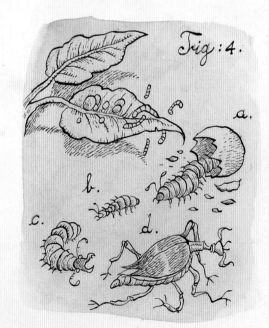

Fig : 4.

a) - Their microscopic eggs are usually found
on spinach leaves.

b) - When you eat spinach, the warmth of your body
will cause little white worms to hatch...

c) - When exposed to your gastric juices,
these little worms will become mortifera.

d) - A mortiferus egg not ingested by a human
and left in a garden will, after seven days, give
rise to a "cutiferum", more commonly known
as a "praying mantis."

Mortifera scour our stomach walls for months, and then take on the appearance of moths. We expel them through our mouths or noses when sneezing.

Fig : 1. *Fig : 2.*

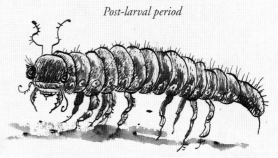

Post-larval period

 Useful Tip

To remain in good health, avoid placing your hand in front of your mouth when you sneeze, the better to rid yourself of these noxious parasites.

You will no doubt be considered ill-mannered, but at least you will be healthy, and never in danger of bellyaches.

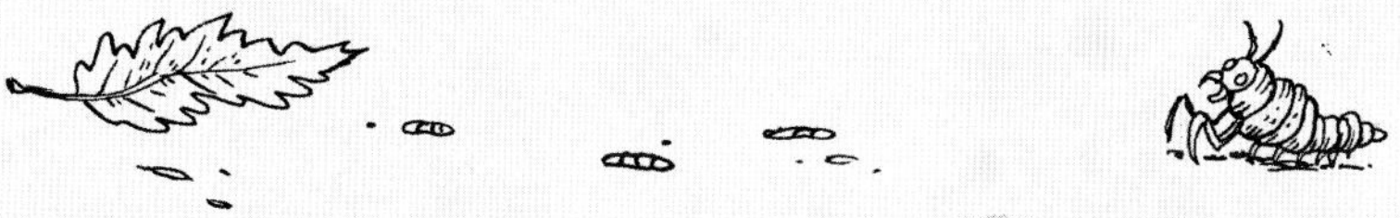

The young mortiferus will soon change, opting either for claws or raptorial forelegs.

Mortiferus developmental process in the digestive tract.

Fig : 3

The shells of their larvae are made of iron molecules.

This is what gives spinach its terrible bitter taste.

Careless, ignorant parents force their children to eat it...

But never fear: a nice thyme infusion will destroy them straightaway.

Then you will expel their dead bodies with a few burps.

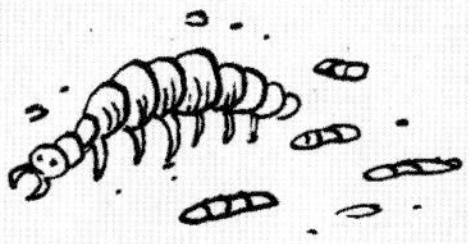

How to Observe Them

Although you can't see them, you can quite easily hear them...

After a big meal, get comfortable in front of the TV, right by your dad.

Press your ear to his big ol' potbelly.

"Boik!" "Gloop!" If you hear strange gurgling sounds...

...then you're probably listening to

a mortiferus feast!

From the Curious and Bizarre Encyclopedia of Cryptozoology, by Billy Fog

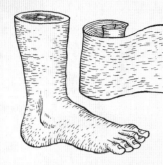

The Game of Billyfoot

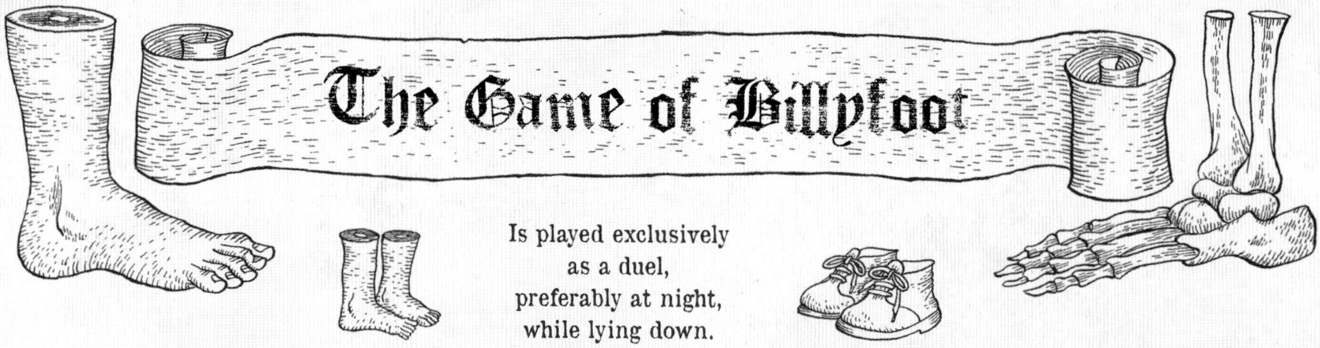

Is played exclusively
as a duel,
preferably at night,
while lying down.

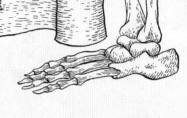

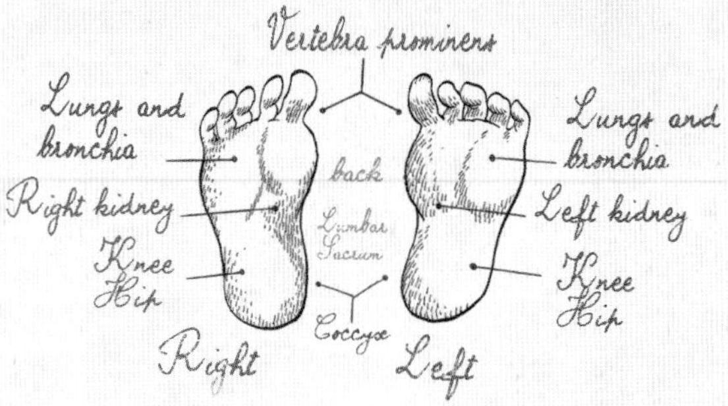

Vertebra prominens

Lungs and bronchia   *Lungs and bronchia*

Right kidney   *back*   *Left kidney*

Lumbar Sacrum

Knee   *Knee*
Hip   *Hip*

Coccyx

Right   *Left*

BENEFITS:

Playing the game of "Billyfoot" on a regular or daily basis stimulates various pressure points on the bottom of your foot, insuring health and well-being.

- Rules -

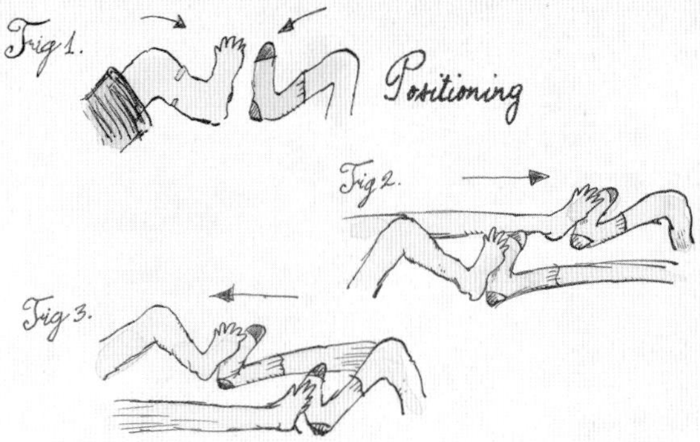

1 - Place the bottoms of your bare feet (socks are also permitted) against your opponent's.

2 - Starting position:
older player's left leg bent, older player's right leg straight.

3 - Object: push hard enough to bend both your opponent's legs. In case of foot slippage, resume the starting position, and reset score to zero.

4 - The first player to get the most points wins.

Fig.1   *Positioning*

Fig.2

Fig.3

- Winner's Prize -

The loser must obey the winner for an entire day, from the first glimmers of dawn to sunset. The loser must be utterly devoted, and obey all the winner's wishes without complaint, on pain of burning in hell for all eternity.

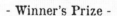

SPECIAL TIPS:

a) *Playing "Billyfoot" with an older brother is highly discouraged, especially one with malicious intent.*
b) *Best played, if possible, with a fragile and impressionable younger sister.*

The Super Hoodie

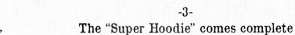

-1-
Knitted with yarn spun
from an Ophiuchus cocoon.
(Which account for the horizontal stripes.)

Fig: 1.

Fig: 2.

-2-
The "Super Hoodie" isn't scratchy.
It cannot be torn or pierced,
and is immune to wear and tear.
(Stains just slide right off it.)

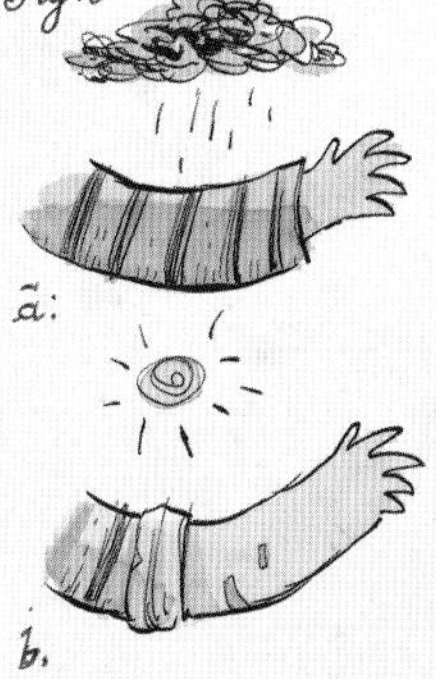

Fig: 3

-3-
The "Super Hoodie" comes complete
with a super hood
that protects from rain, snow, and cold.
(When you're hot, you can roll up the sleeves of the "Super Hoodie."
And roll them back down when you're cold!)

a:

b.

-4-
The super hood makes you invisible.

Fig: 5.

Fig: 4.

-5-
It also serves as a
backpack or pocket
when your pants
pockets are full.

-6-
It can turn into a cape, to help
you run faster..

Fig: 6.

-7-
It commands the winds, to help
you fly higher.

Fig: 7.

-8-
Lastly, the super hood allows the "Super
Hoodie" to be hung on the coat rack.

Cool!

They call me Billy Fog.
I like night and solitude, rain and melancholy...

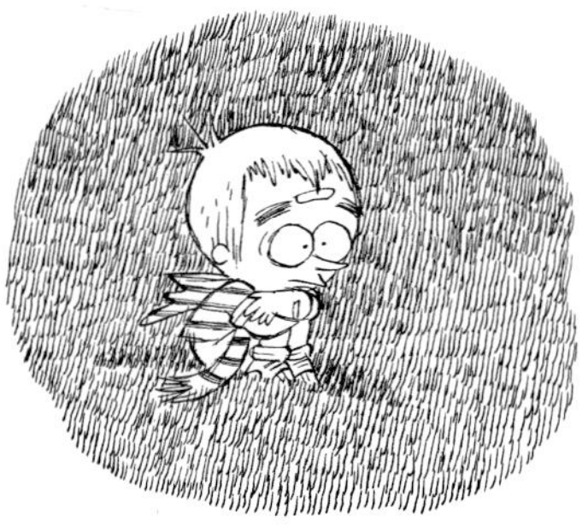

But I'm scared of death.

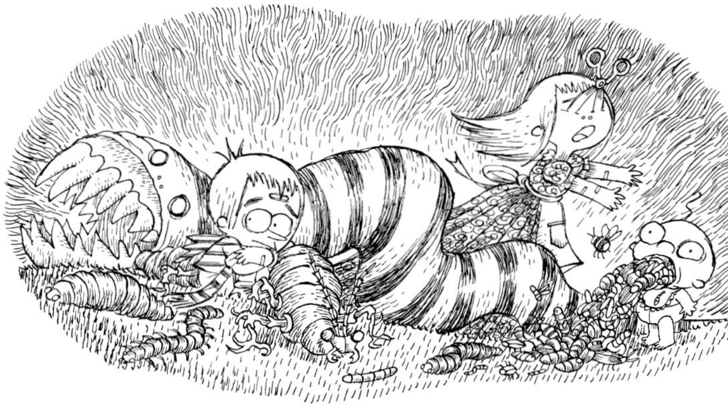

Why'd Tarzan have to go away?

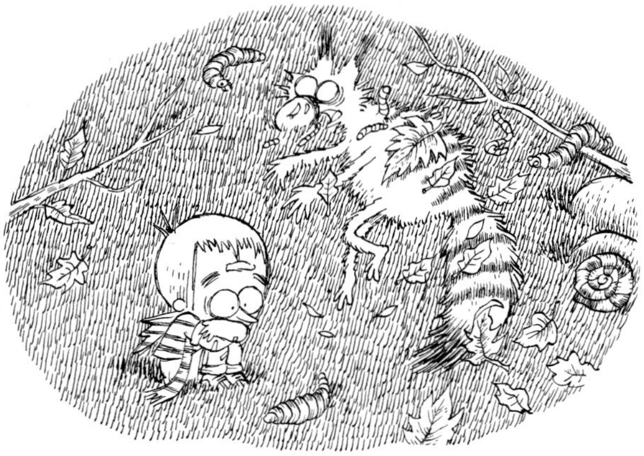

It's so mysterious! No one really knows what it is.

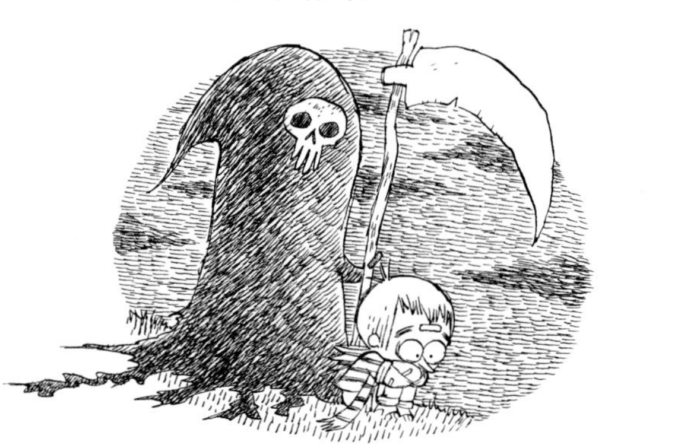

That's what's so terrifying.

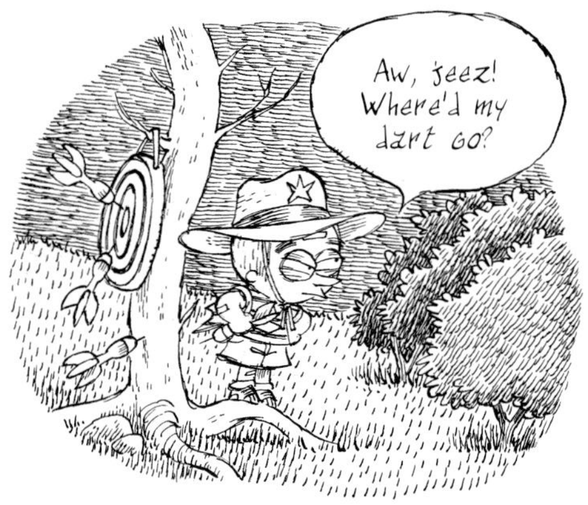
Aw, jeez! Where'd my dart go?

Plus, to tell the truth... death's never very pretty.

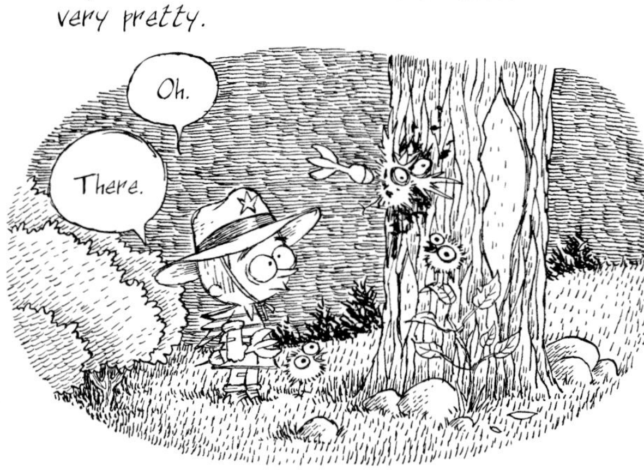
Oh.
There.

In theory, old people are closer to death than we are. Sometimes, they smell weird...

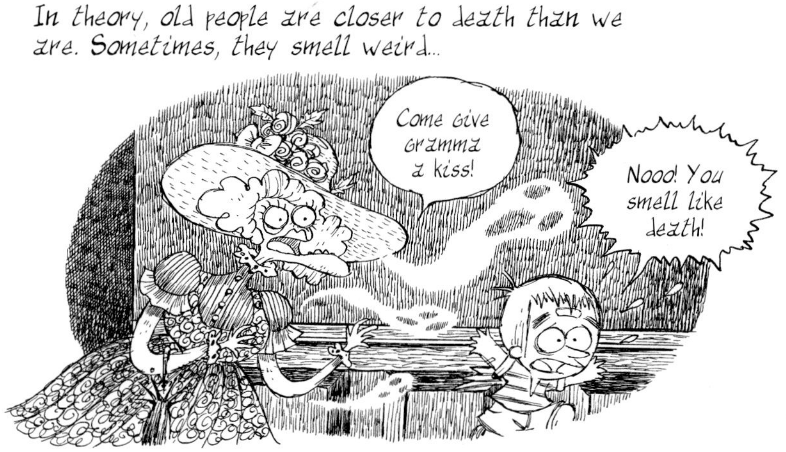
Come give gramma a kiss!
Nooo! You smell like death!

A smell like a warning that seems to say:

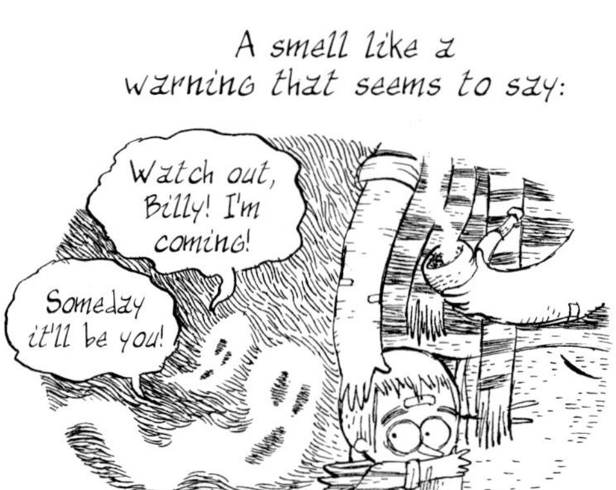
Watch out, Billy! I'm coming!
Someday it'll be you!

What does it look like? It has many faces. It's fiendishly inventive.

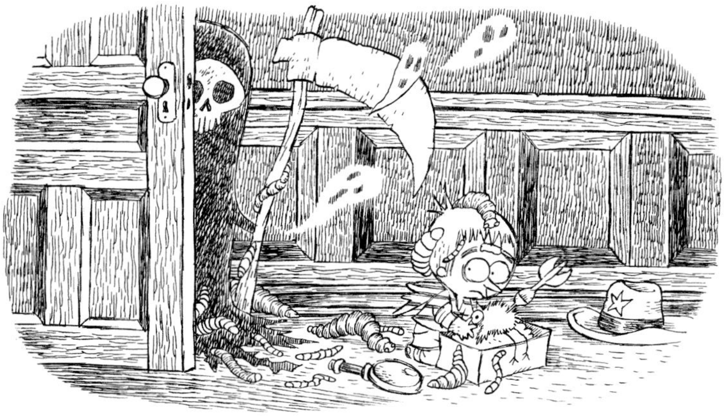

Sometimes it's a big white worm, plump and soft.

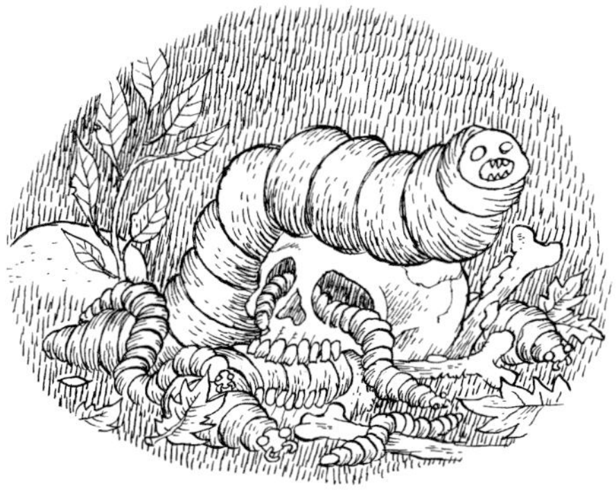

Or the sad swinging of a hangman's rope.

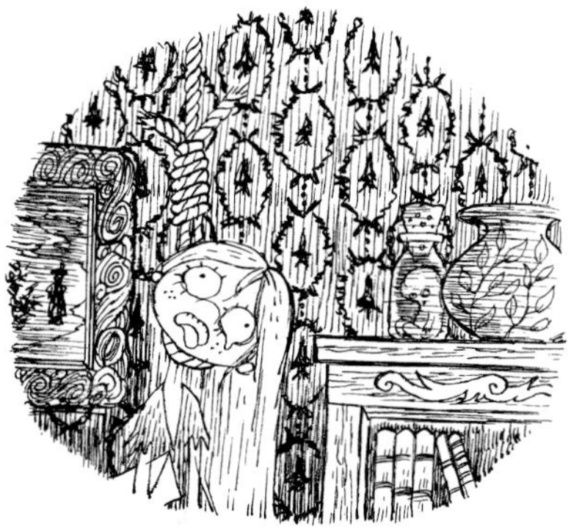

Sometimes it's a blazing fire, and swirling ashes.

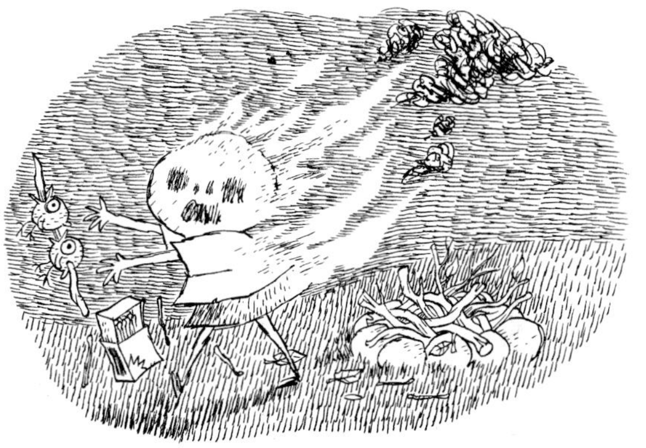

Or a sinister accident and a split skull.

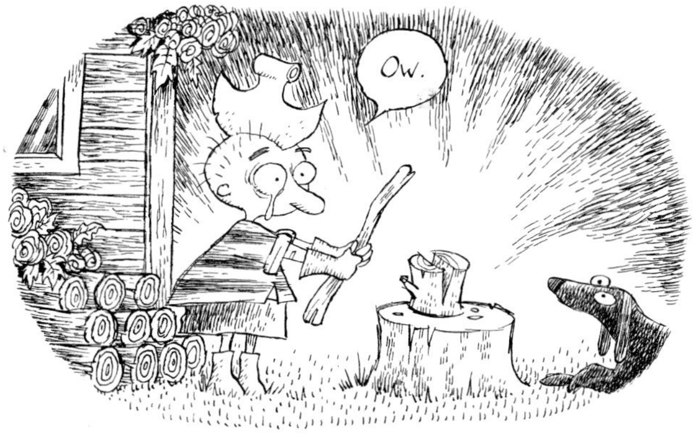
Ow.

Is death sneaky? It sleeps in all of us.

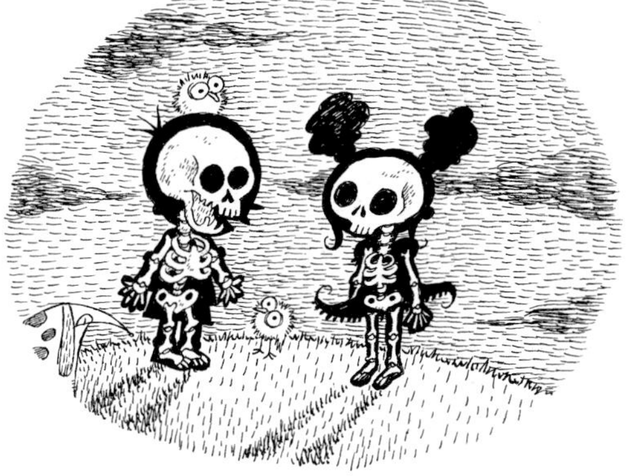

Like a growing larva that will leave its cocoon when the time comes.

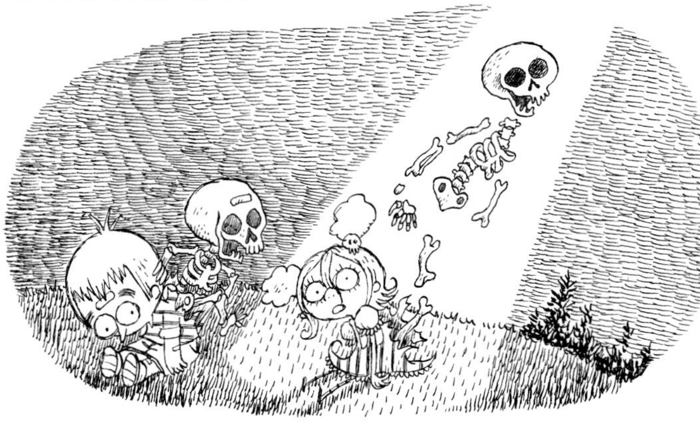

It can come for you at anytime: big or little, young or old, good or evil.

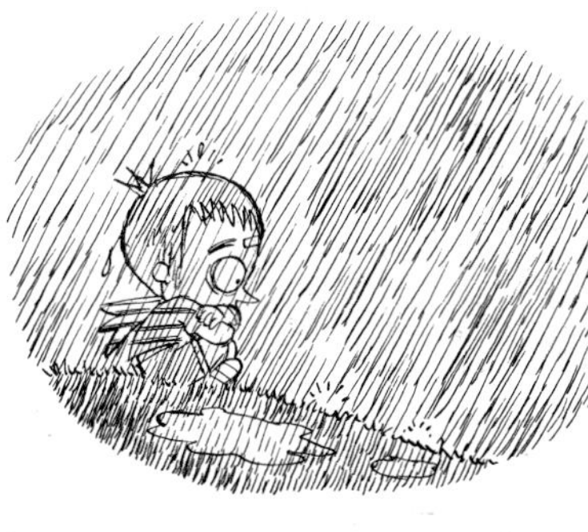

We are all equal in the face of death.

The Little Knife Girl

or
the true story of Mary Emily James

Do you know the story
of Mary Emily James,
"the little knife girl"?

She was born quite long ago,
in a peaceful little town.

They say she would have been the most
unremarkable little girl if, upon emerging
from her mother's belly,
she hadn't pulled a knife out of nowhere
and tried to disfigure her wet nurse.

Mary Emmy was immediately
put in an orphanage.
But her misdeeds didn't stop there…

She was often found
in the kitchen, curled up
in a drawer, among enormous knives
with razor-sharp blades.

Dreadful murders became
a daily obsession for little Mary.
She butchered as others breathe:
slowly, calmly, constantly.

When other children
were still playing with dolls or marbles,
she was playing with knives.

Monday: the neighbor's dog.
Tuesday: the gardener's cat.
Wednesday: the gardener. Thursday…

It was too much. Infuriated by the atrocities,
the director of the orphanage
abandoned her, without regrets, atop a hill
while she was sleeping.

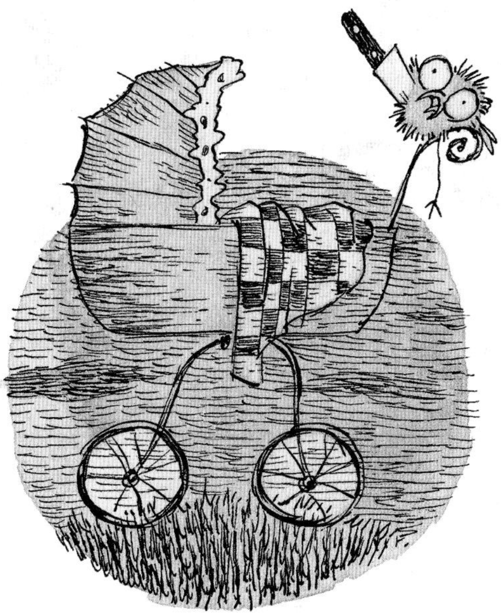

But Mary Emily James fascinated people
as much as she terrified them.
The next morning, she was discreetly taken in
by Professor MacPetterson,
an eminent expert in "maniac psychiatry."

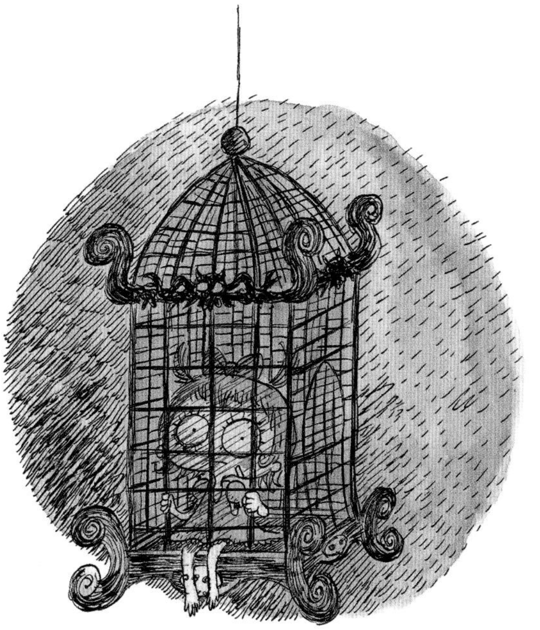

No scientist could ever hope to find
a better subject for study!
What curious composure!
What an unfathomable obsession!

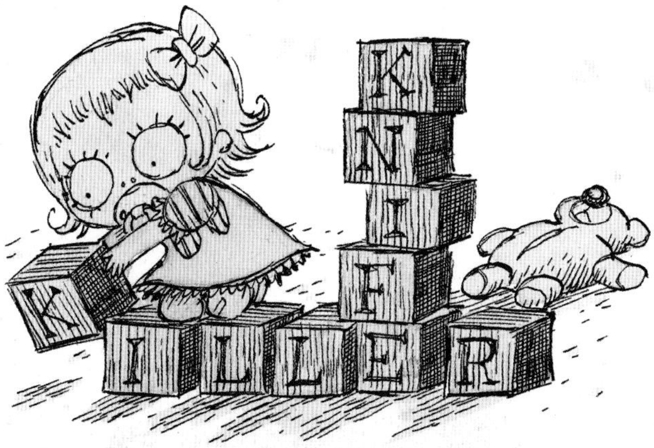
KNIFE
KILLER

The little killer was very quiet and cooperative.
In the mornings, she carried out
her theory exercises diligently.

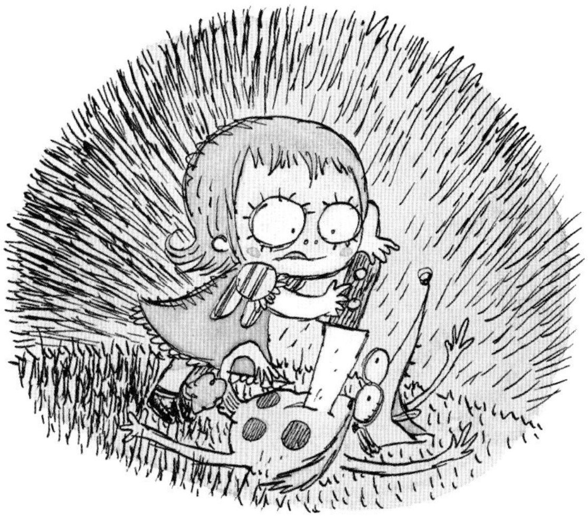

And in the afternoon, applied herself feverishly
to more practical activities.

At Sunday dinner, she would
always carve the chicken.
MacPetterson was quite proud
of his little guinea pig.

And although he experienced a few
harmless little run-ins with her,
he grew fond of her and, with time,
came to think of her as a daughter.

The years went by.
Mary Emmy became a pretty young woman,
with no shortage of suitors.

But she was shy and reserved,
and really quite difficult.

Patrick was far too foolish,
with bad breath to boot.

Wigbert was handsome,
but talked too much.

Percy was quieter,
but his slight squint annoyed her.

Peter was too tall.

Tobias, too fat.

Wigram, too thin.

And Graham, too ugly.

But Charles-Philbert was perfect!
Mary had found her cup of tea at last!
Love! An entirely new feeling for her!

Mary, pathologically shy,
was overcome with hysterical joy,
and chanced to declare her love with a
clumsy, unconsidered gesture.

For the first time in her short life,
Mary Emily James wept.

She wept so hard, so long,
that she had no more tears left.

Guilty and despairing, she sought to punish herself,
and began to scarify herself, carving the sweet name
of her lost love into her flesh.

"C-H-A-R-L-E-S – P-H-I-L-B-E-R-T":
quite a long name for such a short arm!
Mary Emmy fell dead from blood loss
before even finishing the first "L."

Crazed with grief, Professor MacPetterson
made a cross from two knives.

And the next day died too,
while showering her little grave
with roses red as blood.

Impetuous night lovers,
if one summer's eve…

On a walk in the dark
you should perchance perceive…

At the small of your back
A thing like a prickle
Whilst a bright drop of scarlet
Wells towards a trickle…

Pray that it's just
a ravenous skeeter
Pray it's no sharpened
ice-cold boy skewer…

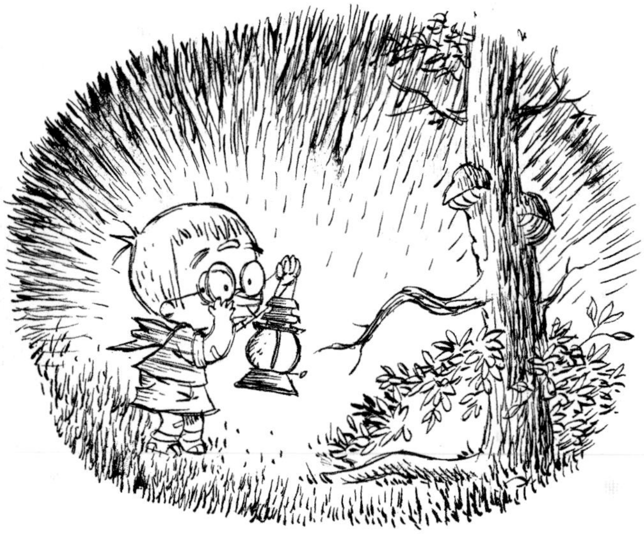

Pray it's a sharp poking branch
that's to blame...

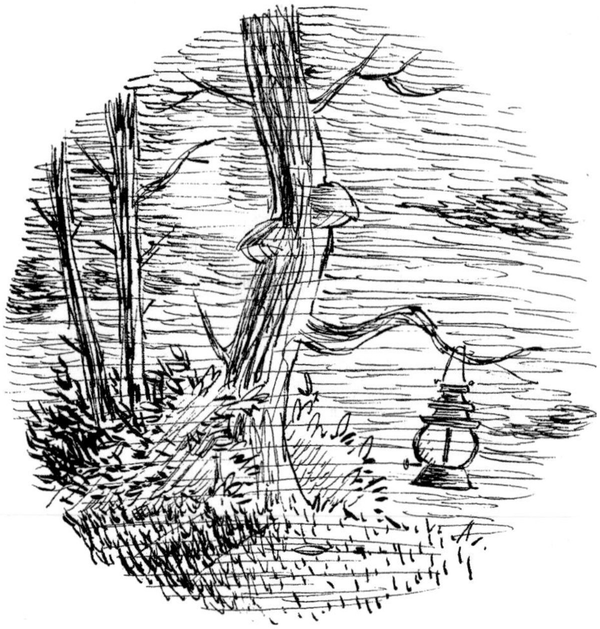

And not the wee murderess,
Mary Emily James...

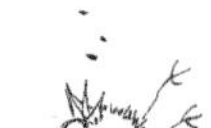

The End

The little vampiress
who didn't want to hurt anyone

In the depths of the shadows
Where shineth no light
Seemed to hover two arrows
Tipped with arrowheads bright.

Whetted ivory incisors,
No arrowheads they,
I was left none the wiser
For their turning away.

The pale creature had spared us
Her dagger-sharp bite
And with fleetness nefarious
Had taken her flight.

Pacifist vampire!
Heaven thanks thee.
Your restraint we admire,
For leaving us be.

Neither human nor mammal
Have your fangs led astray
But their pearly enamel
Never will stay.

Hunger will rack you
When your discipline fails
Your own hand you'll gnaw
through
To your own entrails.

On the floor you expire
Blood seeps from your limbs.

Your presence, O' vampire

In memory dims.

"In the depths of the shadows,
where shineth no light, seemed to hover two arrows,
tipped with arrowheads bright."

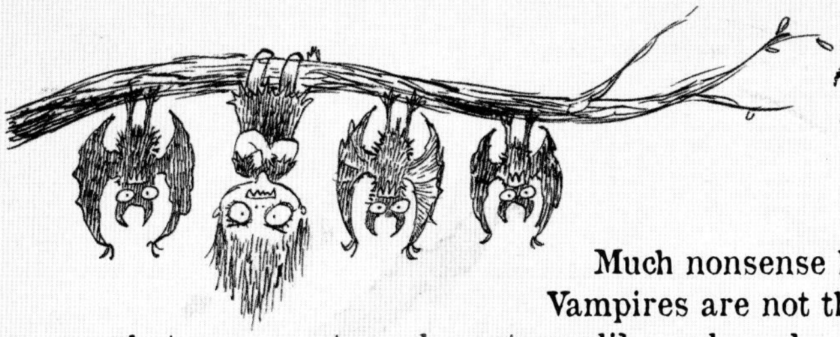

Vampires

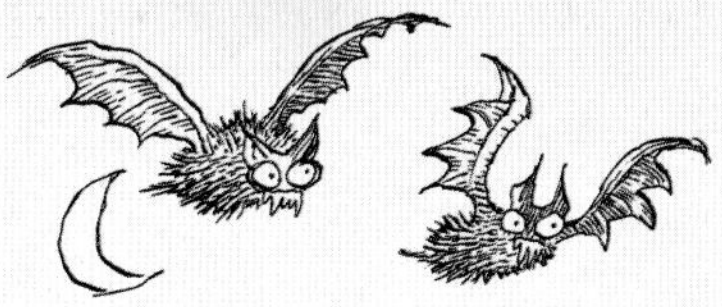

Much nonsense has been bandied about on the subject.
Vampires are not the much maligned abominations of legend, but mere nocturnal creatures like owls and possums. They are narcissistic, love looking at themselves in the mirror, collect crucifixes, and go crazy for garlic dishes.

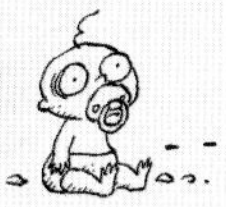

ORIGINS

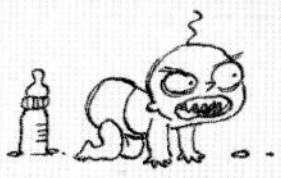

- They say restless children who refuse to go to bed on time will grow up to become compulsive noctambulists, and then, bit by bit, little vampires allergic to the light of day.
- Vampires prefer cozy wardrobes to dusty coffins.

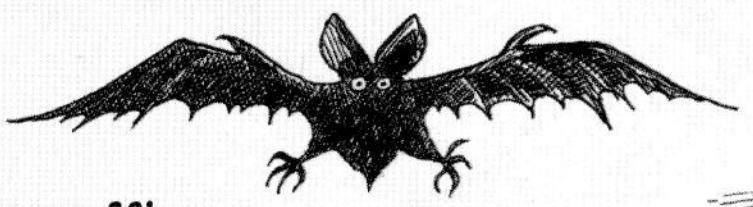

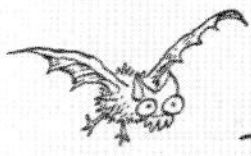

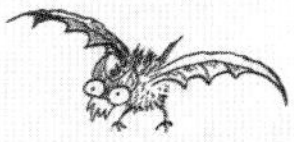

Beware

Never surround yourself with garlic cloves!
Contrary to common wisdom, this attracts them!
Garlic is their FAVORITE CANDY…

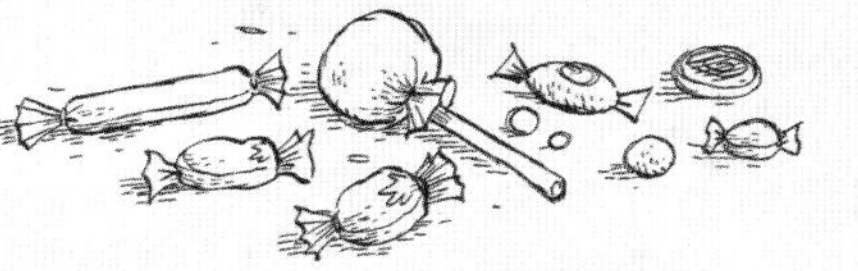

Fig.1

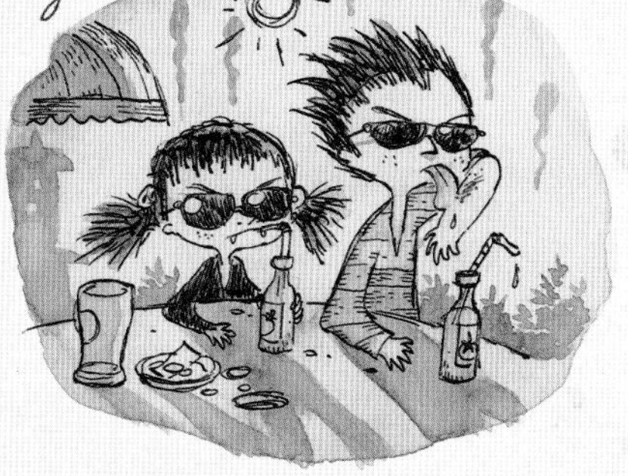

A) How to recognize them

They are pale, dressed in black head to toe, wear large sunglasses, and drink tomato juice.

Their breath smells strongly of garlic, and they can't keep from licking their scabs.

Their prominent canines, and their incisors, which cause them to LISP…

B) Are They Evil?

Not any more than most humans...
In case of danger, the best weapons remain altruism and generosity.
When you meet vampires, make friends:
stick out your hand and give them a drink from your wrist.

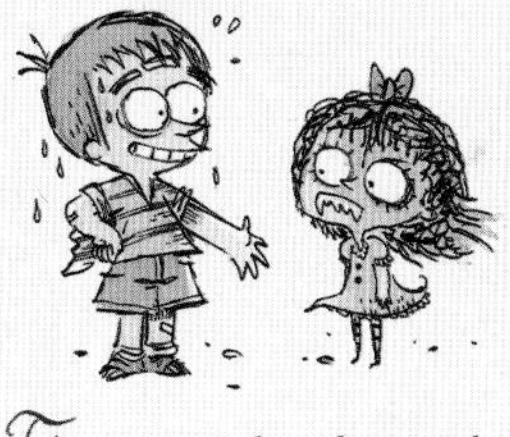

Fig.2 *– Relaxed attitude.*

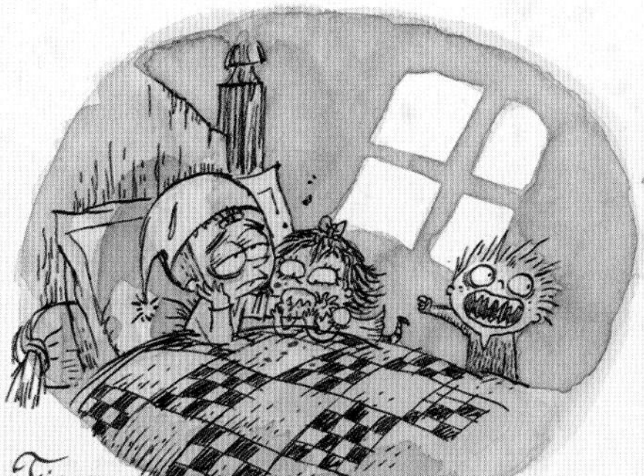

Fig.3

- Vampires are very faithful friends.

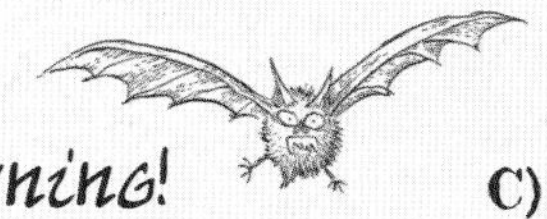

Warning!

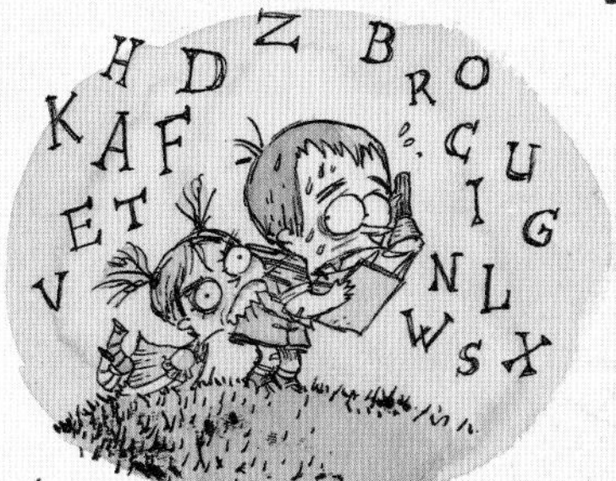

Fig.4

To prevent infection from a vampire bite, say the alphabet three times backwards.

C) How to Defend Yourself Against an Evil Vampire

- The best defense is a good offense: attack! Bite first!
- Then they'll turn back into normal humans like you and me, but they won't be any less dangerous...

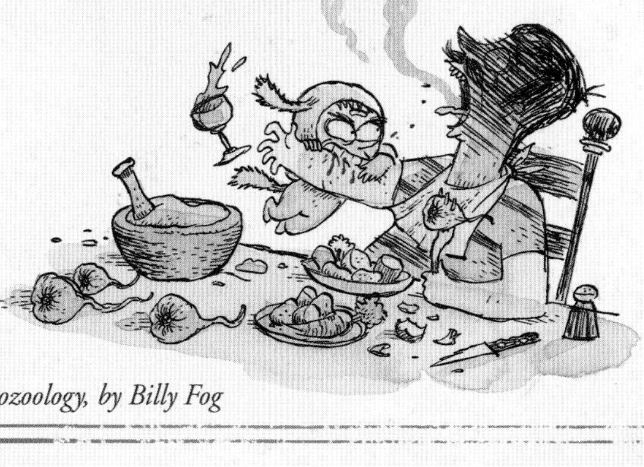

From the Curious and Bizarre Encyclopedia of Cryptozoology, by Billy Fog

The night

I love the night with passion.
I love it the way you love
your country, or your mistress—
with an instinctive love,
a deep, invincible love.

I love it with all my senses:
with my eyes that see it,
with my nose that breathes it,
with my ears, which hear its
silence,

with all my flesh, which its shadows caress.

Larks sing in the sun,

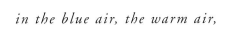

in the blue air, the warm air,

the light air of clear mornings.

But the owl flees through in the night,

a black spot crossing black space,

and joyously, exhilarated by the vast blackness,

lets out his vibrant, sinister cry.

The day fatigues and bores me.
It is ruthless and brutal, boisterous, cruel, raucous

I get up with difficulty,
I get dressed wearily,

I go out regretfully,
and every step, every movement,

every gesture, every word,

every thought exhausts me

as if I were lifting a crushing burden.

But when the sun sets,
a bewildered joy,
a joy from every part of my being
fills me.

I wake up; I come to life.

As the shadows grow,
I feel utterly different,
younger, stronger,

more alert,

happier.

I watch it grow thicker,
the vast, gentle dark that falls
from the sky.

It drowns the city,
an elusive,
inscrutable
wave,

it hides, expunges,
obliterates colors,
shapes;
embraces houses,
monuments,
and living things

with its imperceptible touch.

*Then I want to hoot for joy
like an owl,*

*to dash across the rooftops
like a cat,*

*and an impassioned,
invincible desire to love
lights up in my veins.*

From "Night: A Nightmare," by Guy de Maupassant, 1891.

There's one super power I've always dreamed of having: the ability to turn myself into a skeleton.

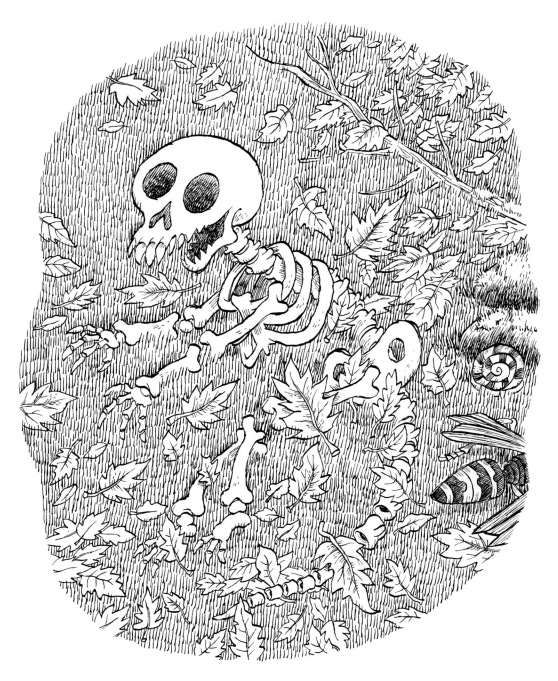

The thought of someday having to do this doesn't exactly fill me with joy...

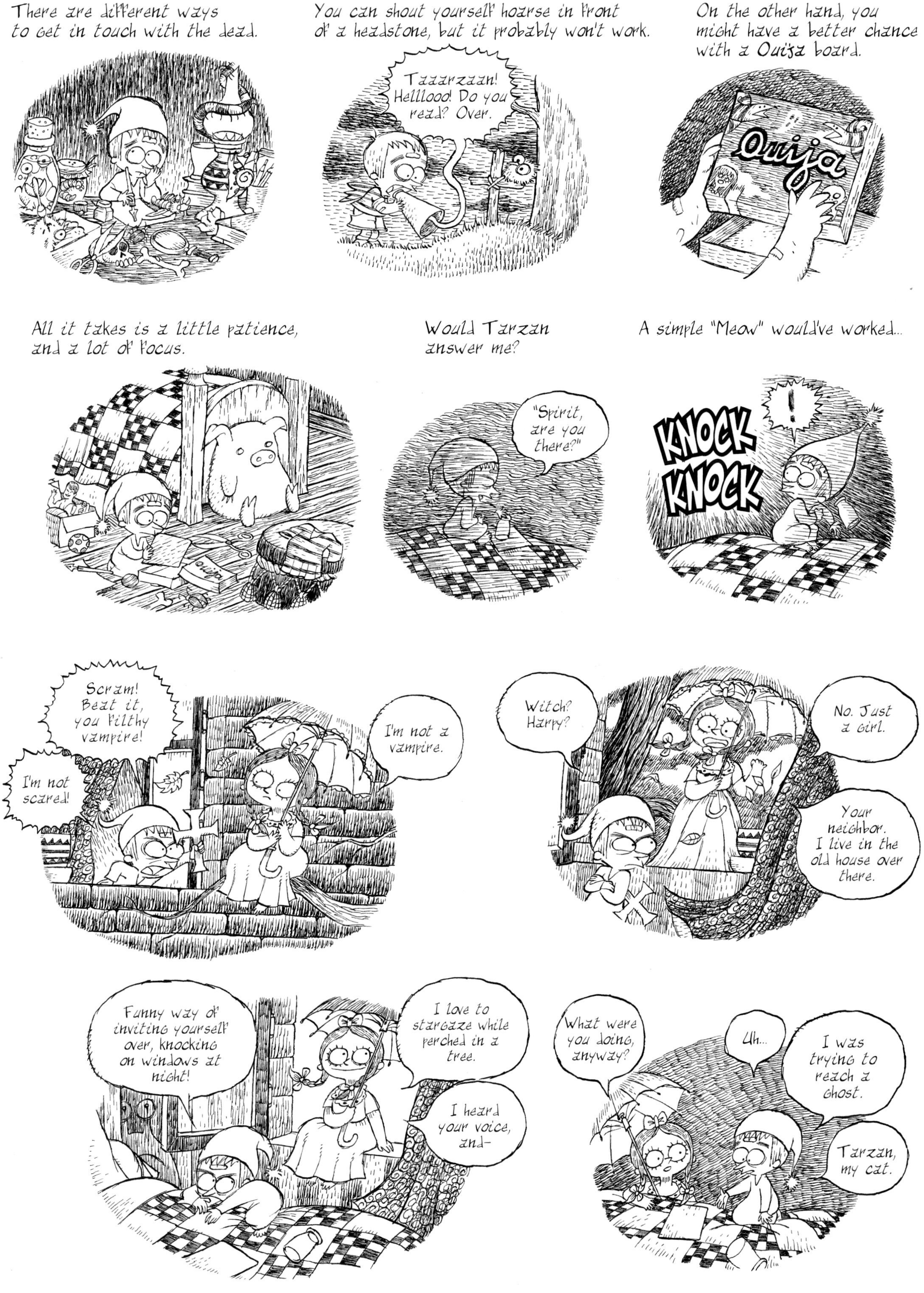
There are different ways to get in touch with the dead.
You can shout yourself hoarse in front of a headstone, but it probably won't work.
Taaarzaan! Hellllooo! Do you read? Over.
On the other hand, you might have a better chance with a Ouija board.
Ouija
All it takes is a little patience, and a lot of focus.
Ouija
Would Tarzan answer me?
"Spirit, are you there?"
A simple "Meow" would've worked...
!
KNOCK KNOCK
Scram! Beat it, you filthy vampire!
I'm not scared!
I'm not a vampire.
Witch? Harpy?
No. Just a girl.
Your neighbor. I live in the old house over there.
Funny way of inviting yourself over, knocking on windows at night!
I love to stargaze while perched in a tree.
I heard your voice, and-
What were you doing, anyway?
Uh...
I was trying to reach a ghost.
Tarzan, my cat.

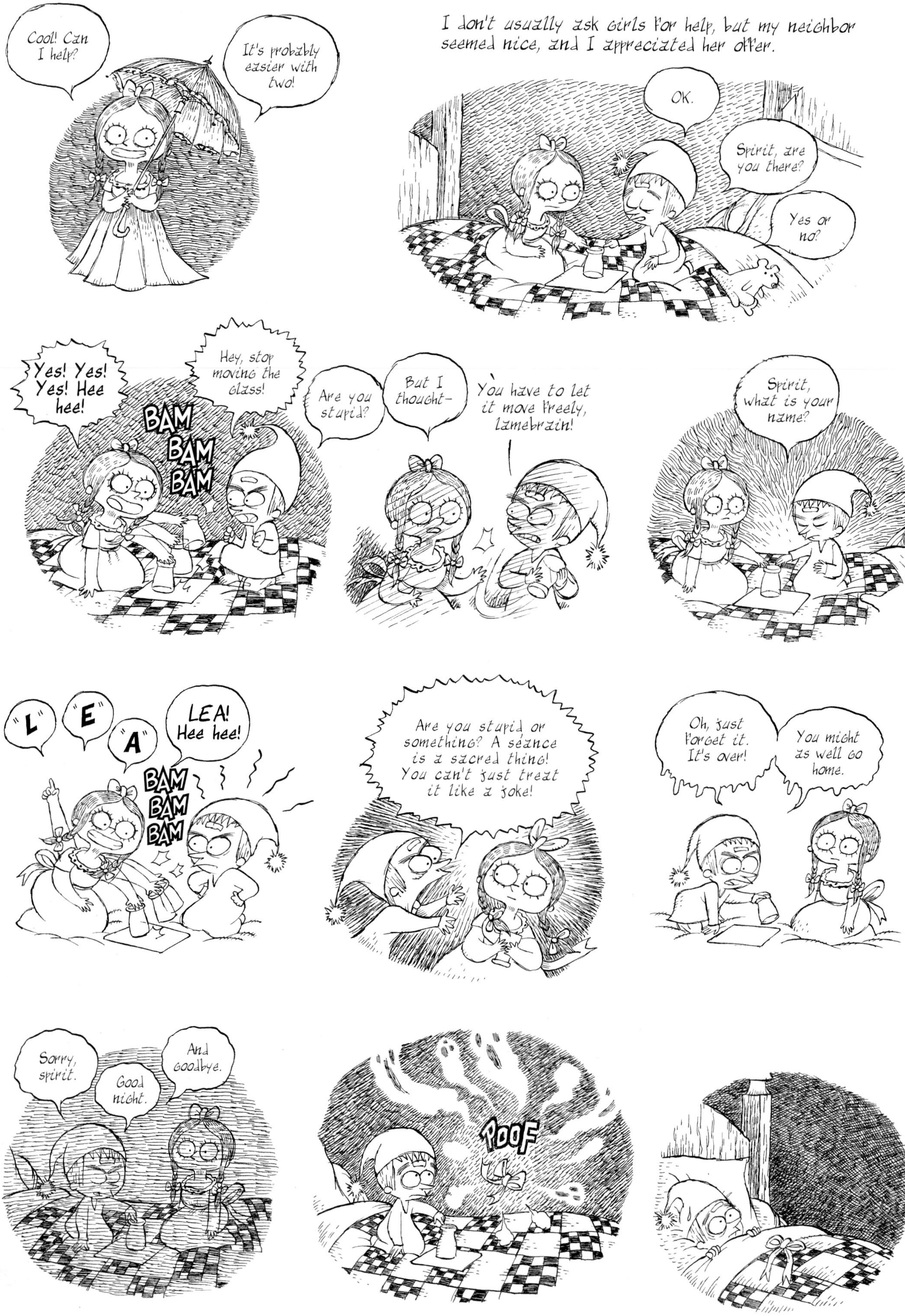
Cool! Can I help?
It's probably easier with two!
I don't usually ask girls for help, but my neighbor seemed nice, and I appreciated her offer.
OK.
Spirit, are you there?
Yes or no?
Yes! Yes! Yes! Hee hee!
BAM BAM BAM
Hey, stop moving the glass!
Are you stupid?
But I thought-
You have to let it move freely, lamebrain!
Spirit, what is your name?
"L"
"E"
"A"
LEA! Hee hee!
BAM BAM BAM
Are you stupid or something? A séance is a sacred thing! You can't just treat it like a joke!
Oh, just forget it. It's over!
You might as well go home.
Sorry, spirit.
Good night.
And goodbye.
POOF

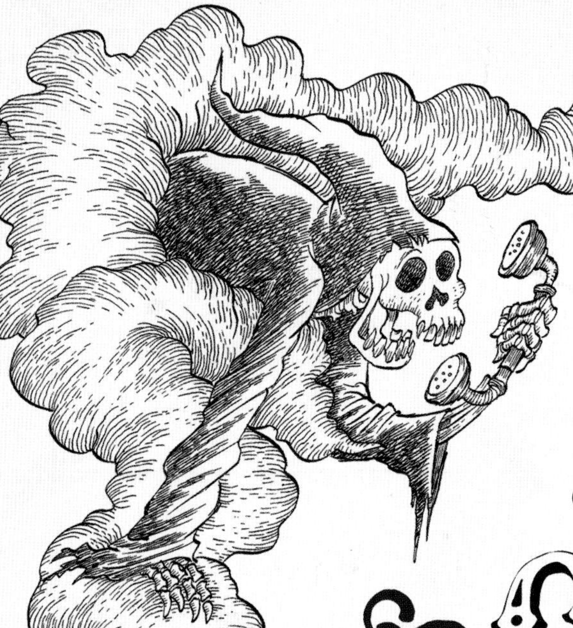

Haven't heard from the dearly departed for a while?
Worried? Want more than anything to hear from them again?
No problem!
Summon them with the

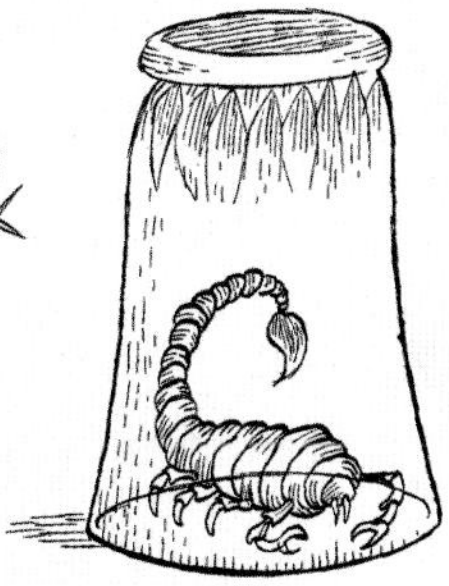

Incredible OUIJA TALKING BOARD!

The fantastic Ouija box contains:

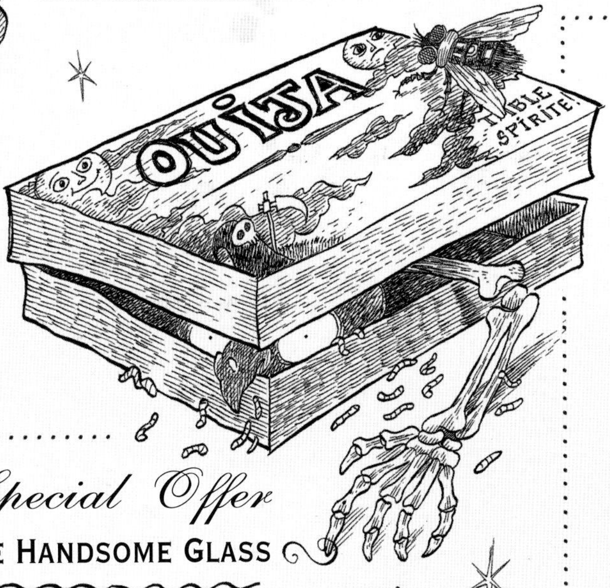

OUIJA
TABLE SPIRITE!

ONE MONOCHROME DUAL-FUNCTION TALKING BOARD

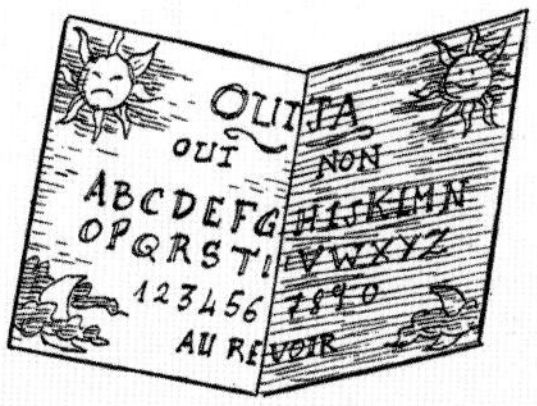

OUIJA
OUI
NON
ABCDEFGHIJKLMN
OPQRSTUVWXYZ
1234567890
AU REVOIR

- **Lightweight**, foldable, easy to carry!

- Brighten your Sunday dinners by using your TALKING BOARD as a striking **placemat**!

Special Offer
ONE HANDSOME GLASS

Sturdy yet **light**,
it handles easily,
and **glides** over the bumpiest parlor tables without leaving a single scratch.

Cozy and comfortable: ghosts go gaga for it!

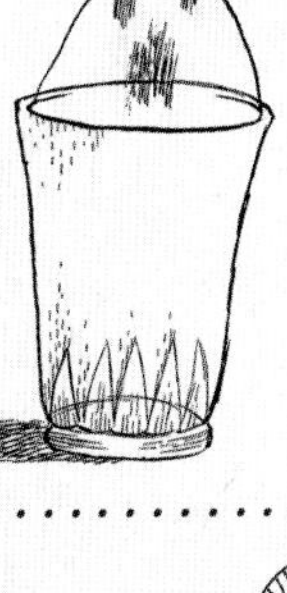

ETERNAL SEPARATIONS: A THING OF THE PAST!

Never again will you feel alone!
It's as easy as
PICKING UP THE PHONE!

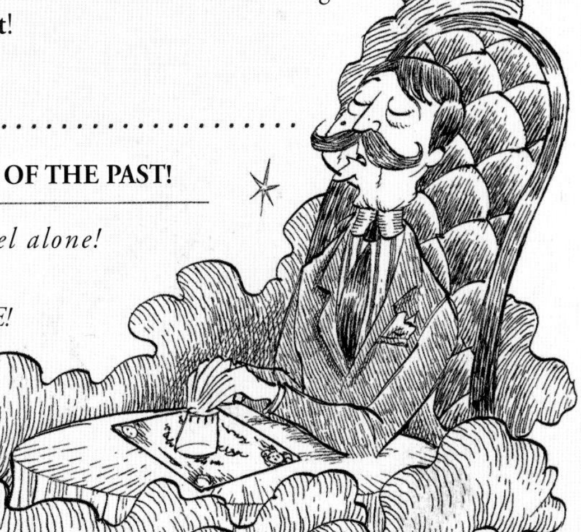

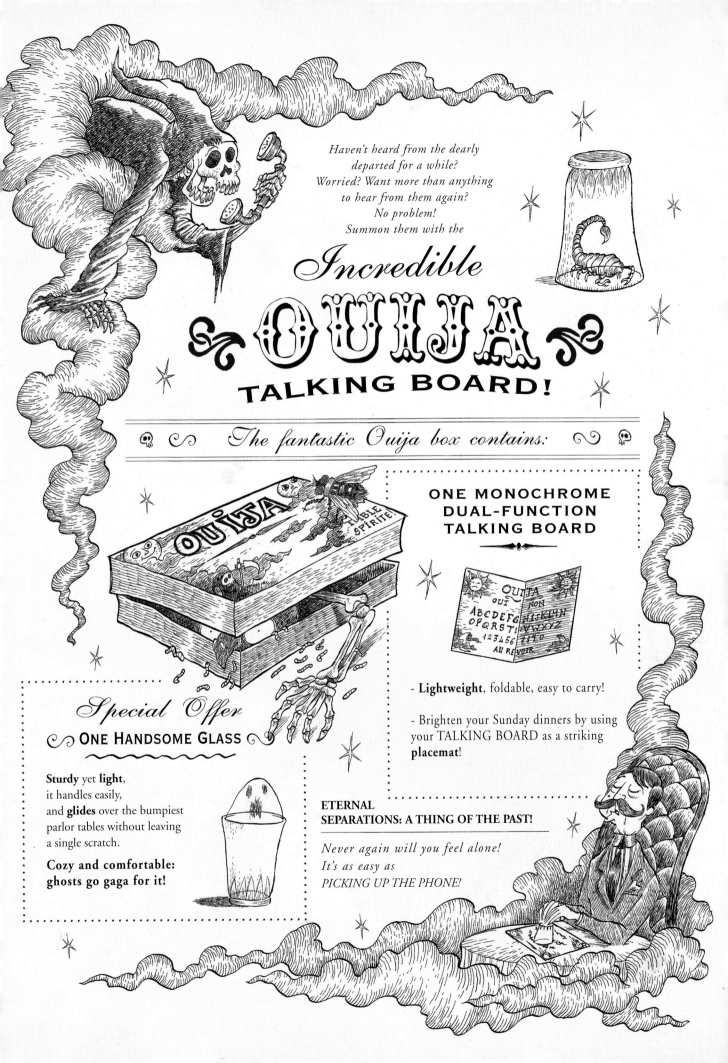

SPECIAL SECTION: PARAPSYCHOLOGY

"I listen to the bird not for its song, but for the silence that follows." – NOGUCHI YONENRO

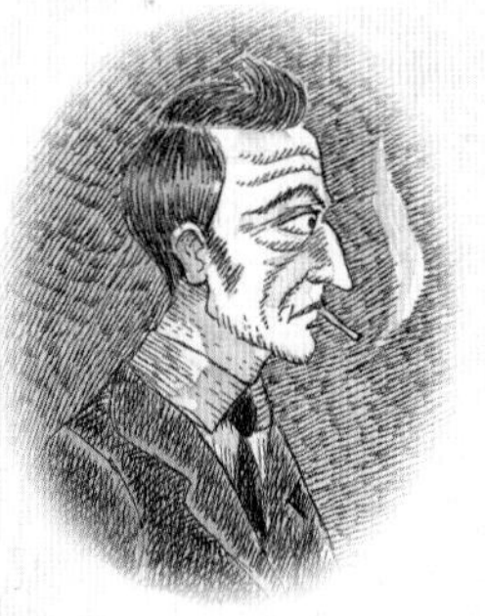

A useful and captivating special section by our mysterious Mr. **HARRY PRICE, the celebrated ghost hunter.**

THE ORIGINS of Ouija are as obscure as those of spiritualism itself. It seems this means was invented quite long ago to receive messages from Beyond.

– LEXICON –

OUIJA:
Planchette adorned with numbers and letters. A fine tool for conversing with spirits of all sorts (the deceased, or otherwise).

MEDIUM:
A very sensitive person able to pick up extrasensory vibrations from the invisible world. The medium is a sort of go-between, a liaison between the material and immaterial worlds.

GUIDE:
Designated person who asks questions and reads the replies aloud.

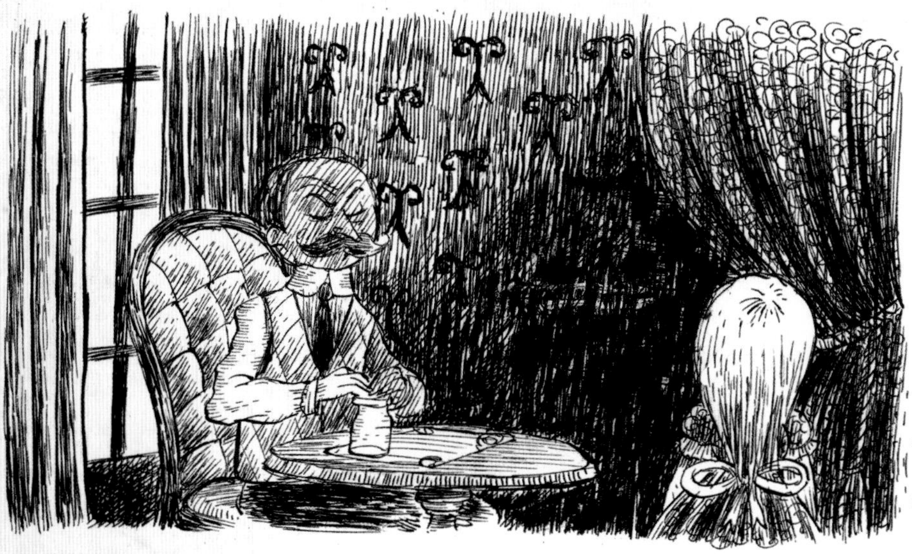

Spiritualism is a healthy activity popular with the smart set.

TECHNICAL ADVICE

You may experience a minor vibrating sensation in your fingertips, as well as a light frisson or cold draft. Don't panic: fluid is passing between you and the spirit.**These are the beginnings of contact.**

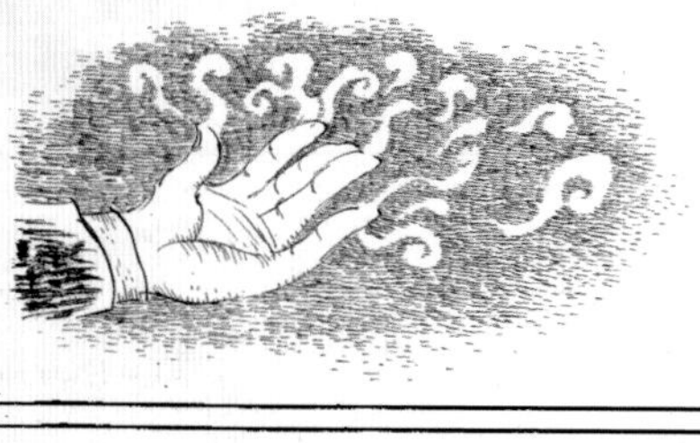

Now you can ask your question.
The glass will begin to *move*, urged on by the spirit within…

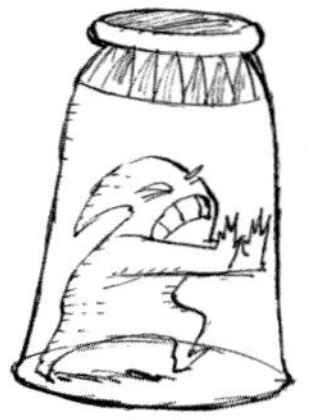

Give it free rein. Do not press on the glass, so as not to exhaust or upset the spirit. The guide should enunciate each letter and number slowly and clearly, to **inform the spirit of their position.**

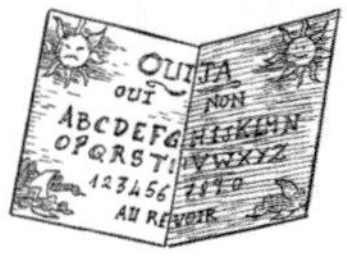
OUIJA
OUI
NON
AU REVOIR

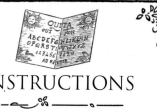

INSTRUCTIONS

*1 - A **pedestal table** is the preferred base. (A round table with a single foot or central column.)*

*2 - Set the **Ouija** board on it, as well as a fairly light glass.*

3 - Solitary use is forbidden if you are not an expert; nor should groups ever exceed 10 people. You must then choose a medium and a guide (who will sit to the medium's right).

*4 - Spiritualism séances should usually take place at night, for spirits rest by day. Low, diffuse lighting is preferred (so as not to seem threatening to spirits, or draw mosquitoes). You should be able to see the table clearly. This atmosphere is conducive to relaxation and the concentration necessary for entering into contact with the ethereal plane. However, take care that no areas fall **completely into shadow!***

*5 - Place your right **index** finger on the glass. Or, if you are alone (and an expert), the thumb, index, and middle fingers of both your hands.*

*6 - Observe a moment of **silence**, then cordially invite the spirit in by speaking the celebrated words:*

"SPIRIT, ARE YOU THERE?"

7 - Be patient, and don't hesitate to try the séance again later if nothing happens.

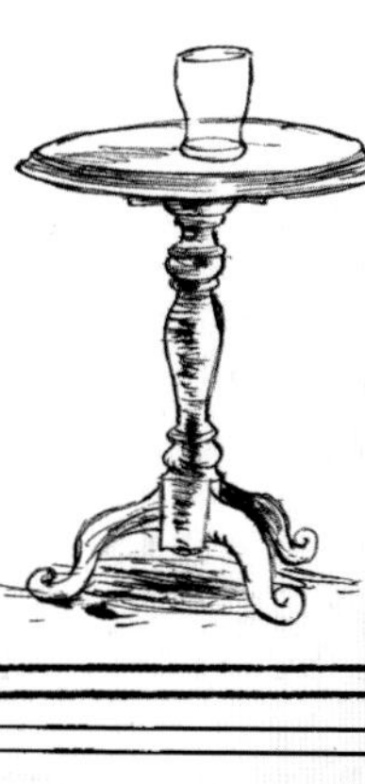

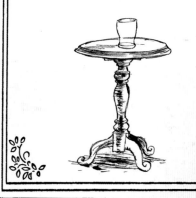

OUIJA

"If no one answers me, then I haven't made myself heard." - ELSA TRIOLET

Allan Kardec (1804-1869)

Real name: Hippolyte Léon Denizard Rivail. One of Ouija's main proponents. Philosopher and educator by profession, he was the founder of Spiritism, and contributed greatly to spreading it worldwide.

WARNINGS
& SPECIAL RECOMMENDATIONS

[S]PIRITUALISM is an act of communication between two parallel [w]orlds. It is a natural act. But beware: [IT] **IS NOT A GAME!** Indeed, it can [be] quite dangerous if used for en[ter]tainment, or for evil ends. Make [su]re all participants have good in[te]ntions, and above all, remember:

[TH]E QUALITY [OF] THE ANSWERS [DE]PENDS ON [TH]E QUALITY OF [TH]E QUESTIONS!

[Th]e energy of the medium (the **FLUID**) [en]ables spirits to *move the glass* over [th]e letters of the **TALKING BOARD,** [in] order to compose words and phrases.

[W]ith practice, participants will, bit by [bi]t, be able to take their hand from the [gl]ass, which will then move *without [an]y physical contact*. This method is [gr]ueling for the medium, and uses *a [gr]eat deal of energy*.

[Es]chewing this [pr]ocedure is pre[fe]rable and will [sp]are you incon[ve]nience. Just rest [yo]ur finger lightly [on] the glass.

THESE RULES MUST BE FOLLOWED

❋ *Your motives must be pure! Know that this ancient practice will not give you any special powers.*

❋ *Don't think spirits are here to solve your problems. They come simply to have a little chat. If your motives are impure, you run the risk of attracting unscrupulous spirits out to take advantage of you.*

❋ *In the event the situation should get out of hand, remember: you are the master of your own home.*

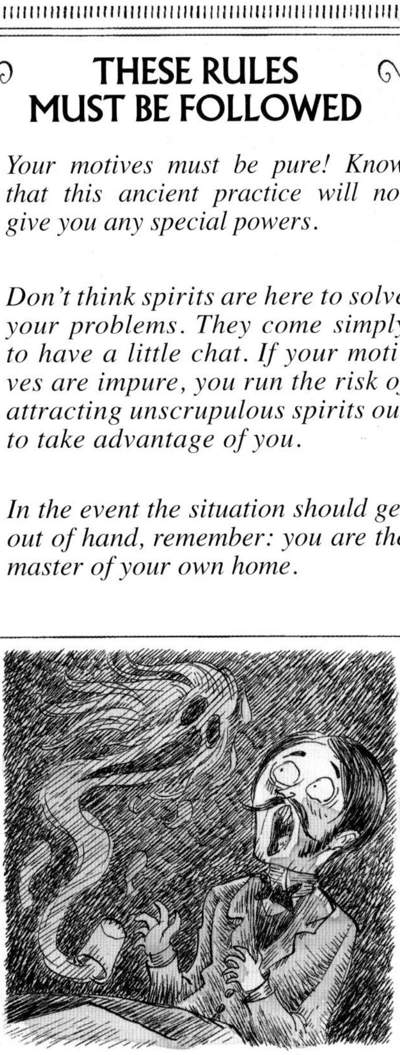

CLOSING A SÉANCE

Always remember to thank the spirit and bid it goodbye, both in your head and aloud. Then, slowly, gradually break the link with the other participants by lifting your hands from the table in unison.

Advice from Harry Price

A nice chamomile tea with rose petals and a sprinkling of lavender blossoms is recommended to help you relax your psychic and mental self. Your astral body will be purified, and afterwards, the pleasant, restful night will leave you full of energy, well-disposed toward another séance at some future date.

Best of luck!

NEXT WEEK: BACK FROM HIS JAUNT IN SCOTLAND, HARRY PRICE TELLS US ALL TALES OF HAUNTED CASTLES!

The Little Scissor Girl

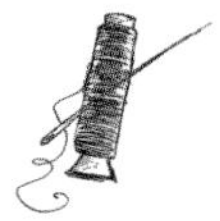

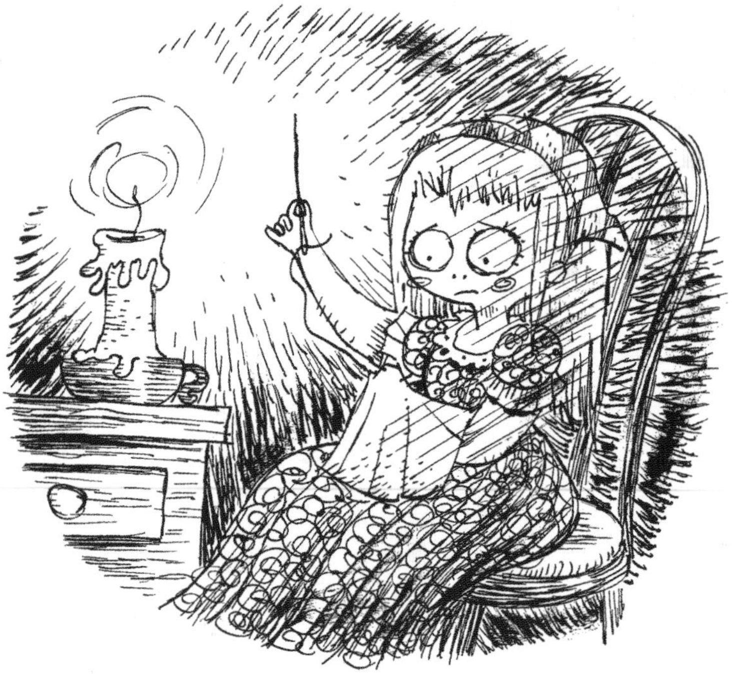

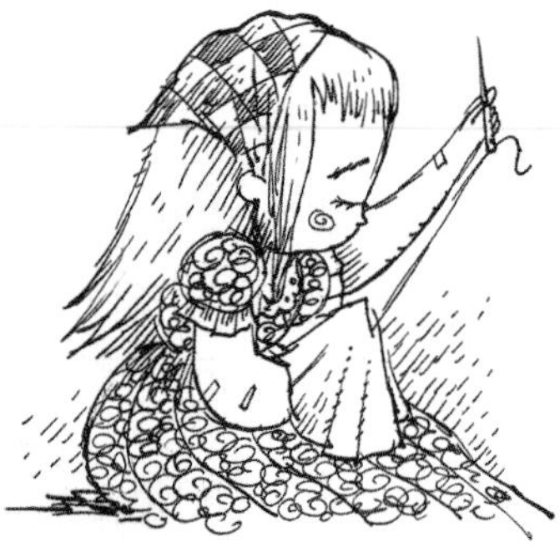

On the cloth of white muslin
Fell in tangles and pools
The long thread of hempen
Unreeled from its spools.

Frail fingers ungainly!
With bright pinpricks dotted
All places where plainly
Her red blood had clotted.

Each task a tormenting
Station of the cross,
She worked, unrelenting,
For she was her own boss.

To seam-stressing driven
By accounts in arrears,
Her glum life was woven
In sorrows and tears.

Steel needles, insidiously,
her fingers would prick
with each stitch, perfidiously
Through yards of fabric.

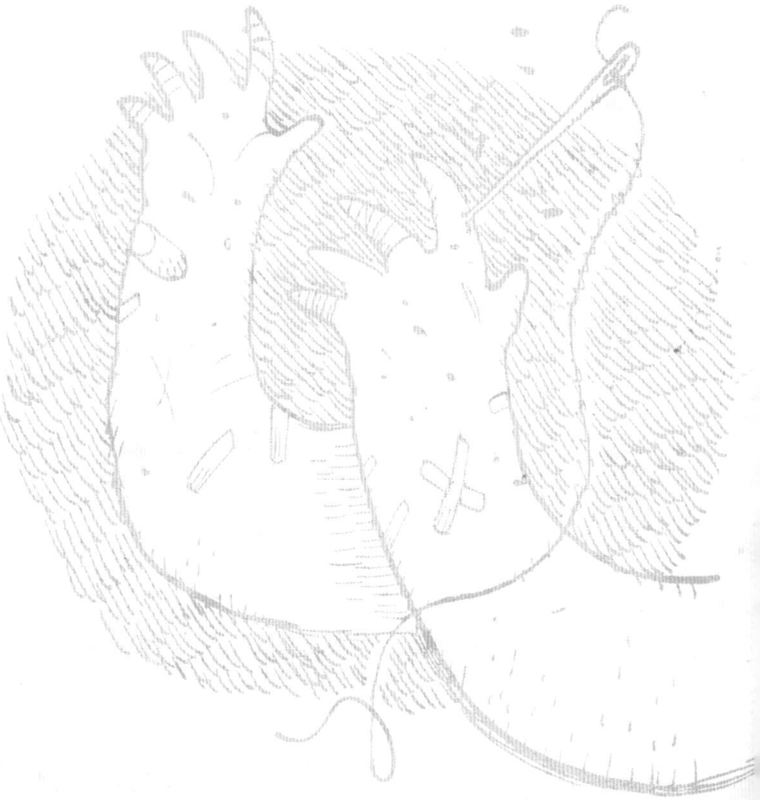

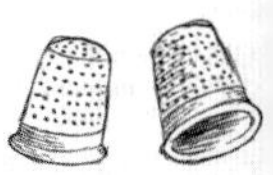

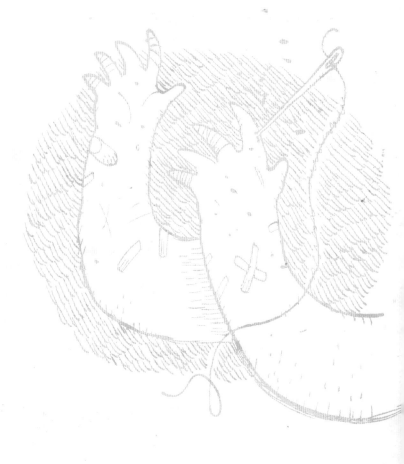

Patch, embroider, crochet,
She toiled all through the night,
O'er silk, satin, lamé
By her dim candlelight.

She lifted her scissors,
But the sharp, pointed blades
slipped, proving more traitors
than tools of the trade.

That vile-beaked bird
To her pain and surprise
Faceward, undeterred
Flew and pecked out her eyes.

On the cloth of white muslin
Fell in tangles and pools
The long thread of hempen
Unreeled from its spools.

Ghosts have both feet in the grave, and their heads in the clouds... They must know a lot about death.

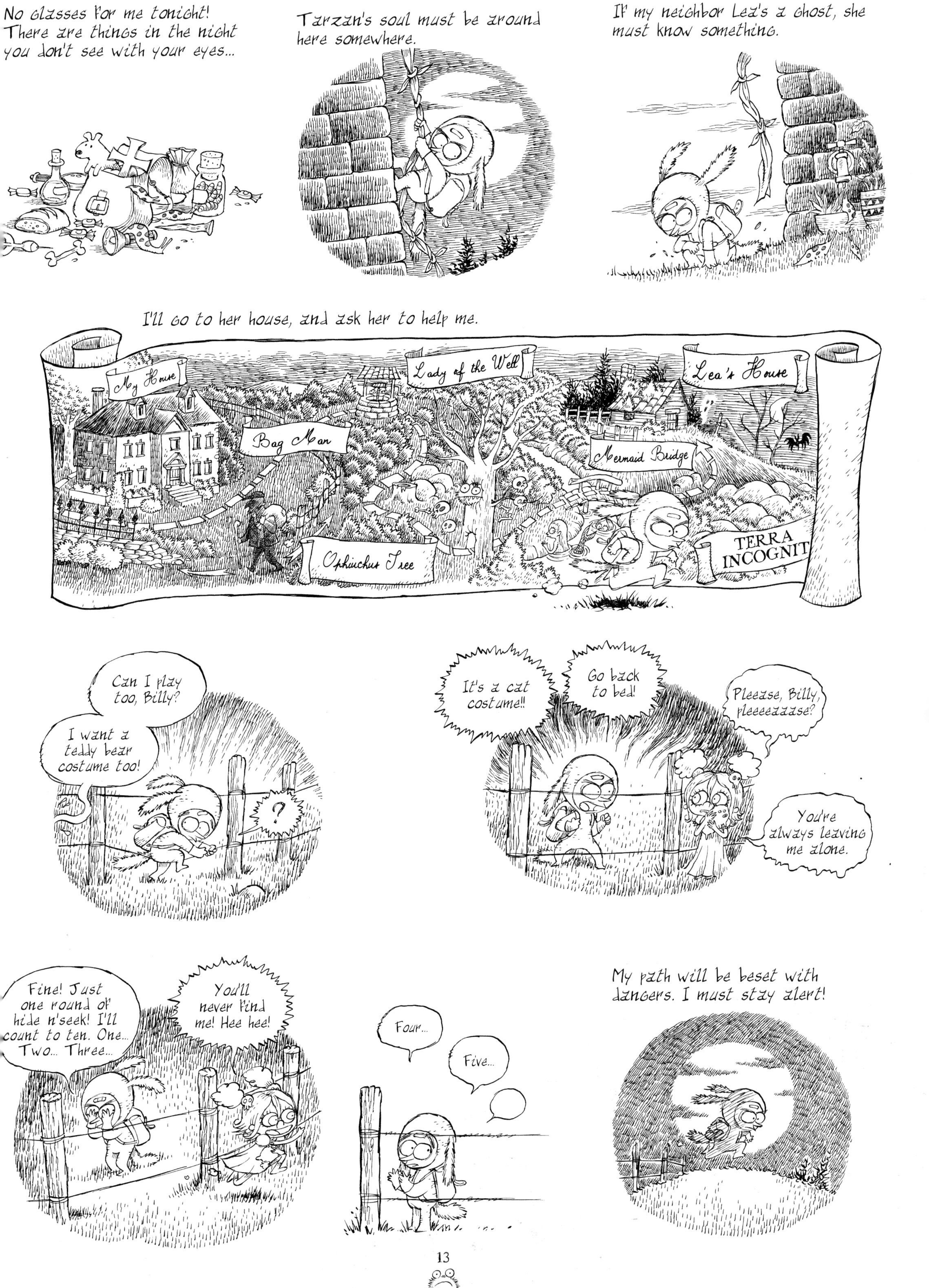
No glasses for me tonight! There are things in the night you don't see with your eyes...
Tarzan's soul must be around here somewhere.
If my neighbor Lea's a ghost, she must know something.
I'll go to her house, and ask her to help me.
My House
Lady of the Well
Lea's House
Bag Man
Mermaid Bridge
Ophiuchus Tree
TERRA INCOGNIT
Can I play too, Billy?
I want a teddy bear costume too!
?
It's a cat costume!!
Go back to bed!
Pleease, Billy, pleeeeeaaase?
You're always leaving me alone.
Fine! Just one round of hide n'seek! I'll count to ten. One... Two... Three...
You'll never find me! Hee hee!
Four...
Five...
My path will be beset with dangers. I must stay alert!

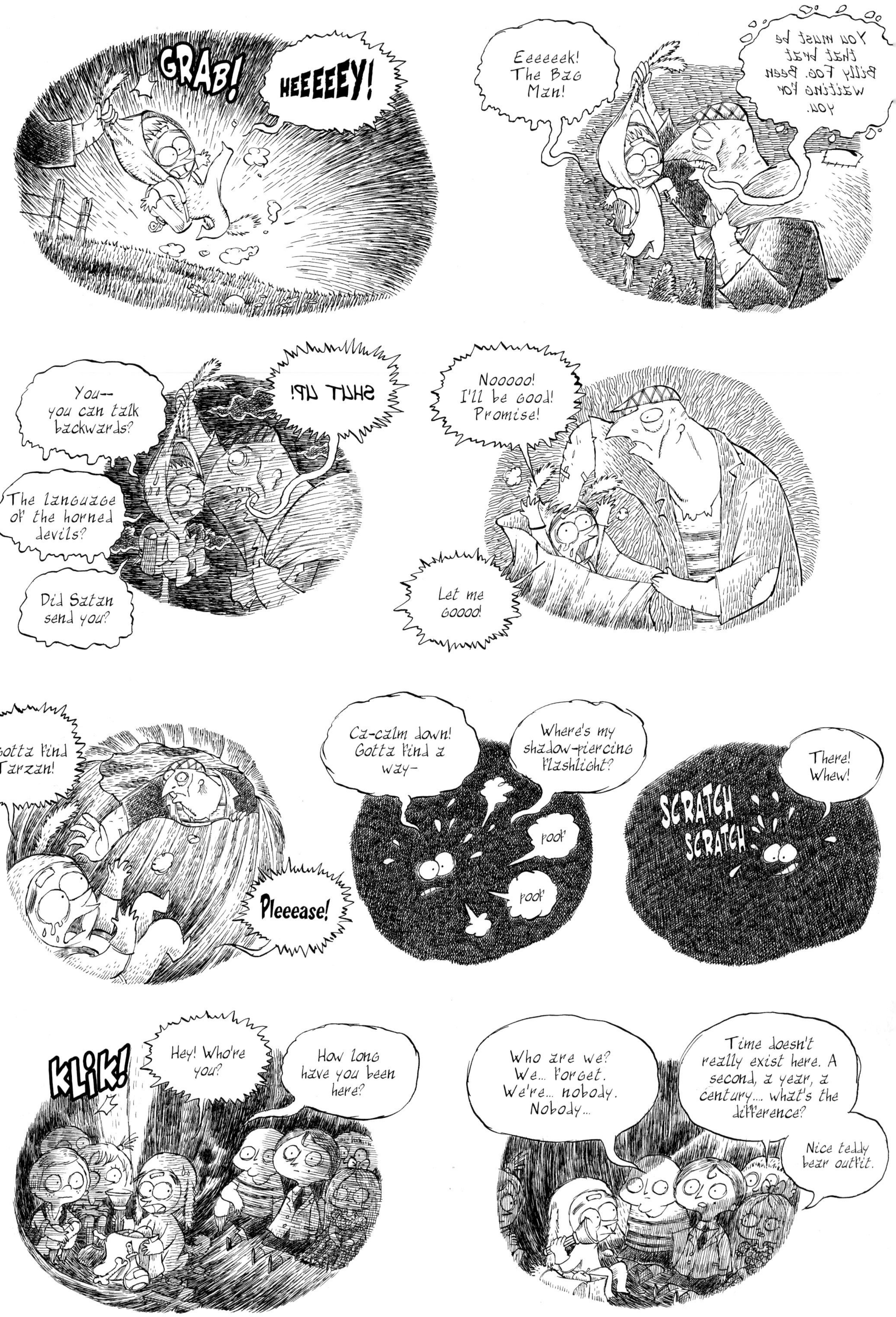
GRAB!
HEEEEEY!
Eeeeeek! The Bag Man!
You must be that brat Billy Foo. Been waiting for you.
You-- you can talk backwards?
SHUT UP!
The language of the horned devils?
Did Satan send you?
Nooooo! I'll be good! Promise!
Let me goooo!
I gotta find Tarzan!
Pleeease!
Ca-calm down! Gotta find a way-
Where's my shadow-piercing flashlight?
poof
poof
SCRATCH SCRATCH
There! Whew!
KLIK!
Hey! Who're you?
How long have you been here?
Who are we? We... forget. We're... nobody. Nobody...
Time doesn't really exist here. A second, a year, a century... what's the difference?
Nice teddy bear outfit.

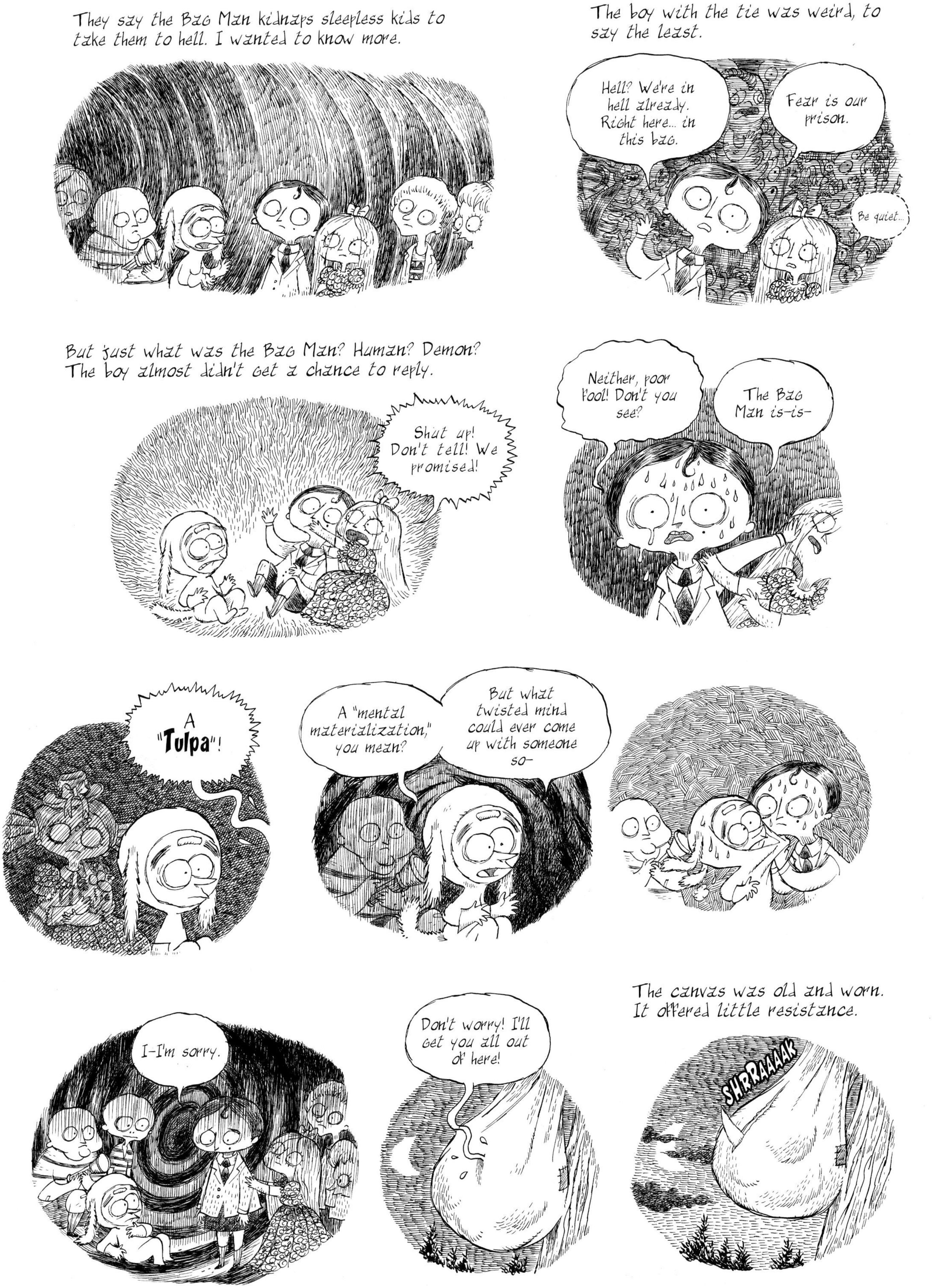
They say the Bag Man kidnaps sleepless kids to take them to hell. I wanted to know more.
The boy with the tie was weird, to say the least.
Hell? We're in hell already. Right here... in this bag.
Fear is our prison.
Be quiet...
But just what was the Bag Man? Human? Demon? The boy almost didn't get a chance to reply.
Shut up! Don't tell! We promised!
Neither, poor fool! Don't you see?
The Bag Man is–is–
A "Tulpa"!
A "mental materialization," you mean?
But what twisted mind could ever come up with someone so–
I–I'm sorry.
Don't worry! I'll get you all out of here!
The canvas was old and worn. It offered little resistance.
SHRRAAAK

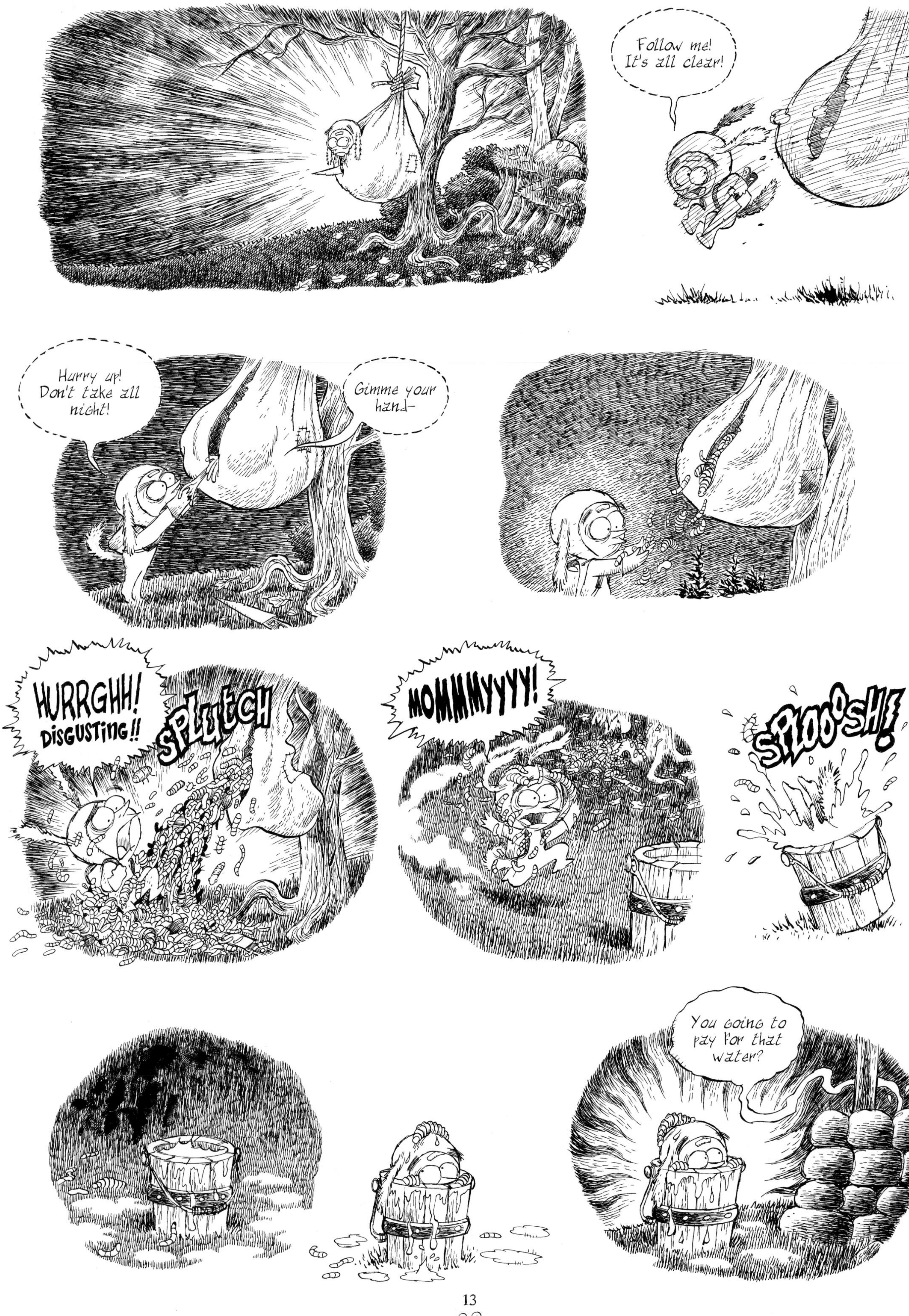
Follow me! It's all clear!
Harry up! Don't take all night!
Gimme your hand-
HURRGHH! DISGUSTING!!
SPLUTCH
MOMMMYYYY!
SPLOOOSH!
You going to pay for that water?

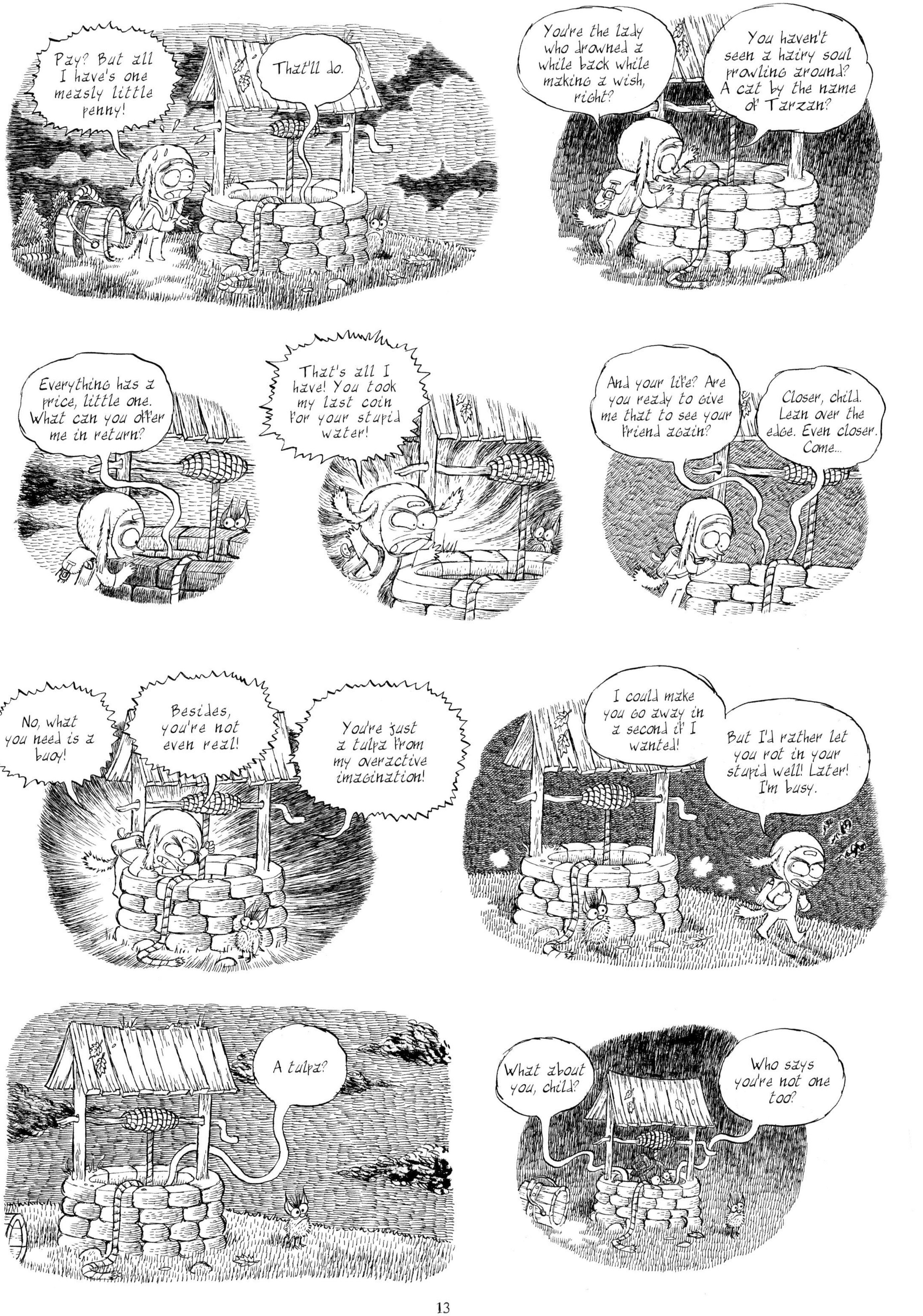

Pay? But all I have's one measly little penny!
That'll do.
You're the lady who drowned a while back while making a wish, right?
You haven't seen a hairy soul prowling around? A cat by the name of Tarzan?
Everything has a price, little one. What can you offer me in return?
That's all I have! You took my last coin for your stupid water!
And your life? Are you ready to give me that to see your friend again?
Closer, child. Lean over the edge. Even closer. Come...
No, what you need is a buoy!
Besides, you're not even real!
You're just a tulpa from my overactive imagination!
I could make you go away in a second if I wanted!
But I'd rather let you rot in your stupid well! Later! I'm busy.
A tulpa?
What about you, child?
Who says you're not one too?

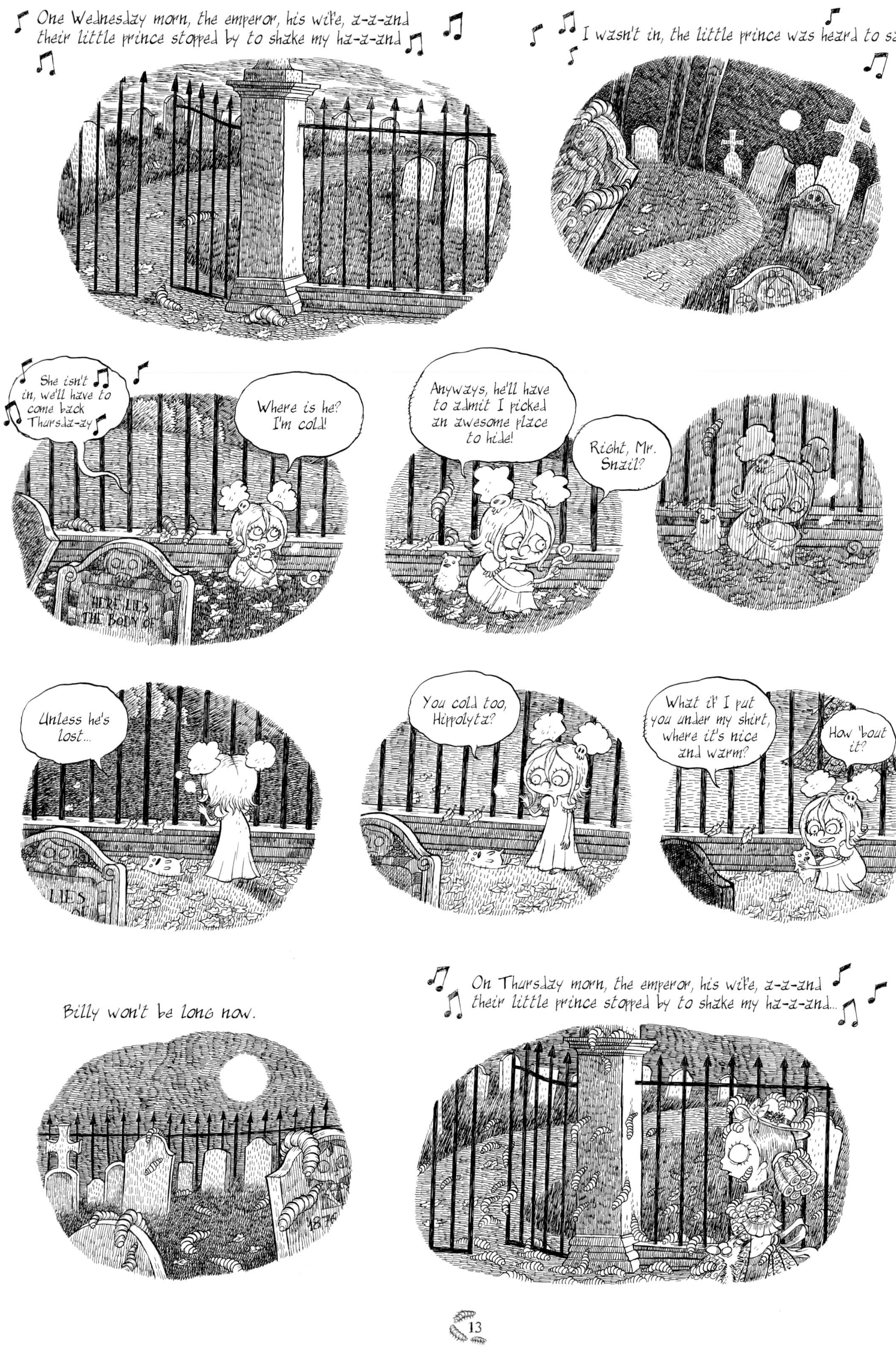

One Wednesday morn, the emperor, his wife, a-a-and their little prince stopped by to shake my ha-a-and
I wasn't in, the little prince was heard to sa-a-
She isn't in, we'll have to come back Thursda-ay
Where is he? I'm cold!
HERE LIES THE BODY OF
Anyways, he'll have to admit I picked an awesome place to hide!
Right, Mr. Snail?
Unless he's lost...
LIES
You cold too, Hippolyta?
What if I put you under my shirt, where it's nice and warm?
How 'bout it?
Billy won't be long now.
On Thursday morn, the emperor, his wife, a-a-and their little prince stopped by to shake my ha-a-and...

"You're not even real! You're just a tulpa from my overactive imagination!"
Heh, heh! Lady of the Well! That sure shut her up!

Billy Fog

Tulpas

Are "ethereal materializations" of conscious or unconscious thoughts...
An ignoramus will, despite him or herself, materialize selfishness, envy, and anxiety,
thus becoming indirectly responsible for the world's ills.
We are constantly creating tulpas.

Positive Tulpas (*Amoris Beatus*)

When people dear to us (friends, parents) are in pain or going through a rough patch, just think about them very hard and try to feel all the love you have for them as clearly as you can.

TAB. I

Sincerity — *Naïveté* — *Love* — *Loyalty* — *Peace*

Some people call these "wishes" or "prayers."

Negative Tulpas (*Tormento Jinxum*)

More often, when racked with anger, fear, or frustration, we are far likelier to have bad thoughts.

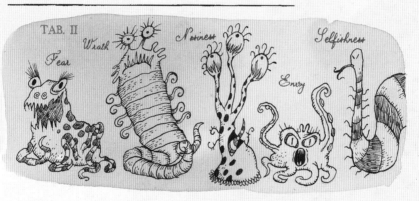

TAB. II

Fear — *Wrath* — *Noxiness* — *Envy* — *Selfishness*

Believers call these "devils" or "curses." Others call them the "evil eye" or "ill fate."

 Tulpas originate in the soul, then emanate from the brain...

How to Materialize a Tulpa

a. Put a plastic bag on your head.

b. Concentrate really hard on a bad thought.

c. Really, really hard.

d. The tulpa, imprisoned in a plastic bag, is ideal for terrifying little sisters.

Warning: Above all, do not pull the bag down over your face, lest you suffocate and die.

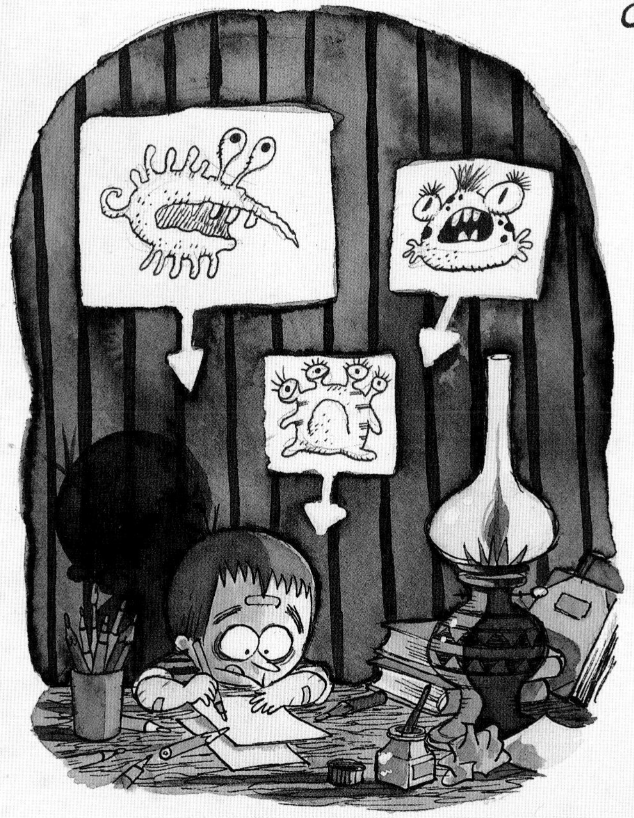

Personal Remarks:

When people are referred to as "lucky"
this in fact means they are well-loved.
Many amoris beatus watch over them.
(myth of the Guardian Angel)

However, bad luck (syn. of "Jinx")
is often tied to someone hated and despised,
on whom a great number of tormento
jinxum are projected.

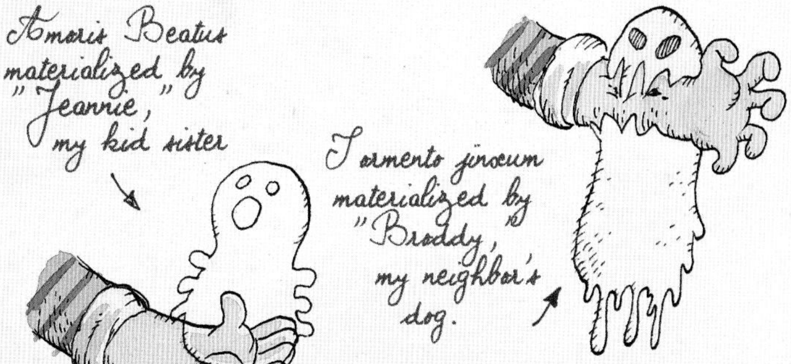
Amoris Beatus materialized by "Jeannie," my kid sister
Tormento jinxum materialized by "Broddy," my neighbor's dog.

How to Get Rid of a Tulpa

It's easy: just materialize its opposite.
(A tormento jinxus of anger
for an amoris beatus of
bravery, for example.)
Flushing a tulpa down the toilet
is highly discouraged.

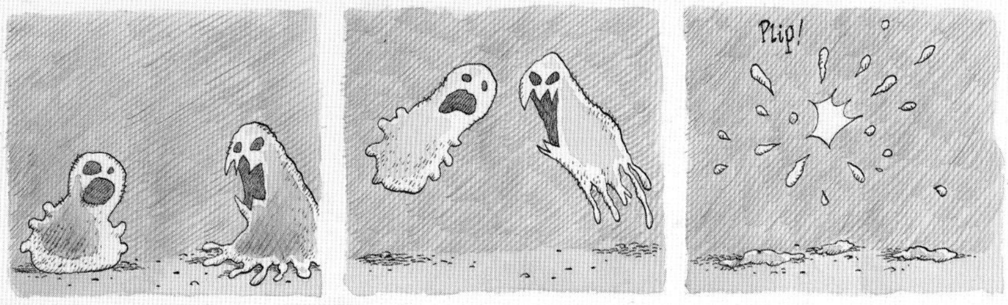
Plip!
a) The two opposites attract each other like magnetic poles. b) They are unavoidably drawn to confrontation. c) ...and mutual annihilation.

When you empty your mind of
thoughts through meditation,
all varieties of Tulpa
will vanish.

Caring for a Tormento Jinxus

Occasionally, a tormento jinxus will turn against its creator.
You can easily lose control of it, which is quite dangerous.
You must learn to control your anger.
(Though fomenting a nice little vengeance can be quite exciting.)
Find it a fairly spacious home in your backyard,
under your bed, or in your closet,
for it grows quite rapidly.

Feeding

A pinch of pride and a crumb of bitterness
daily should do quite nicely.

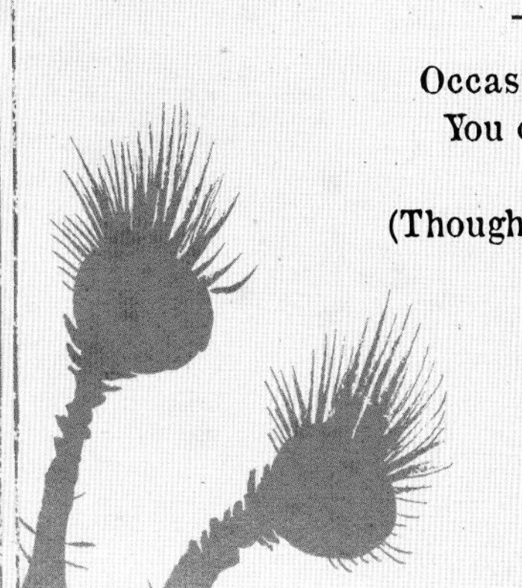

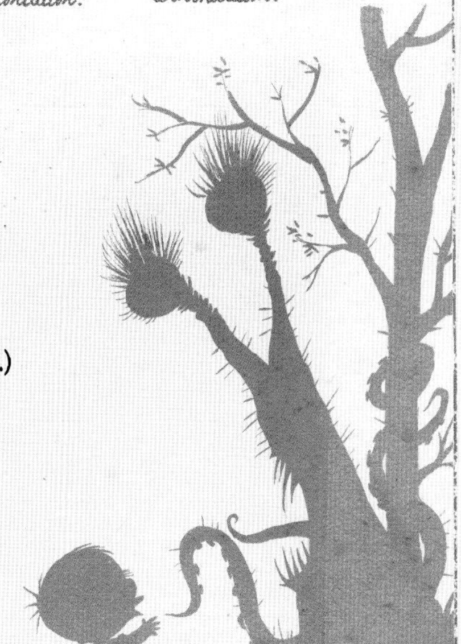

From the Curious and Bizarre Encyclopedia of Cryptozoology, by Billy Fog

"There exist beliefs, natural and supernatural occult forces…
Man has always been able to observe their causes, consequences, and effects.
You are free to believe as you wish, but for my part, I have been able to verify the authenticity of
certain phenomena. Here are a few."

Harry Price

SUPERSTITIONS

"Superstition is to religion what astrology is to astronomy: the mad daughter of a wise mother." – VOLTAIRE

IF A DOG WEEPS

THERE WILL BE A DEATH AMONG YOUR LOVED ONES OR ACQUAINTANCES.

IF YOU FIND A COIN WHILE WALKING DOWN THE STREET,

PISS ON IT

BEFORE PICKING IT UP TO

TO KEEP YOUR HAND FROM SWELLING.

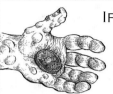

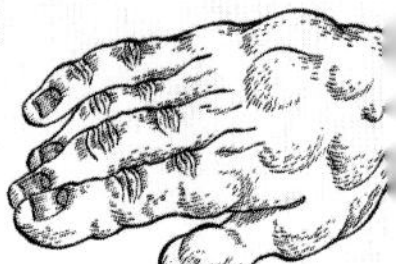

At *twilight* time, ***never*** say, "Good Evening," to people you ***run into***, for if they are ***dead***, they can give your voice to the ***Devil***, who will then come and ***take you away.***

NEVER STARE

too deeply into a *well:*

the DEVIL waits at the bottom

If you brush the hair of someone

who is brushing someone else's hair

THE **YOUNGEST**

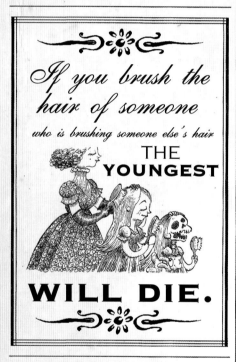

WILL DIE.

NEVER DRINK STRAIGHT FROM THE TAP!

A grass snake could come out and bite you on the mouth. *Use a glass!*

A DROWNED MAN will start ***bleeding*** should a **loved one** find him on the shore.

A BASIL

seed will give rise to a tall, beautiful plant if sown while murmuring INSULTS & CURSES.

Scattering COARSE SALT in a corner of your house

wards off evil spirits.

DO NOT COUNT STARS IN THE SKY

IT WILL **GIVE YOU WARTS.**

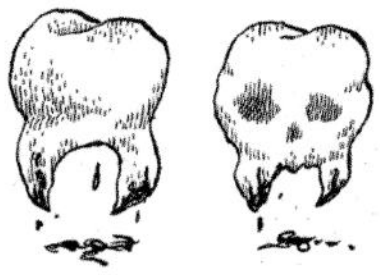

DREAMING OF LOSING YOUR TEETH

presages the death of a loved one.

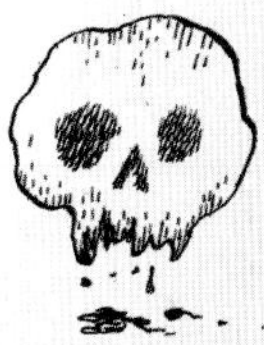

SUPERSTITIONS

"Superstition is the poetry of life; that is why it is good for a poet to be superstitious." – GOETHE

PLUNGE
A BLACK CAT
into a font of holy water.

If he struggles,
he's possessed by the Devil.

If he doesn't,
he's a good-for-nothing.

ALWAYS close the door to your house at night if you're inside, for an evil spirit could throw rocks that will cause you pain.

To never again know fear or fright, it is recommended to carry on your person a pin *used to hold closed the shroud of one who has died.*

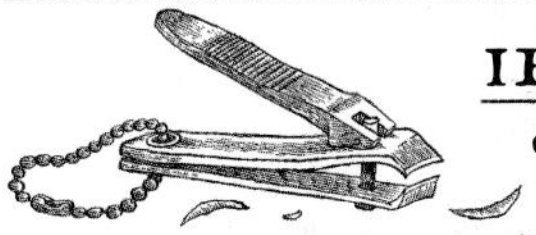

IF YOU EAT A MAGPIE'S BRAINS,
or cut your toenails at night, you may go mad.

Grimace sparingly! If the wind changes, your face could freeze like that *forever!!*

If you smell something bad by night, don't mention it,

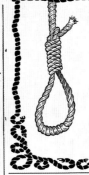

or your nose **WILL ROT.**

COUNTER-SPELL: STICK YOUR HAND IN YOUR ARMPIT RIGHT AWAY, THEN SNIFF IT.

The hangman's rope is a well-known lucky charm. Carrying one in your pocket is a good cure for toothache. It attracts good luck and keeps away the evil eye.

They say carrying the bone of a frog eaten by ants *will attract the attentions of the one you love.*

👉 COVER YOUR MOUTH with your hand when you sneeze to keep your **soul from getting away.** Cover your mouth when you yawn to keep the **Devil from getting in.**

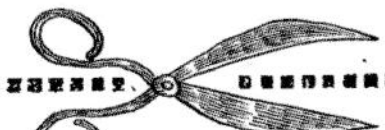

IF A DOG STARES AT YOU
WHILE YOU ARE EATING:

YOU WILL GET
A STYE IN YOUR EYE
(don't lance it).
*COUNTER-SPELL:
TOSS HIM A BITE AND CHASE HIM OFF.*

Throw a bat in the fire to hear appalling insults quite clearly. They also say children who get bat guano on their heads become cantankerous.

A pair of open scissors between box spring and mattress in a child's bed will ward off NIGHTMARES.

A NEW BROOM IN YOUR HOME WARDS OFF EVIL SPIRITS.

EVERYTHING YOU NEED TO KNOW ABOUT COUNTER-SPELLS! (BECOME A SUBSCRIBER! SEE PAGE 28.)

Three hours after midnight, with not a living creature stirring.
Far away in the dark, the clock tower's bell tolls three times.

It is the witching hour...

you are so inclined, then one day I'll tell you how fear ed to get the best of me by putting out my flashlight.

Its accomplice, the woods, deployed a thousand stratagems to make me turn back.

In the deep dark, I couldn't find my "Nightmare whistle."

So I forced myself to laugh out loud and sing at the top of my lungs.

Which, alas, wound up waking up the Ophiuchus!

Clinging tightly to its pelt, I tore out entire tufts of fur, which threw it into a fit of blind rage.

I escaped being eaten alive...

by just a hair.

13

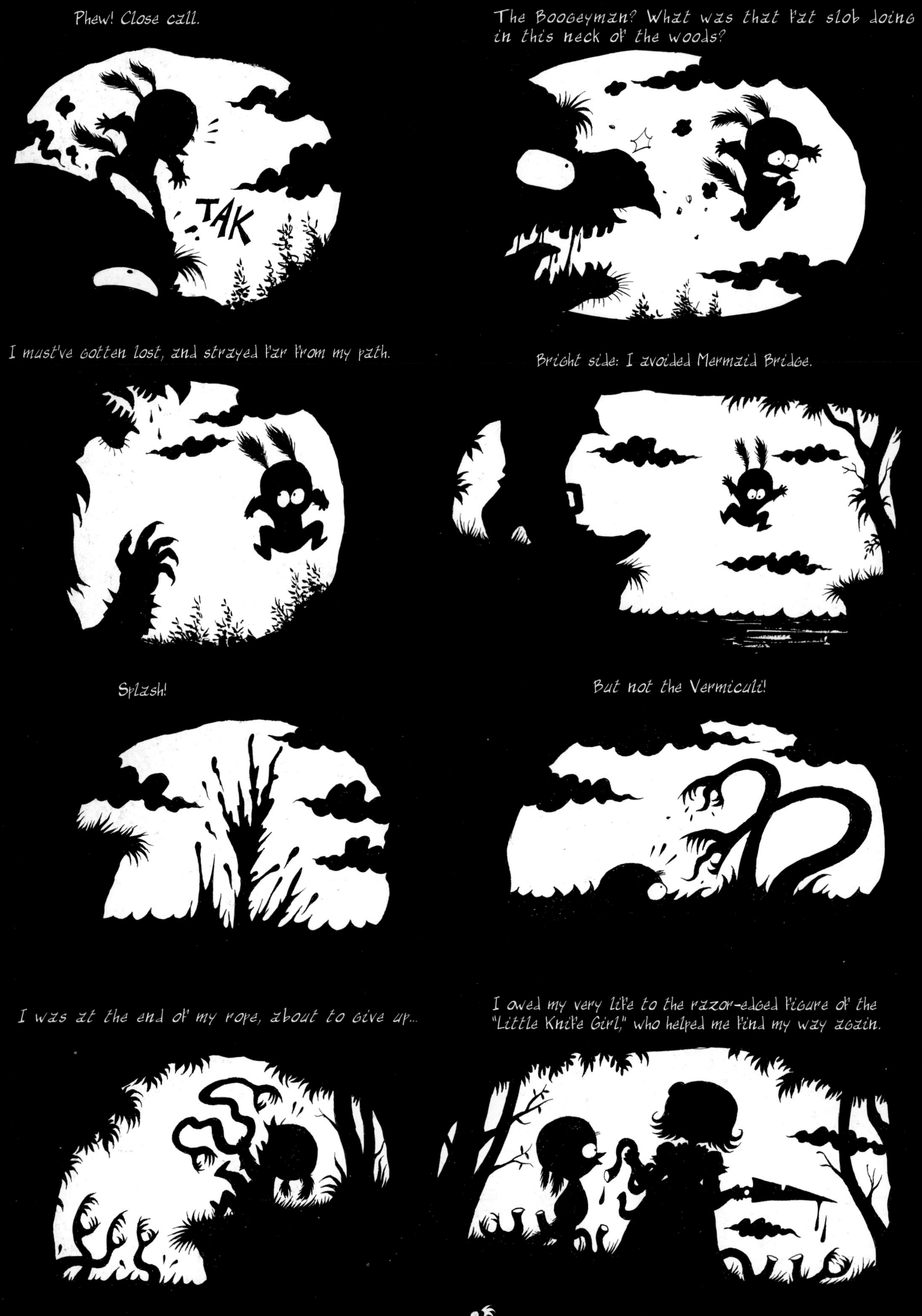
Phew! Close call.
TAK
The Boogeyman? What was that fat slob doing in this neck of the woods?
I must've gotten lost, and strayed far from my path.
Bright side: I avoided Mermaid Bridge.
Splash!
But not the Vermiculi!
I was at the end of my rope, about to give up...
I owed my very life to the razor-edged figure of the "Little Knife Girl," who helped me find my way again.

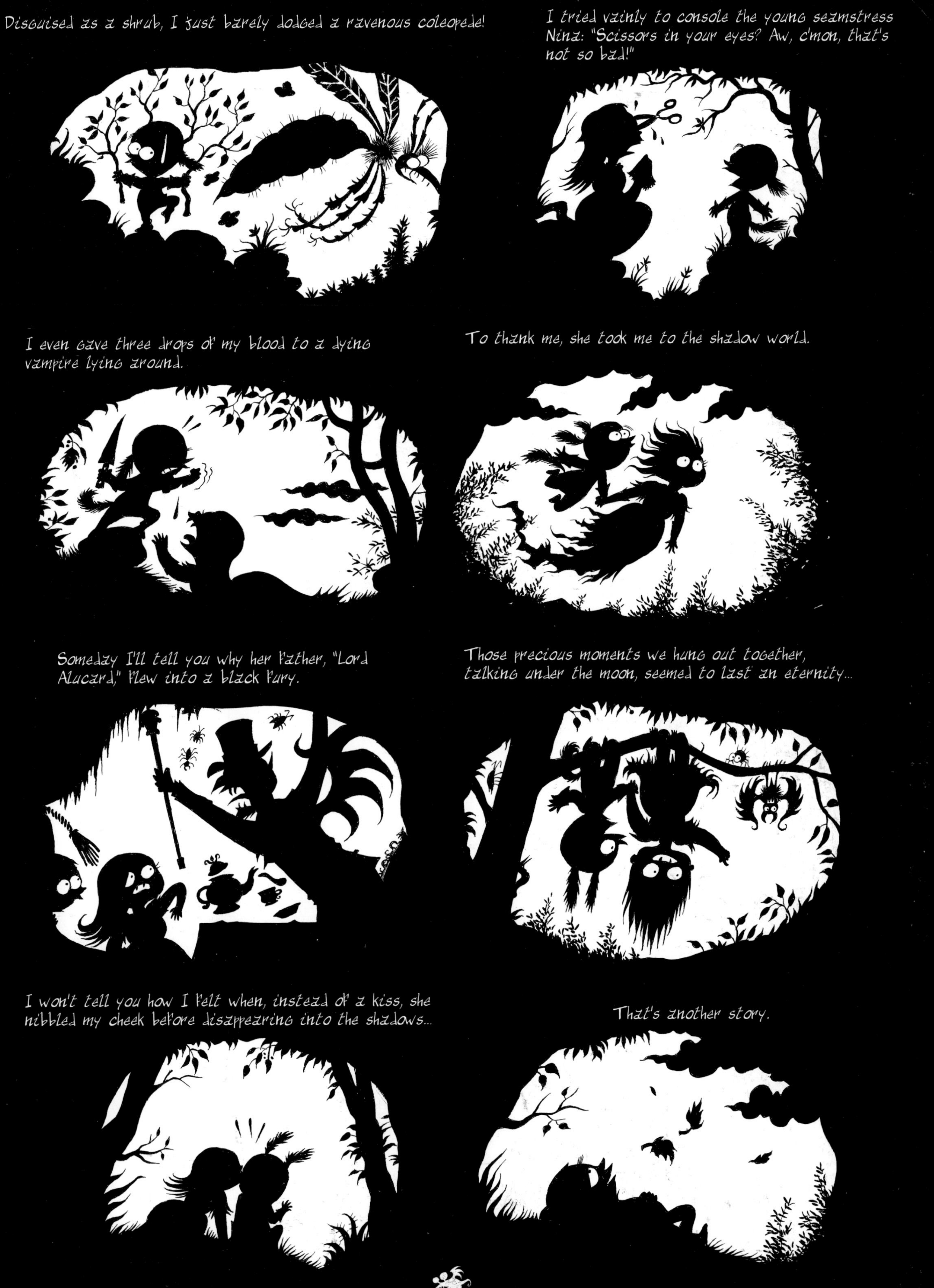

Disguised as a shrub, I just barely dodged a ravenous coleopede!
I tried vainly to console the young seamstress Nina: "Scissors in your eyes? Aw, c'mon, that's not so bad!"
I even gave three drops of my blood to a dying vampire lying around.
To thank me, she took me to the shadow world.
Someday I'll tell you why her father, "Lord Alucard," flew into a black fury.
Those precious moments we hung out together, talking under the moon, seemed to last an eternity...
I won't tell you how I felt when, instead of a kiss, she nibbled my cheek before disappearing into the shadows...
That's another story.

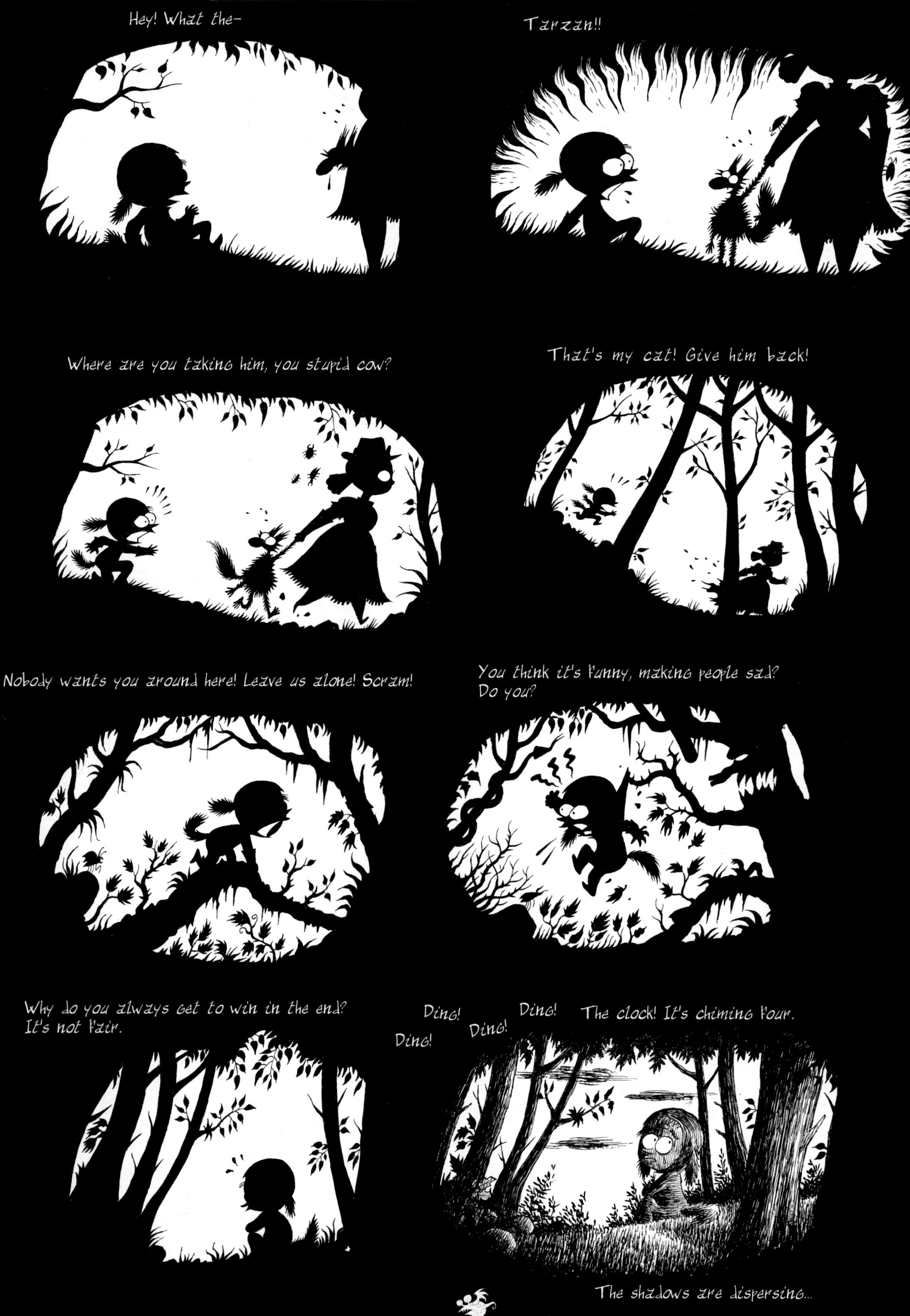
Hey! What the-
Tarzan!!
Where are you taking him, you stupid cow?
That's my cat! Give him back!
Nobody wants you around here! Leave us alone! Scram!
You think it's funny, making people sad? Do you?
Why do you always get to win in the end? It's not fair.
Ding!
Ding!
Ding!
Ding!
The clock! It's chiming four.
The shadows are dispersing...

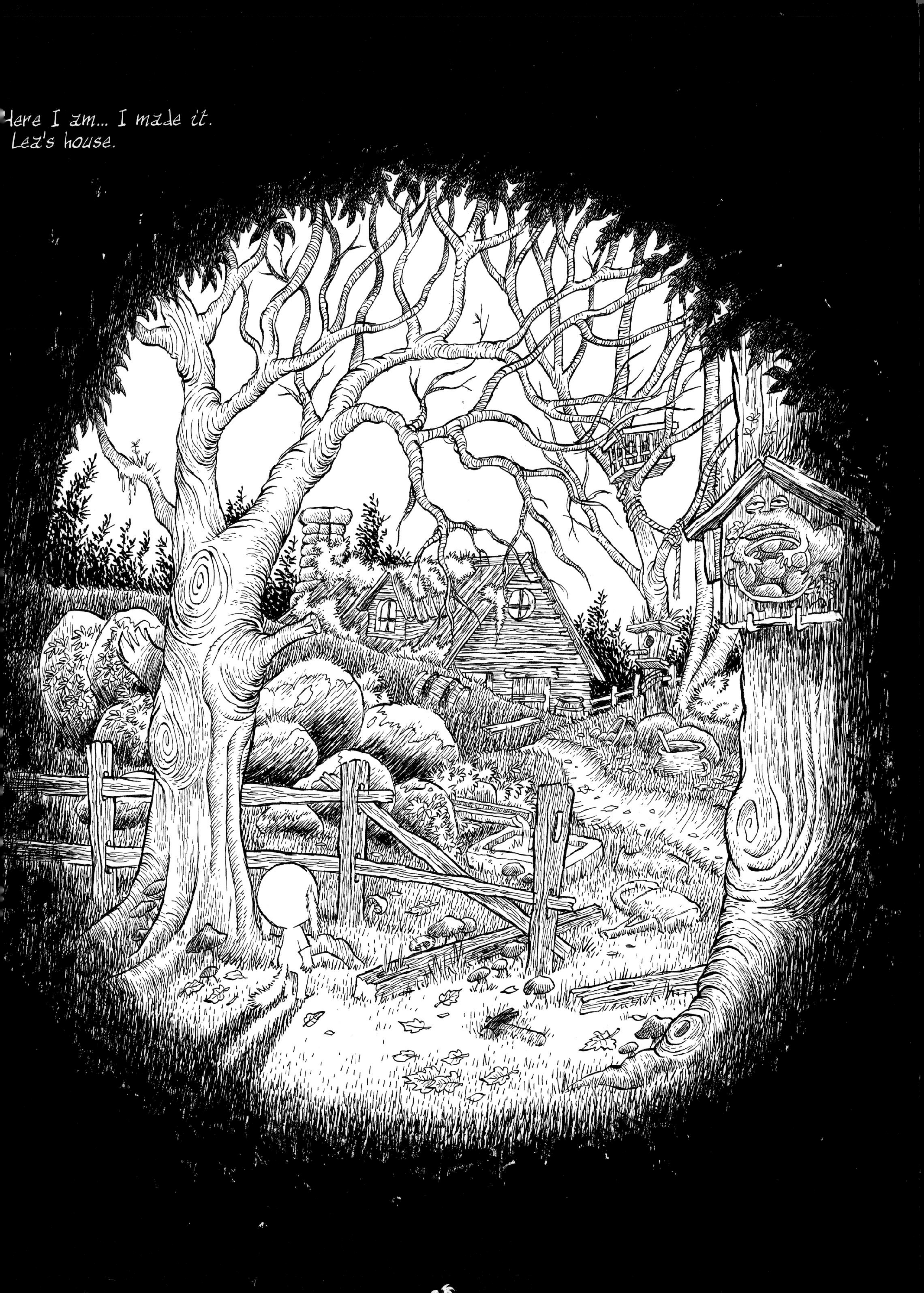
Here I am... I made it.
Lea's house.

SPECIAL SECTION: PARAPSYCHOLOGY

"Ghosts exist. They are parasites of our memory." - ANDRÉE MAILLET

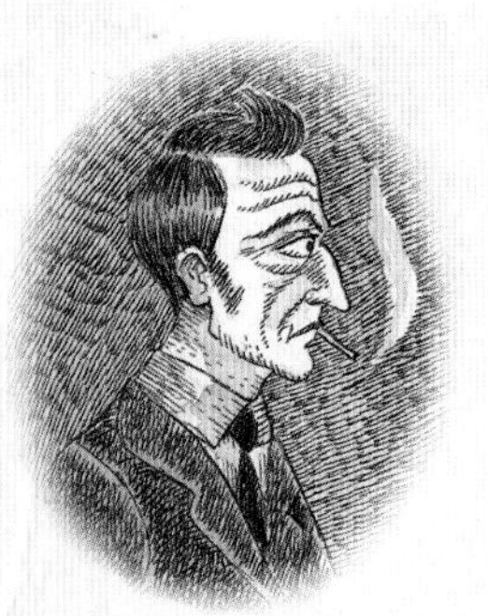

A striking and soundly documented special section by our mysterious Mr. **HARRY PRICE, the celebrated ghost hunter.**

GHOSTS are, as a general rule, apparitions of the deceased who haunt places where they lived, either from an attachment to their past lives, or because of wrongdoing that has pursued them beyond the grave.

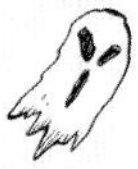

It is not unusual to encounter them on autumn evenings in early November, shortly after All Saints' Day, but also in winter, four weeks before Christmas, during Advent.

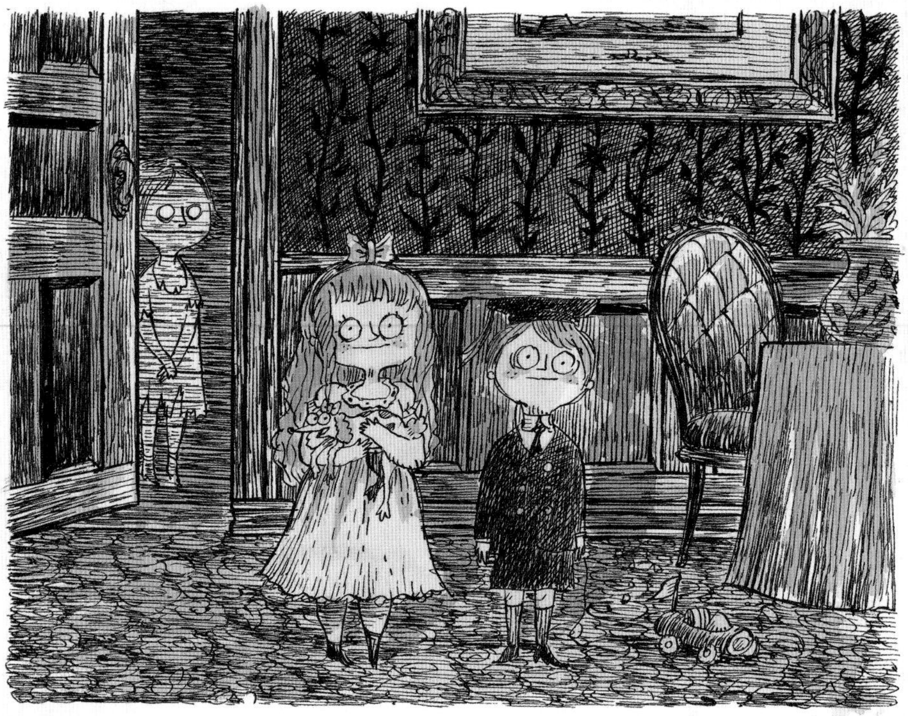

Upper left: apparition of the Sullivan family's youngest son, taken by tuberculosis one year earlier.

There are three main categories of ghost:

SPIRITS

Are invisible and noisily make their presence known, moving or knocking over objects (poltergeists).

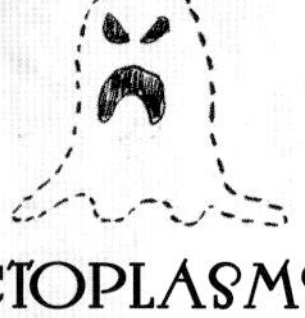

ECTOPLASMS

Slimy-looking creatures of mutable shape.

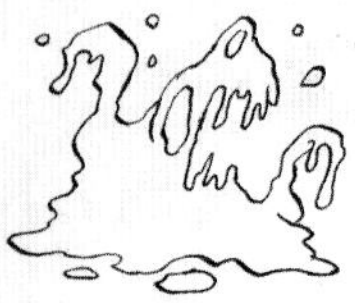

SPECTERS

Transparent or fluorescent humanoid apparitions.

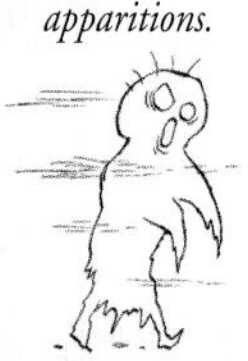

How to Identify Them

Some resemble creatures of flesh and blood in every way. However, strange phenomena surrounding their appearance will serve to tip you off straightaway.

* ***A nasty smell and a sharp drop in temperature*** often precede their appearance.
* They can move about the room and go about their business ***while passing through walls***, without paying you any mind.
* They may sometimes show grave signs of ***injury*** (missing head or legs).
* They never ***blink.***
* They move about by ***floating.***
* Sometimes, on all fours, they climb ***walls or ceilings.***
* Sometimes they ***disappear or alter their appearance*** when stared at directly.

CAUTION:
DO NOT MISTAKE FOR GHOS

ASTRAL BODIES

are not, strictly speaking, ghostly beings, but the result of an astral projection undertaken by a person very much alive.

TULPAS

are materializations of psychic or mental thought. However, take heed: though they are not dead people, they are often no less *surprising*.

REVENANTS

do not belong in the ghost category either. They are animated *dead bodies* (zombies, living dead).

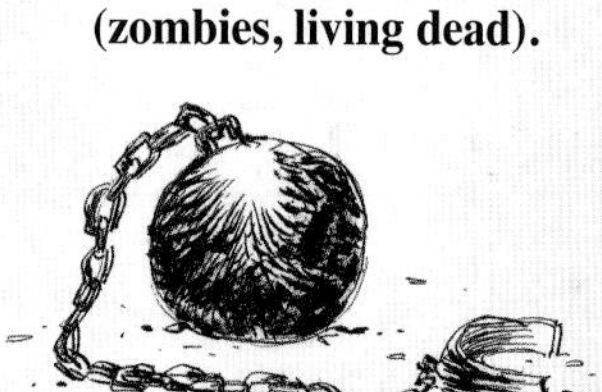

GHOSTS

"The night is conducive to reflection, stillness, fear. In darkness we sleep, we fall silent, and we see ghosts." ~ SIMONE PIUZE

HOW SHOULD YOU BEHAVE IF YOU SEE A GHOST?

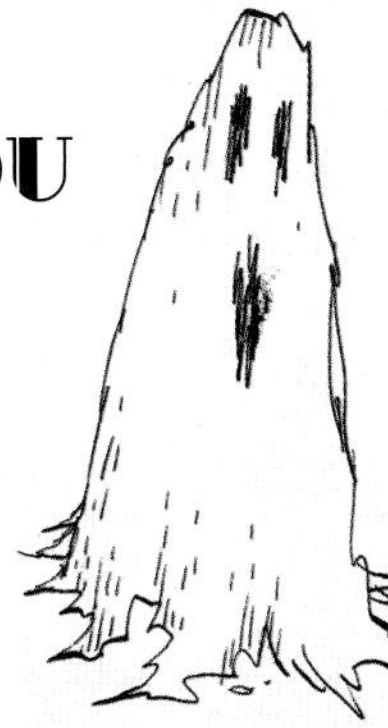

The best thing to do is keep your cool as best you can, since fear excites them.

They are generally bearers of bad tidings. But keep an open mind, and you may profit from the encounter, and sometimes even help them find peace once more.

You are, as a general rule, advised to lend an ear and show altruism. By conversing with them and giving out wise advice (as you would a friend), it is possible to ease their suffering.

However, be a patient counselor! Most ghosts don't know they're dead, and the shock is sometimes distressing. Some truths are hard to hear.

CERTAIN GHOSTS seem to have left an indelible impression on the public. Here are a few:

A FEW EXAMPLES

NEWBORN SPECTERS

If, on rounding a bend, you find a passel of newborns clinging to your ankles, sprinkle them with water while blessing them! These little specters, back from Limbo to clamor for their baptisms, will thank their new godparent before vanishing once more.

WHITE LADIES

Quite possibly, they appear to warn you of some imminent danger. Listen calmly to their advice, and you will avoid mortal peril. Be grateful and spare a thought for the salvation of their souls.

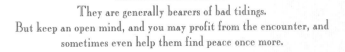

- A Little Gallery of Famous Ghosts -

Lucie

The white lady of the Château de Veauce in Allier. She was locked in the oubliette by a jealous husband in the 16th century.

Marie-Antoinette

Two young English women claim they saw her ghost in August, 1901, in the Petit Trianon in Versailles.

Little Lea

Mischievous by nature, the ghost of little Lea haunts forests in search of someone to play with.

Freddy Jackson

This Royal Air Force pilot appears in a group photo from 1919, two days after his death.

NEXT WEEK: LET HARRY PRICE TEACH YOU FEARSOME AND FORMIDABLE EXORCISM TECHNIQUES!

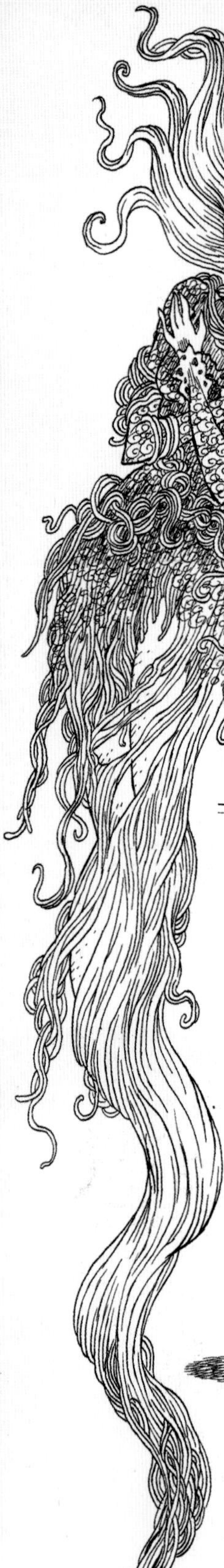

Do shadows of the night
haunt your bad dreams
and make your sleepless nights a veritable hell?
Act now! And find out what's included in the amazing

ALL-IN-ONE KIT *for* GHOST HUNTING

Anti-Ectoplasmic Net

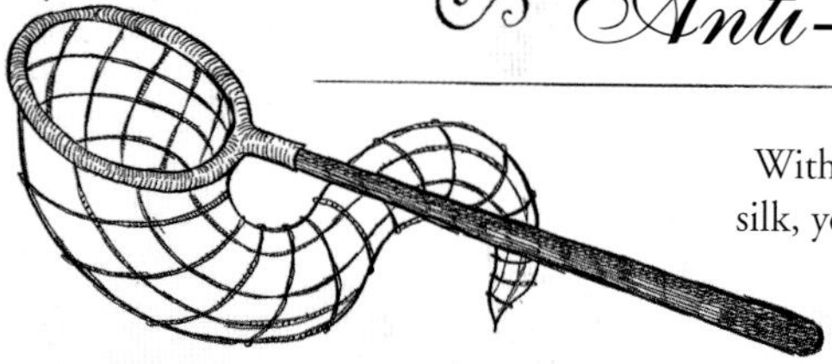

With its elderwood handle and a net woven from tarantula silk, you'll be ready for **real adventures!** Never again will you return empty-handed from the **hunt!**

Shadow Jar

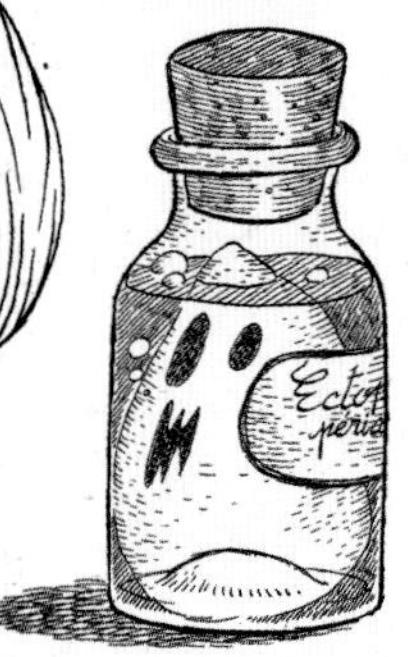

This hermetically sealed jar made from genuine Albanian crystal is **unbreakable**. It guarantees optimal preservation **until the end of time**.

"Ghost Blade" Dagger

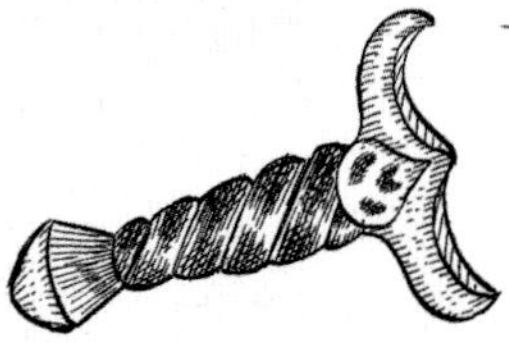

Its astral blade, **invisible** to mortals, will skewer the toughest specters! Ideal for revenants and **rambunctious poltergeists**.

Paralyzing Spray

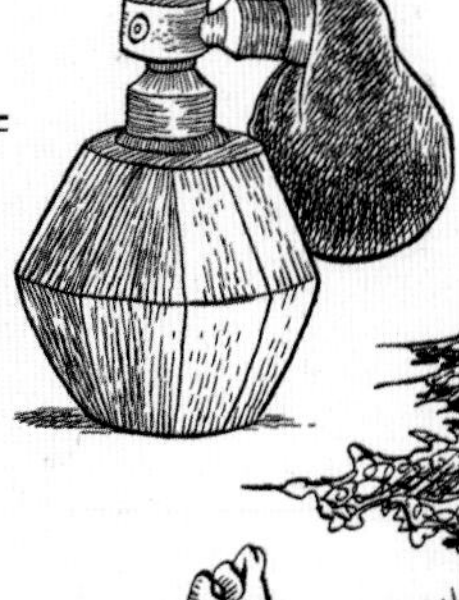

Its holy water solidifies ethereal beings by **instantaneously** paralyzing them!
(Does not work on flesh-and-blood kid sisters.)

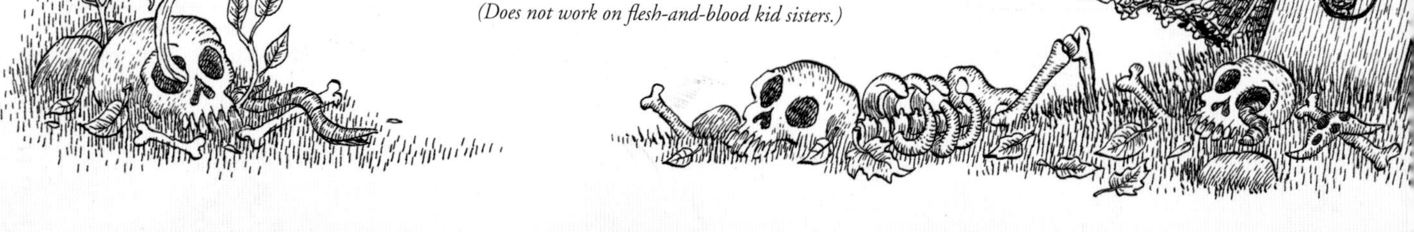

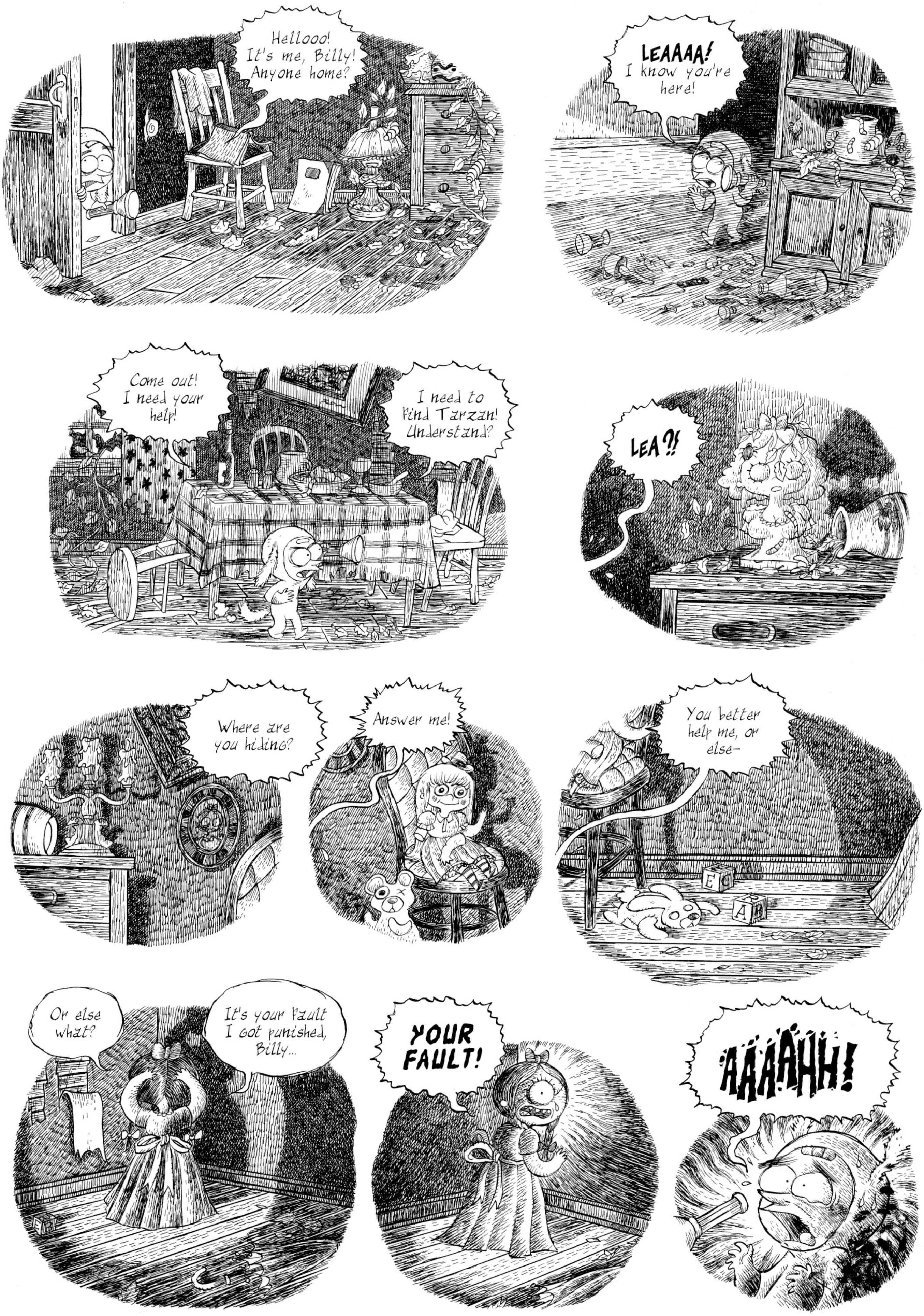
Hellooo! It's me, Billy! Anyone home?
LEAAAA! I know you're here!
Come out! I need your help!
I need to find Tarzan! Understand?
LEA?!
Where are you hiding?
Answer me!
You better help me, or else–
Or else what?
It's your fault I got punished, Billy...
YOUR FAULT!
AAAAHH!

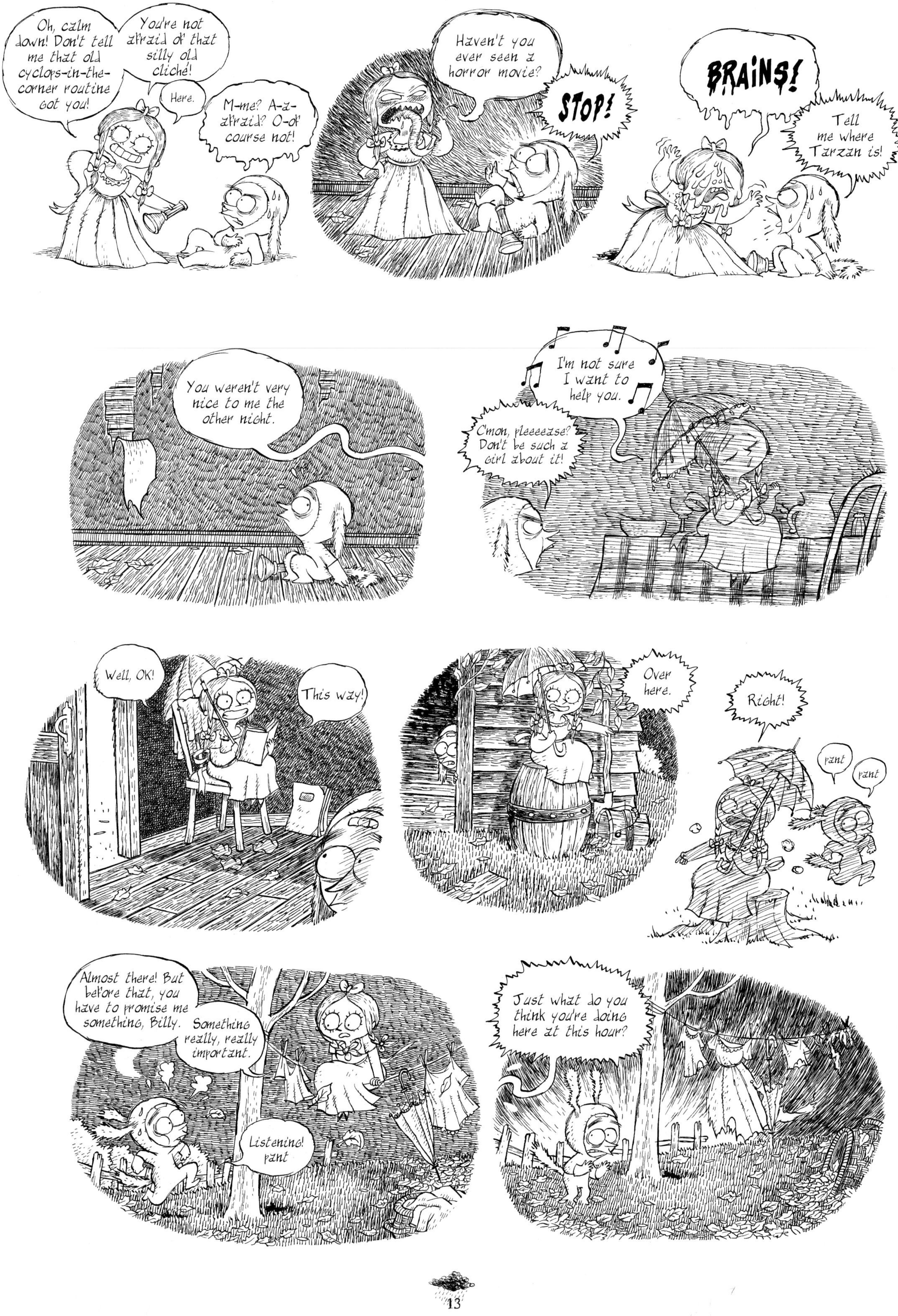
Oh, calm down! Don't tell me that old cyclops-in-the-corner routine got you!
You're not afraid of that silly old cliché!
Here.
M-me? A-a-afraid? O-of course not!
Haven't you ever seen a horror movie?
STOP!
BRAINS!
Tell me where Tarzan is!
You weren't very nice to me the other night.
I'm not sure I want to help you.
C'mon, pleeeeease? Don't be such a girl about it!
Well, OK!
This way!
Over here.
Right!
pant
pant
Almost there! But before that, you have to promise me something, Billy.
Something really, really important.
Listening! pant
Just what do you think you're doing here at this hour?

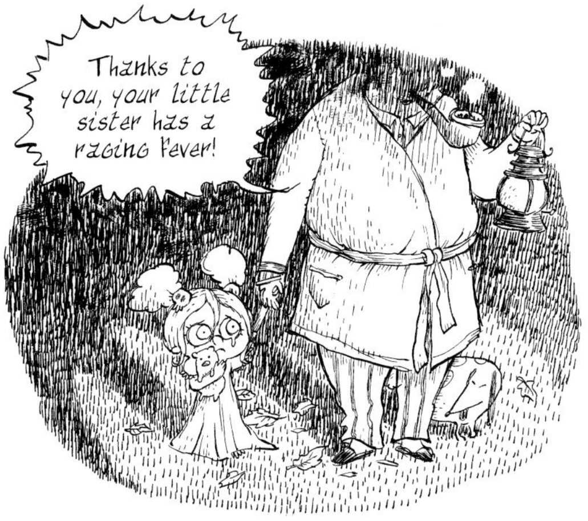
Thanks to you, your little sister has a raging fever!

"You should be in bed right now!" Yadda yadda... Dad was really furious. And so was I.

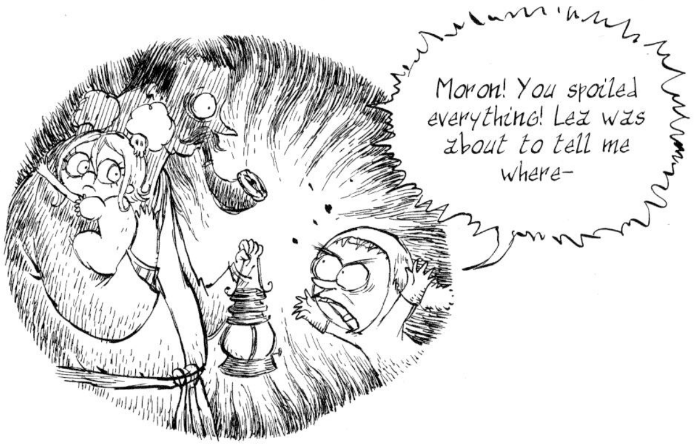
Moron! You spoiled everything! Lez was about to tell me where-

Dad broke in and gave me the spanking of my life. "Don't you take that tone with me! I'm your father!" he bellowed..

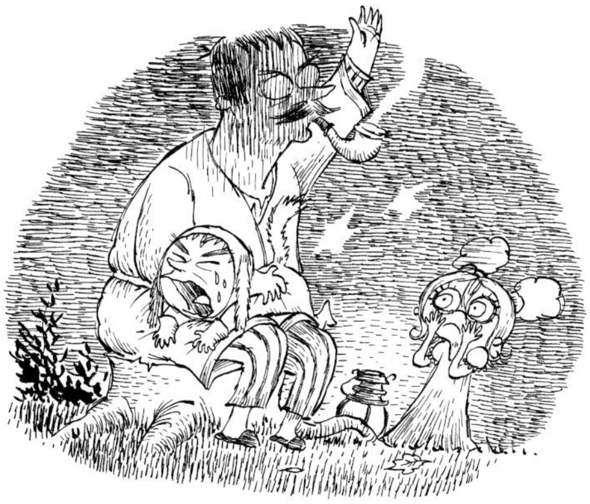

Then he lectured me the whole way back.

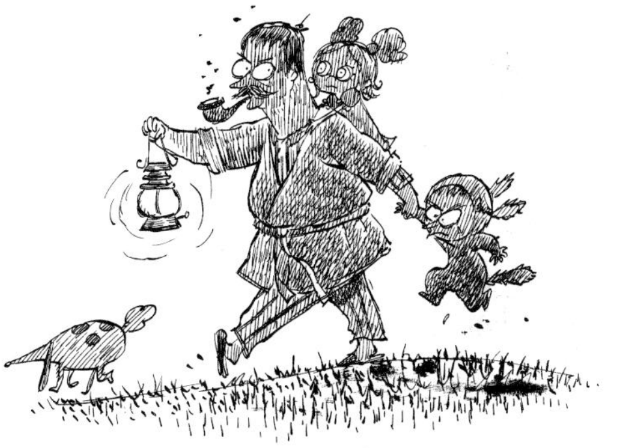

I was grounded. Not allowed to leave my room until he said so..

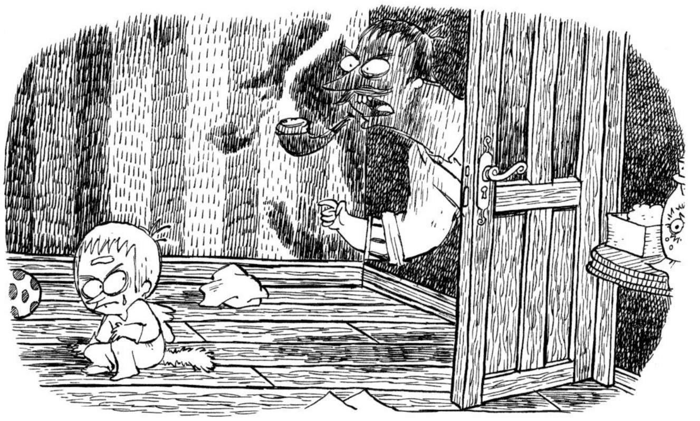

But I couldn't have cared less. Grownups were stupid. They didn't understand anything.

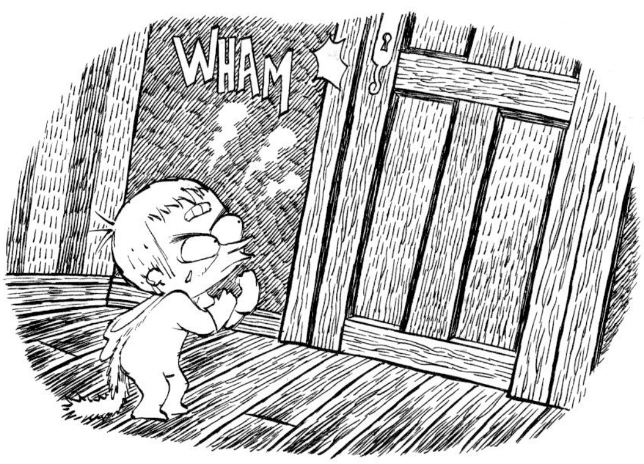
WHAM

They'd forgotten the children they used to be.

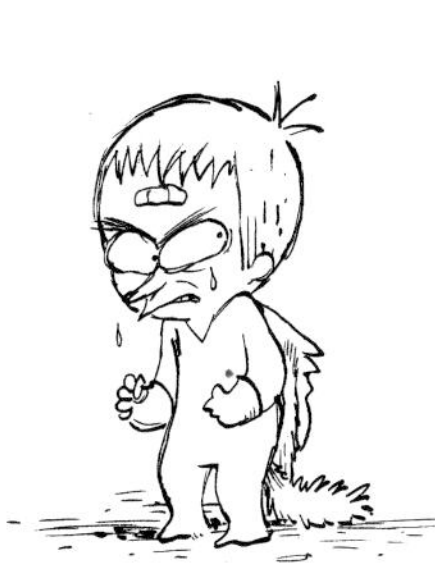

Tarzan...

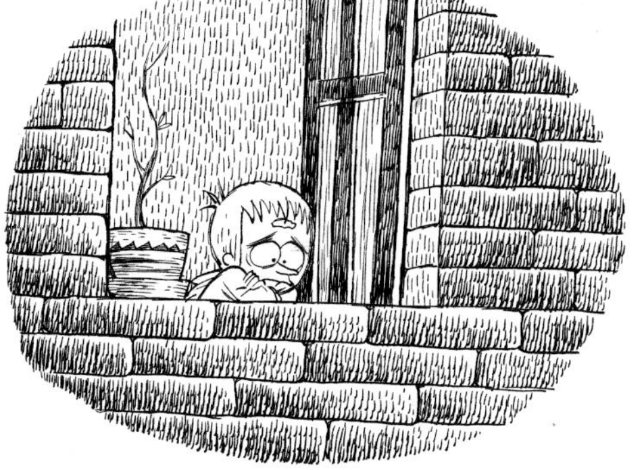

Cats

Half tiger, half ape,
cats have features that are, to say the least, strange.
Black cats are said to keep company with witches,
be incarnations of the Devil himself,
and guide damned souls
to Hell...

One thing is certain:
cats are clean and well-mannered.
Indeed, they take care to bury their calls of nature
so as not to inconvenience others.

*(Their excrement is said to have magical powers,
and nourish plants and the soil.)*

Fig.4   Cattus Griffum . Lib.II   100

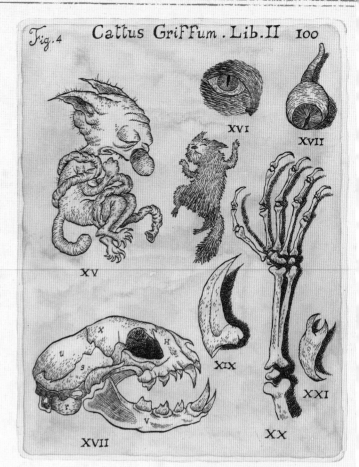

XVI

XVII

XV

XIX

XXI

XVII

XX

A) List of Superpowers

Can leap from
high places, but
not from low
places very well.

See at night thanks
to their dilating
pupils.

Their fur protects them from cold
but also from heat.

Can move about silently thanks to pads on
their paw-bottoms.

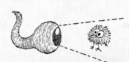

Retractable claws:
a fearsome weapon.

Naturally immune to Vermiculi venom.

Raspy tongues for
brushing fur.

Cleansing saliva so they don't
have to brush their teeth.
(Lucky devils!)

*They are fearsome hunters who
always remember to bring their
masters a gift.*

B) Intimidation Tactics

Formidable and effective!
When they are angry,
they hiss, spit, and arch their backs
raising their hackles
until they resemble actual monsters.

(Gives me the willies!)

How to Handle a Nasty Cat

They are afraid of dogs.

They hate water.

They don't like noise (since their hearing is highly developed).

If you snip their whiskers, they lose their balance.

They don't like being tossed in the air to see if they'll land on their feet.

They just die of fright if you tie a pot to the end of their tail.

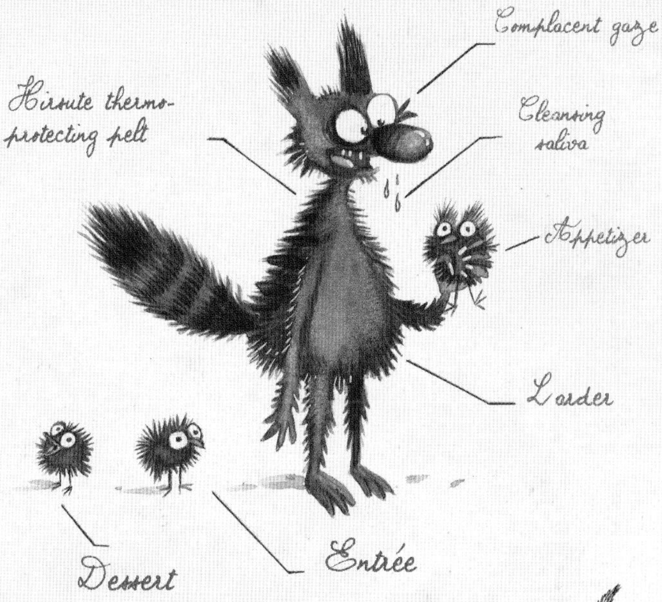
Complacent gaze
Hirsute thermo-protecting pelt
Cleansing saliva
Appetizer
Larder
Dessert
Entrée

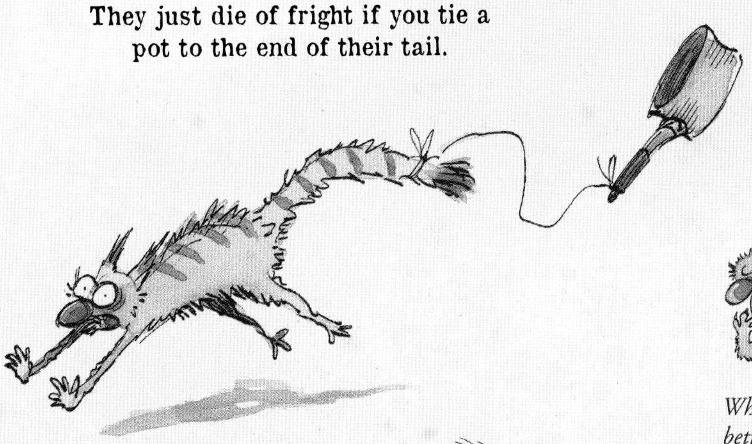

Warning

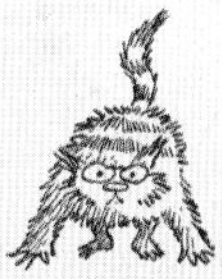

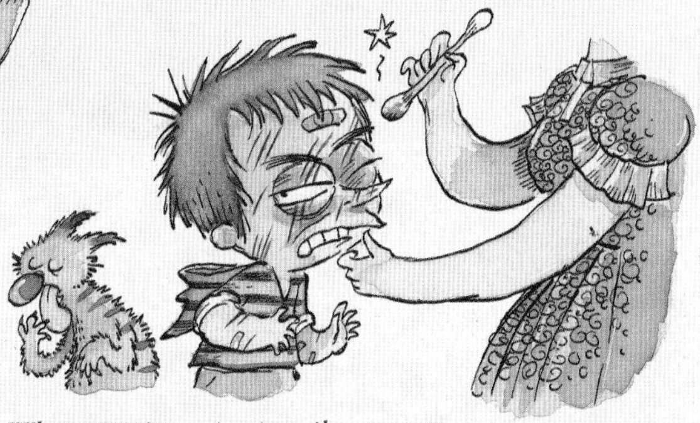

When a cat is waving its tail, better leave it alone. This means it's annoyed. (Not to be confused with dogs, who're the opposite.)

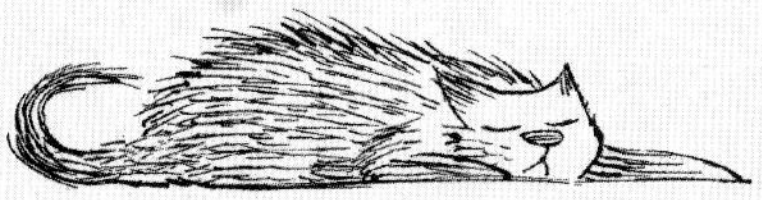

C) Beliefs and Divinatory Signs

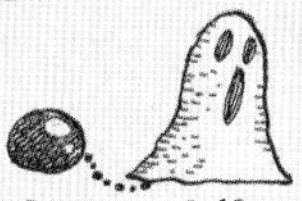

It is said cats can see ghosts and travel on the astral plane while asleep. Which would explain their impressive powers of recovery...

If a cat sneezes once, it's a good sign. However, two sneezes are a sign of sickness or ghostly possession.

If a cat abandons a home, it means great misfortune will strike.

A cat sitting with its back to the fire is a sign of an oncoming storm. (Either that, or its butt's cold.)

If you cross a street right after a black cat, wish any wish and it will come true.

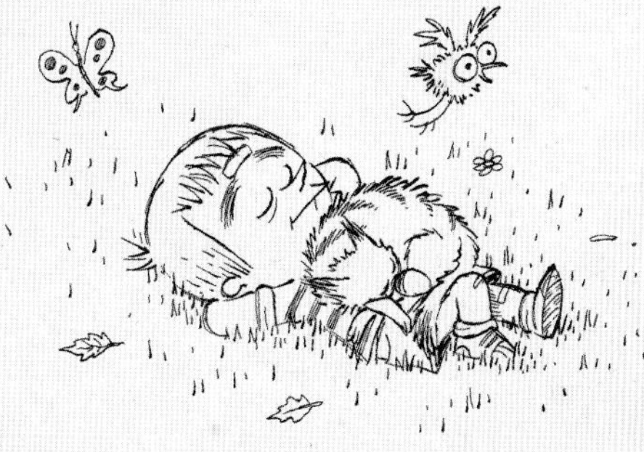

When a cat scratches behind its ear with one paw, rain is on its way.

Stepping on a striped cat's tail is a sign that you will get deep scratches on your ankles.

D) Purring: Meaning and Origin

Where is it from, that strange, incessant sound, like a large tractor?

WHY DO THEY PURR?

Well, duh: just to say they're happy.

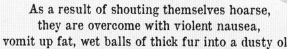

HEALTH BENEFITS (FOR A LONG LIFE):
A purring cat curled up on your belly
twice a day for a week
relieves anxiety and soothes away worry.

E) Reproduction

When mating season is upon us,
cats climb up on the rooftops
and launch into a troubling lament.
Their yowling sounds like
babies whining.

How Do They Reproduce?

As a result of shouting themselves hoarse,
they are overcome with violent nausea,
and vomit up fat, wet balls of thick fur into a dusty old box.

| 10 minutes | 15 days | 3 weeks | 1 month | 2 months |

As the weeks go by, these furballs will grow and develop into cute little kittens.

Cats have their character,
their modesty, their mystery.
When the time comes,
they slip away to die alone,
without bothering a soul...

From the Curious and Bizarre Encyclopedia of Cryptozoology, by Billy Fog

*"I don't know which way my path will wind
But I'll walk it better with your hand in mine."*

Georges Brassens

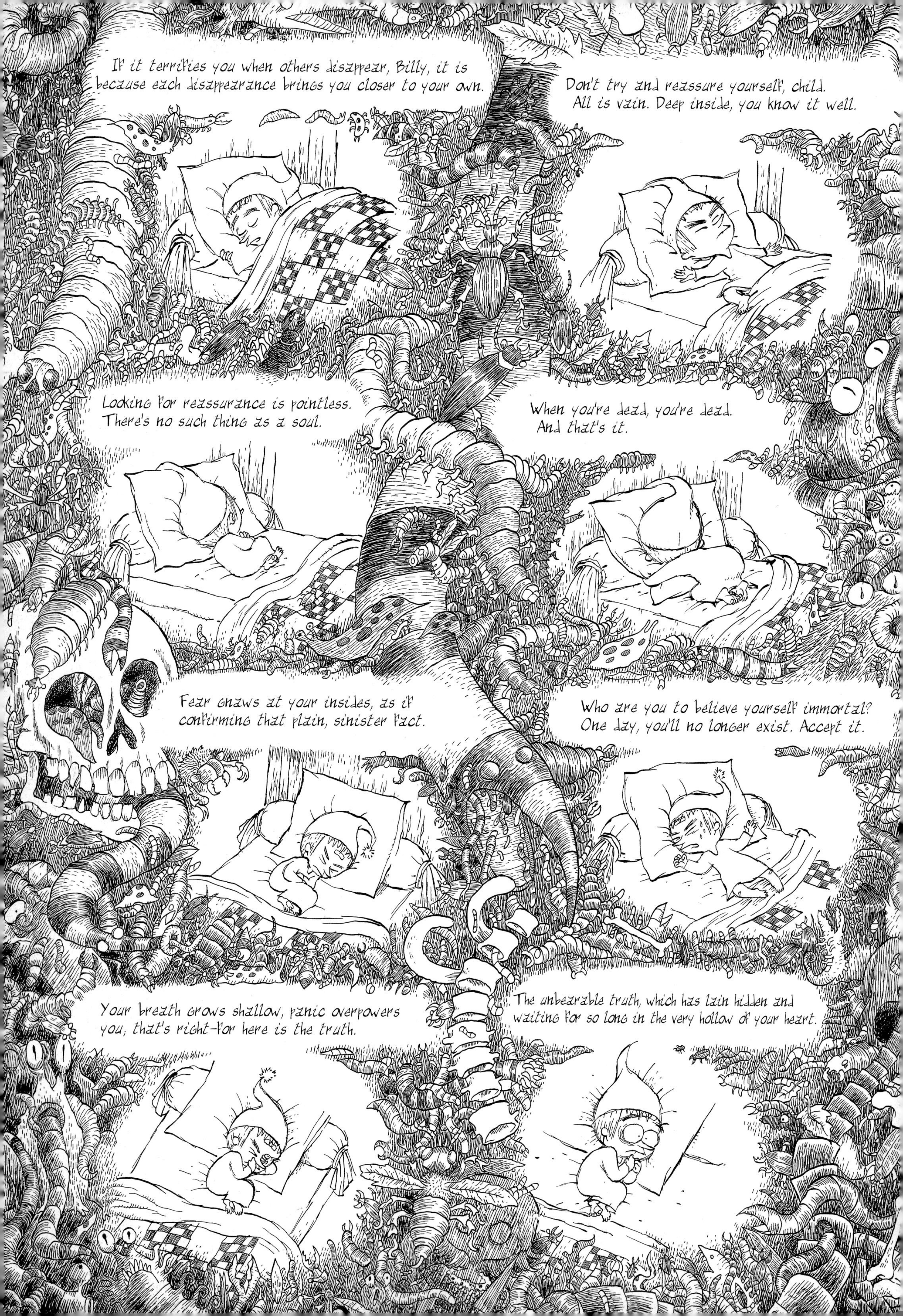
If it terrifies you when others disappear, Billy, it is because each disappearance brings you closer to your own.
Don't try and reassure yourself, child. All is vain. Deep inside, you know it well.
Looking for reassurance is pointless. There's no such thing as a soul.
When you're dead, you're dead. And that's it.
Fear gnaws at your insides, as if confirming that plain, sinister fact.
Who are you to believe yourself immortal? One day, you'll no longer exist. Accept it.
Your breath grows shallow, panic overpowers you; that's right—for here is the truth.
The unbearable truth, which has lain hidden and waiting for so long in the very hollow of your heart.

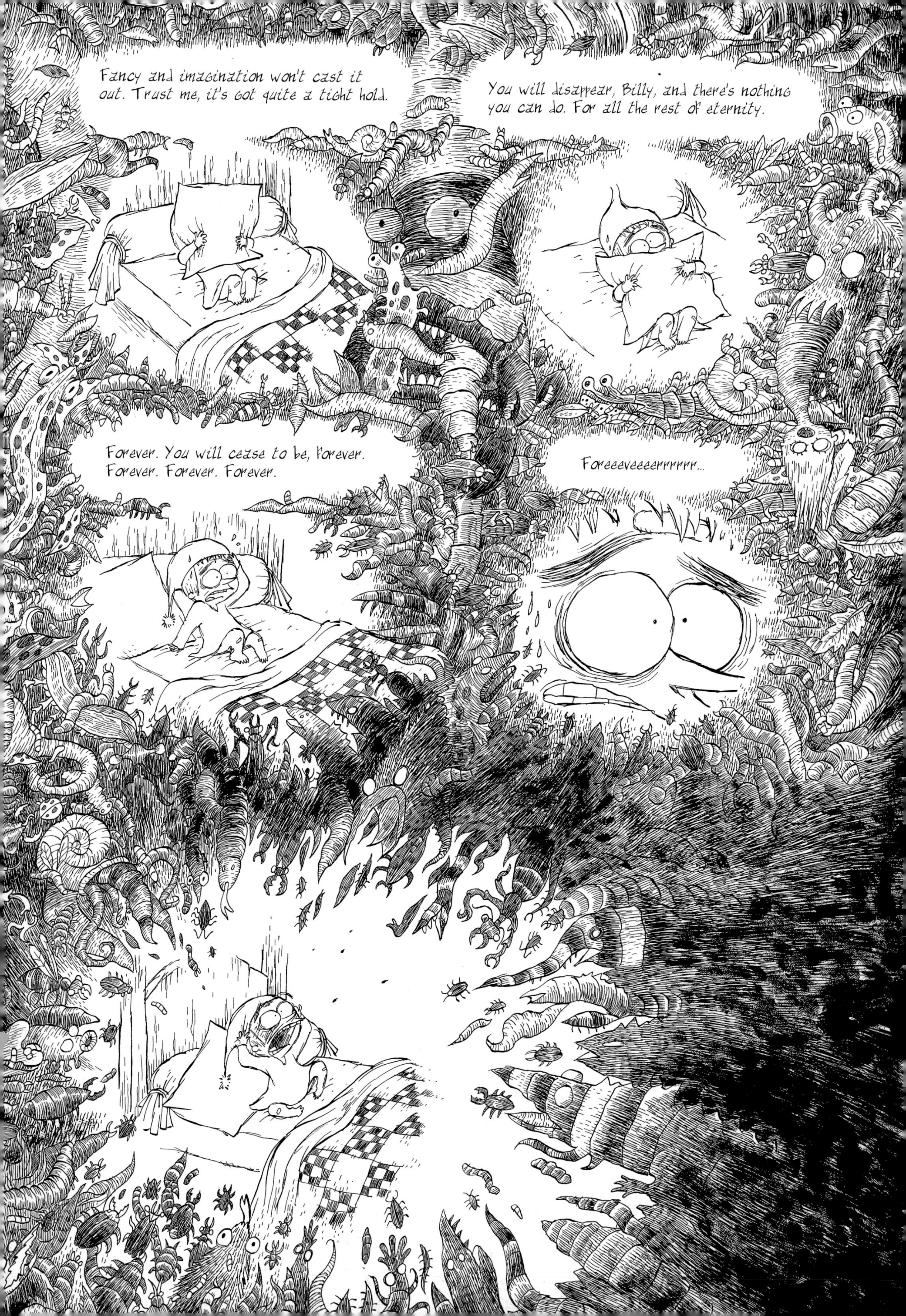
Fancy and imagination won't cast it out. Trust me, it's got quite a tight hold.
You will disappear, Billy, and there's nothing you can do. For all the rest of eternity.
Forever. You will cease to be, forever. Forever. Forever. Forever.
Foreeeveeeeerrrrrr...

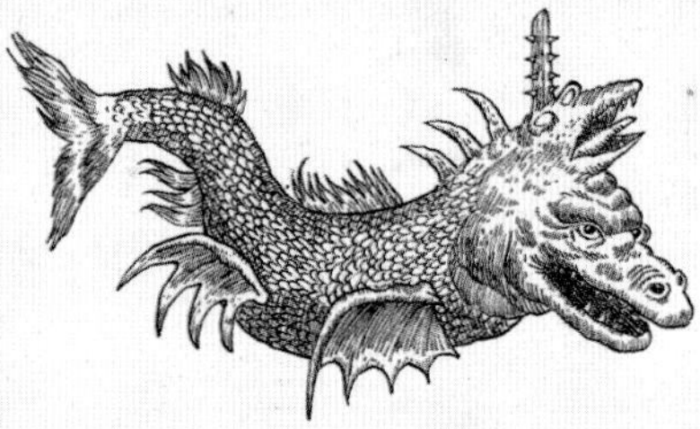

Nightmares

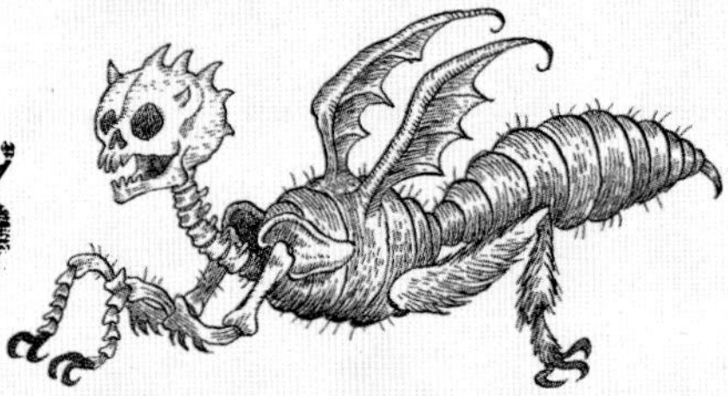

(n.m.) literally, "night spirit of torment"

Nightmares are the sons of shadows, the children of fear and obsession.
Belonging to the Tulpa family,
nightmares usually materialize after nightfall, in children's rooms.
They lurk in the shadows and wait till the hour is late
before coming out and terrorizing sleepers.

☾TAB. XIX☽ INCUBUS NOCTURNIS

Polymorphic nightmare appearing during REM sleep

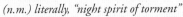

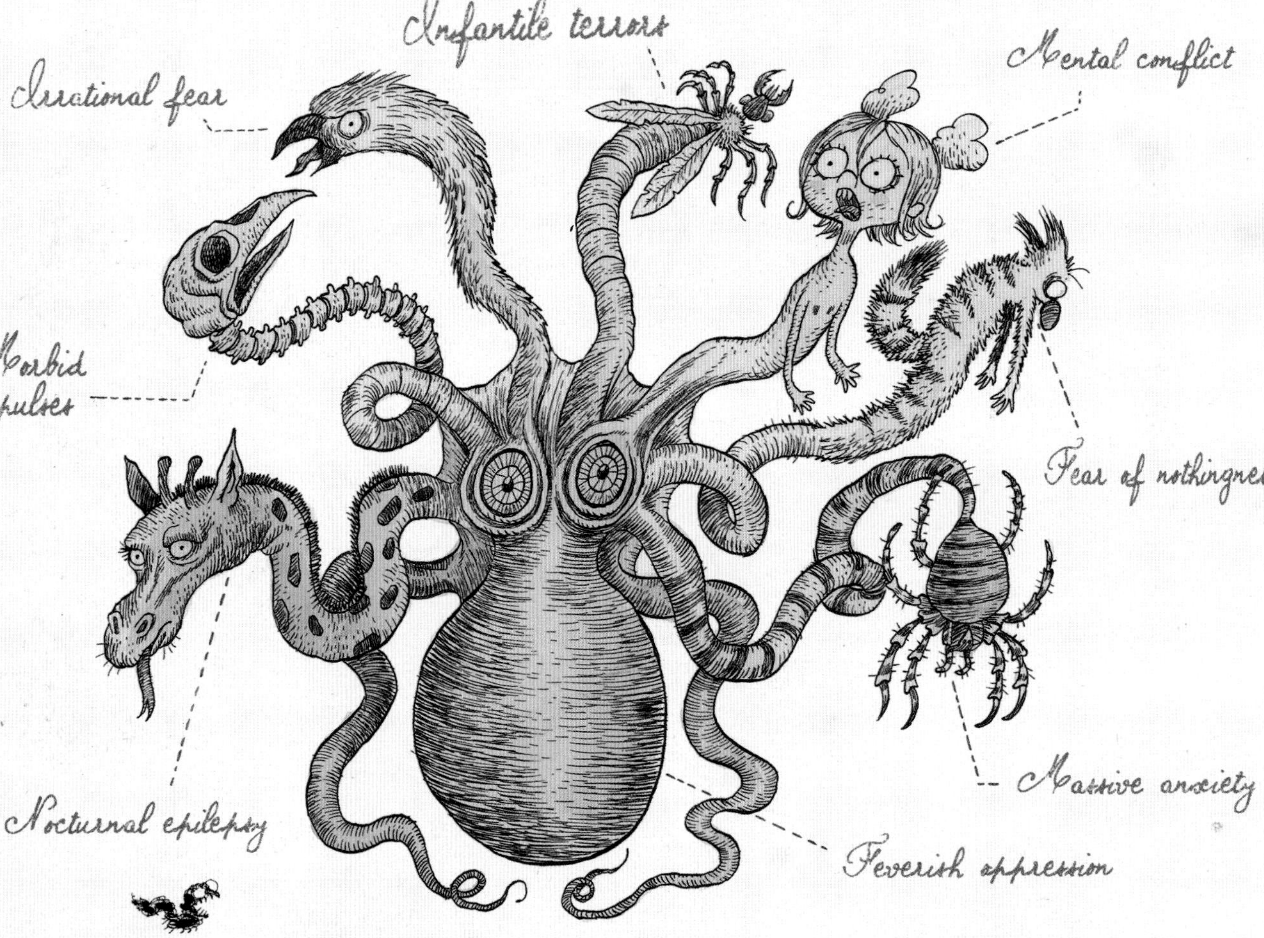
Infantile terrors
Irrational fear
Mental conflict
Morbid impulses
Fear of nothingness
Nocturnal epilepsy
Massive anxiety
Feverish oppression

They rise up as soon as you close your eyes
and shoot tiny microscopic darts
into the pupils of insomniacs
to make them close their eyes.

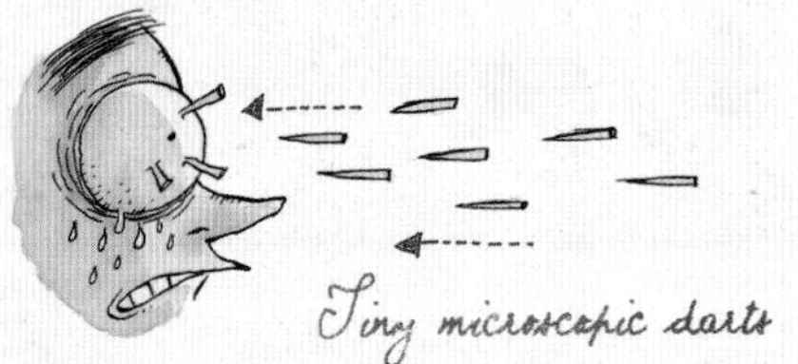
Tiny microscopic darts

(Certain nightmares also use grains of sand.)

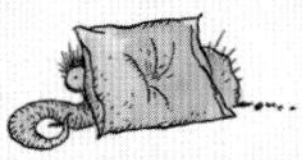

Favorite Hiding Spots:

- *Under beds.*
- *In closets.*
- *Under pillows.*
- *Behind curtains.*

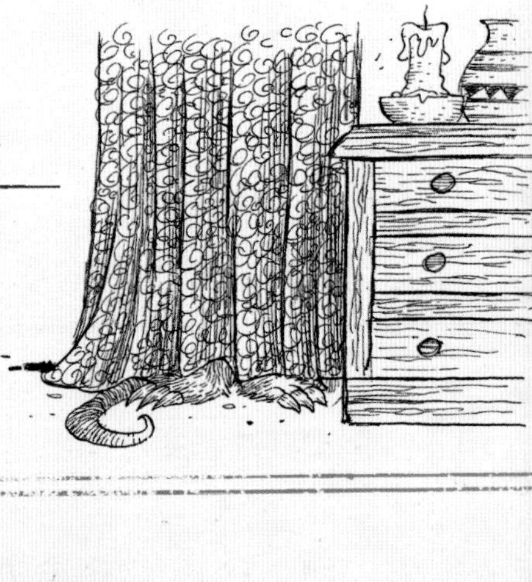

Warning

White light from a bedside lamp
keeps them back, but doesn't banish them.

However, the yellowish glow from a candle
or an old oil lamp attracts them.

There is a nightmare for every fear that a small child can feel.
Their goal: to stimulate our phobias so our hearts race and our bodies sweat.
Nightmares adore a cold sweat, and relish licking up the drops with their long raspy tongues.

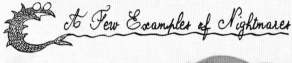 A Few Examples of Nightmares

a. *A baby with crab claws*
who walks on walls.

b. *Having a centipede instead of legs.*

d. *Vomiting wasps.*

c. *Your mother with a wolf's head.*

e. *Having a big sister.*

Nightmares come in many shapes. They adapt themselves to the fears of their prey.
Ex.: Teacher, spider, monster, wolf, or sometimes, in cases of high fever, a mixture of all of these.

 Recommendations

Take a dozen deep breathes to avoid giving in to panic.
Then try to think of something funny.
Laugh very loudly in the dark; laughter's positive energy keeps them back.

If that doesn't do it, wake your parents up in the middle of the night
so they'll chase the nightmares out the window.
But a mom and a dad sleeping after
a long day of work may be hard to wake.

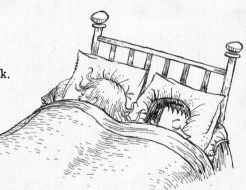

From the Curious and Bizarre Encyclopedia of Cryptozoology, by Billy Fog

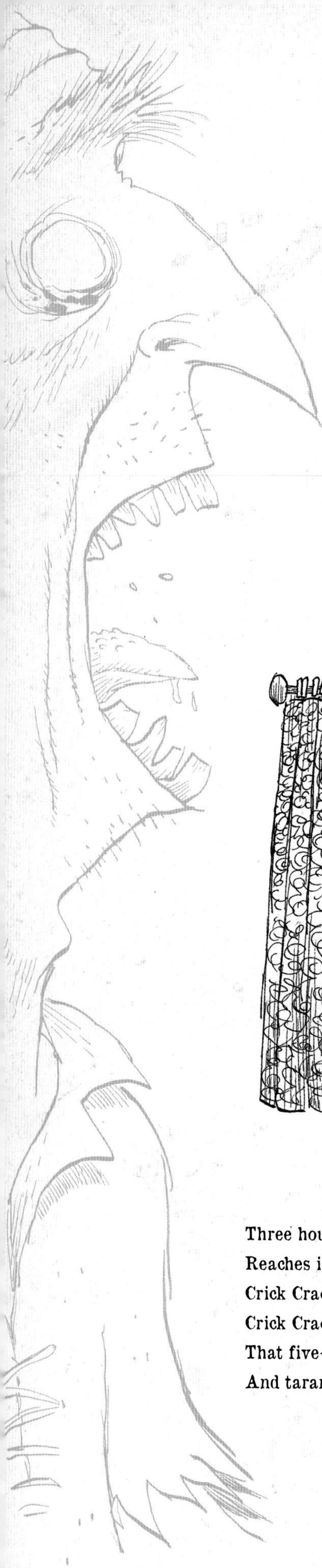

The Boogeyman

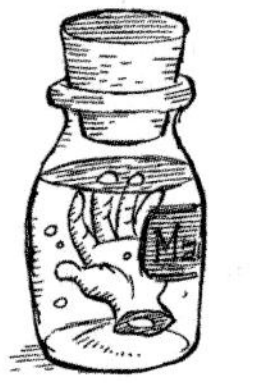

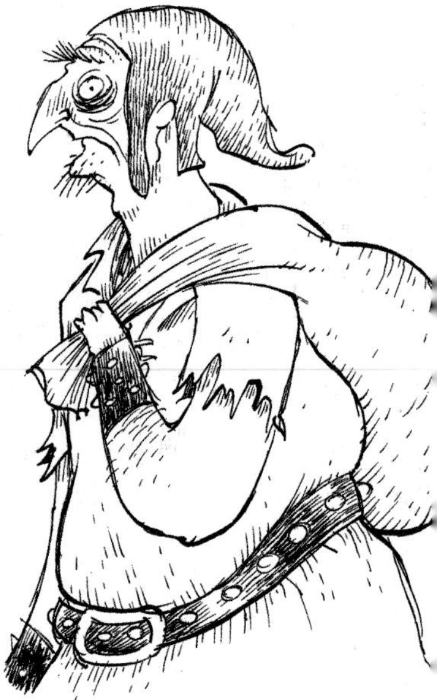

Three hours after midnight, and the living asleep,
The bell tolls the hour in the dark of nights deep.
Crick Crack Crunch! Hear that unearthly din!
Crick Crack Crunch! And you shiver within.
The Boogeyman cometh, his great tongue a-lollin',
In the morning you'll find that your hands he has stolen.

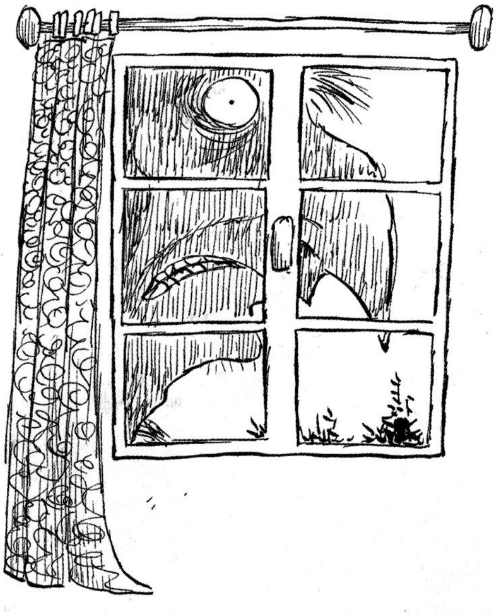

Three hours after midnight, his hunger to slake,
He peers in your window, checks if you're awake.
Crick Crack Crunch! O, the sound of your doom!
Crick Crack Crunch! You're alone in your room!
Every minute that passes fills you with despair.
Quick! Hide your hands while you've still got a pair.

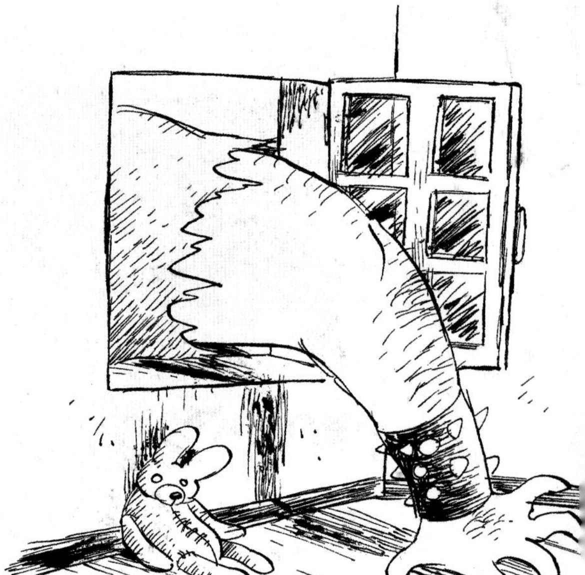

Three hours after midnight, and a great hairy arm
Reaches into your bedroom to do you great harm.
Crick Crack Crunch! O'er the floorboards it errs.
Crick Crack Crunch! It's too late for your prayers.
That five-legged spider creeps up to your bed
And tarantula-terrible, fills you with dread.

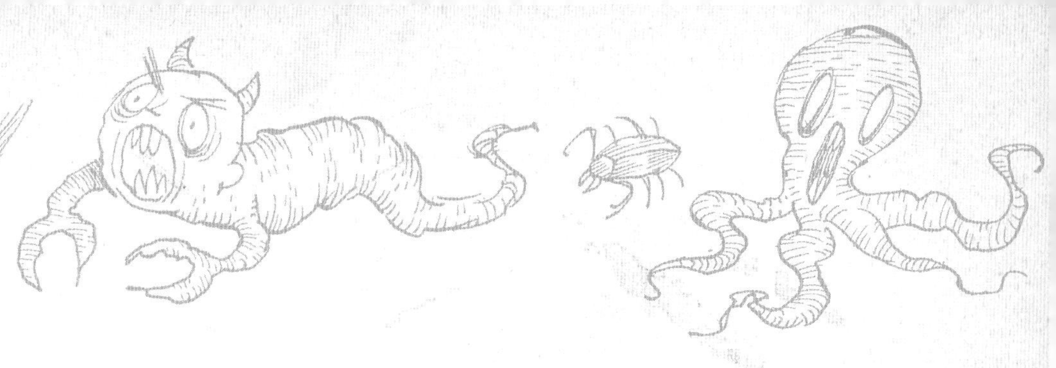

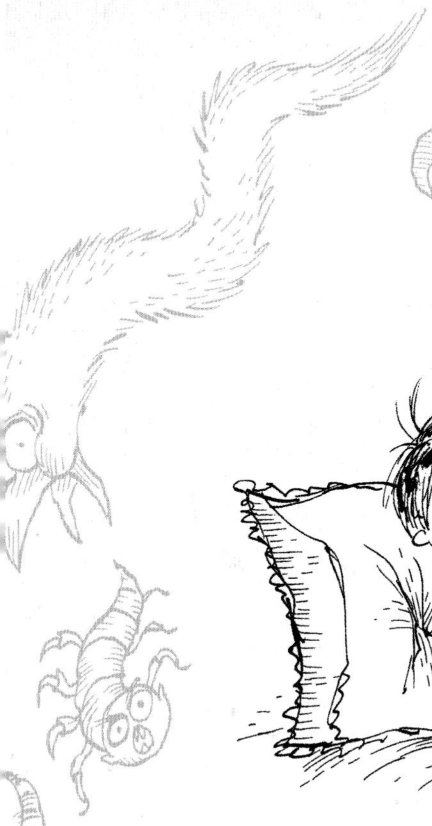

He gurgles, he snickers, he gnashes and tears,
You scream and you plead: he's the stuff of nightmares,
In a cold sweat you wriggle and struggle and fight,
'Gainst his chewing and gnawing with all of your might.

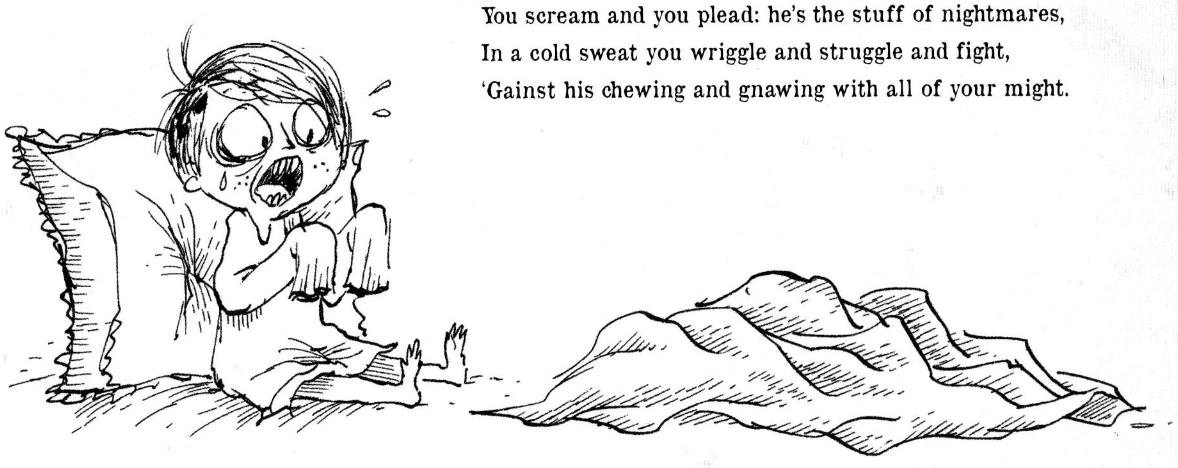

Crick Crack Crunch! Did the Boogeyman sup?
Crick Crack Crunch! Is his belly full up?

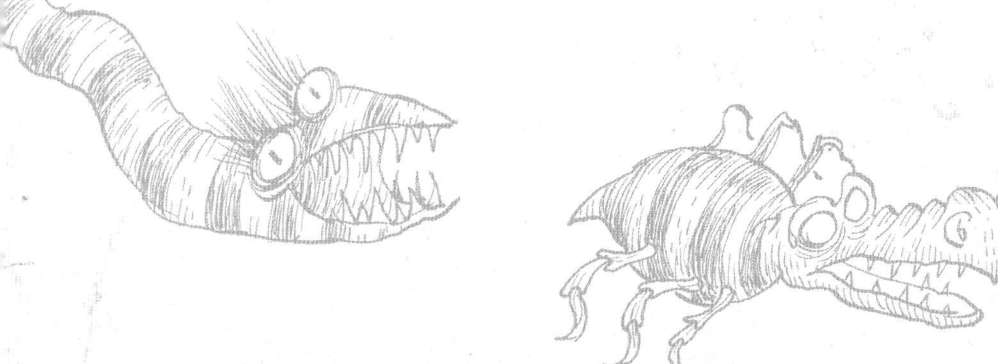

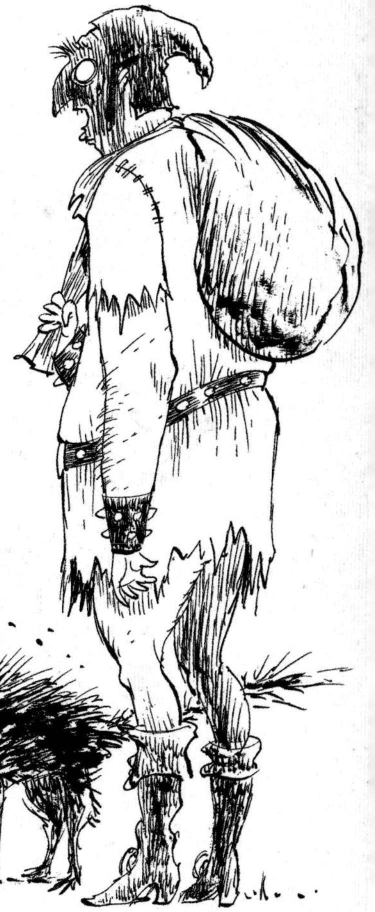

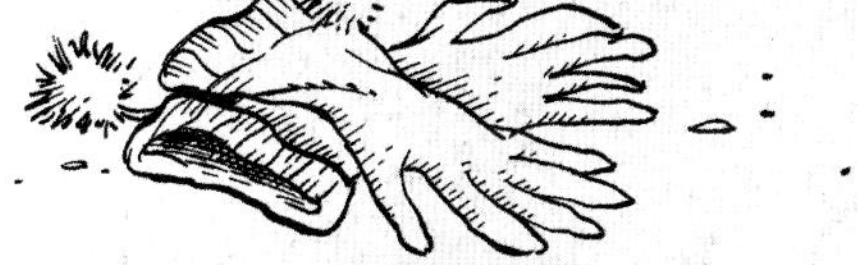

Insomniac kids, if to nightmares you're prone,
Protect your hands whene'er you sleep alone.
Keep them under the sheets, under wraps snug and tight,
Lest you feel the crick-crack of the Boogeyman's bite.

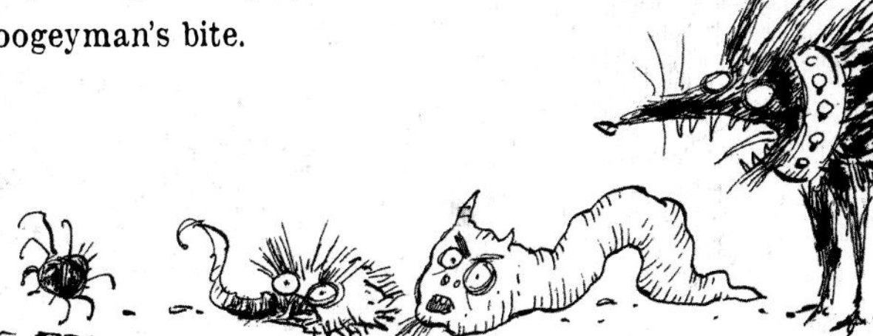

"I haven't been very good this year, especially not to Jeannie
(my sister). I've been kind of mean to her.
I don't know why, since actually,
I love her a lot."

- Billy Fog

Kid Sisters
pueris filiae fraternum

Of all the creatures catalogued in the Encyclopedia of Cryptozoology, the "kid sister" is without a doubt the strangest and most complex...

Contrary to common belief, "kid sisters" are not delivered one fine morning via stork.

Even if your parents maintain they are born from rosebuds, this is baloney. Question them, and you will see from their embarrassed faces that these are lies meant to keep you from being terrified!

For kid sisters grow and mutate in our mothers' bellies... Over the course of several months, like little vampires, they nibble on the food inside mothers' stomachs.

A pregnant mother is always hungry, and often tired (for that very reason).

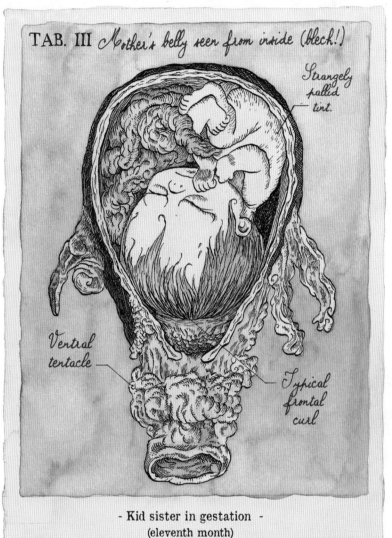

TAB. III *Mother's belly seen from inside (blech!)*

Strangely pallid tint.

Ventral tentacle

Typical frontal curl

- Kid sister in gestation -
(eleventh month)

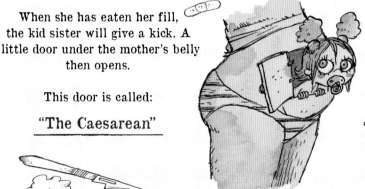

When she has eaten her fill, the kid sister will give a kick. A little door under the mother's belly then opens.

This door is called:

"The Caesarean"

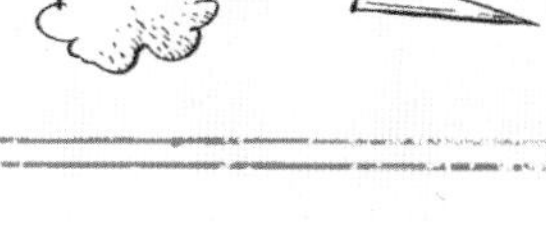

*Doctors (pediatricians) then put kid sisters in jars so they can finish mutating peacefully on a shelf somewhere in a dark place.
(Ex. cellar, attic…)*

Beware

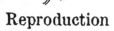

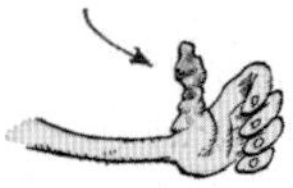

thumb after being sucked

a. Her saliva has acid.

Blond locks

b. Her pigtails are extrasensory antennae.

super long optic nerve
vacuous grin

c. Her eyes can see in the dark.

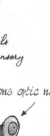

Shark teeth

d. Her strident cry can pierce eardrums.

e. Her pretty little mittens

f. ...turn into fearsome claws!

- Reproduction -

It is the father who plants the seed...

Fig: 1. Nuptial display

Puer Feminum Fraternae

Seeds for kid sisters or kid brothers are found in a special store.

Kid Sister Seeds
Sale
I want that one!

- Instructions -

1. Take one seed before each meal with a tall glass of saltwater.

2. Kid sister seeds are a terribly bitter pill to swallow, and often cause bad nausea. Recommendation: a side of strawberries will make it easier.

3. Repeat this process tirelessly, until you no longer throw up the ingested seed.

4. When you become irritable, you will know you are ... Pregnant!

Problems and solutions

♦ If your mother has too much trouble swallowing her kid sister seed, give her a nice Ferrero Rocher (into which you have previously slipped a seed). She will have a hard time saying no, since moms love chocolate.

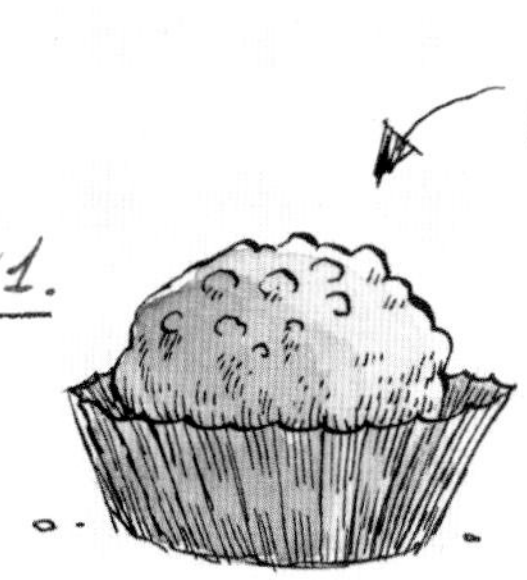

Fig 1.

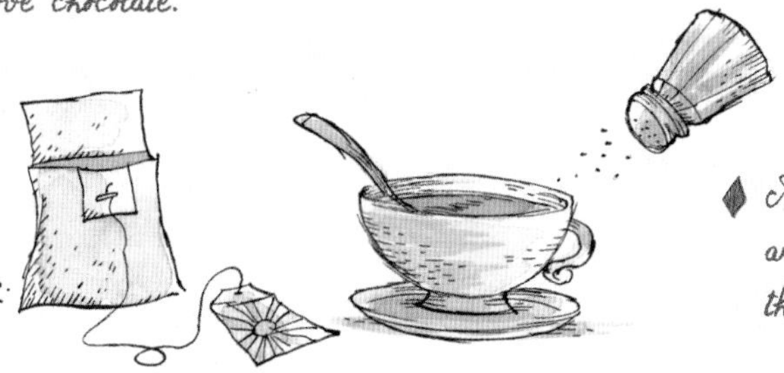

Fig 2.

♦ Add a little salt to her tea, and tell her it's an ancient Japanese infusion that helps break down the fats in chocolate.

♦ Sodium chloride (salt), required for the little embryo's development, will soon produce results.

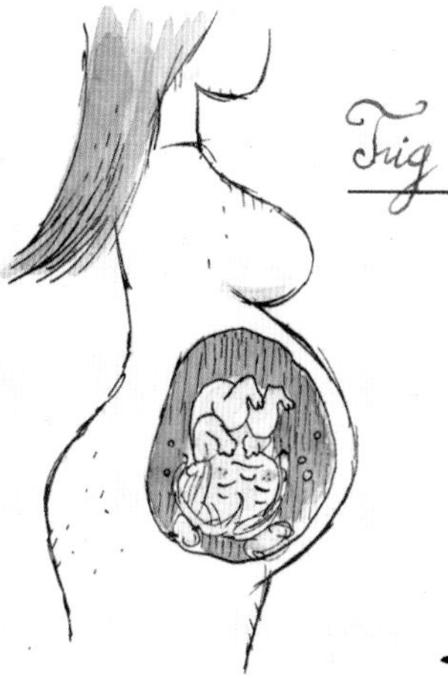

Fig 3.

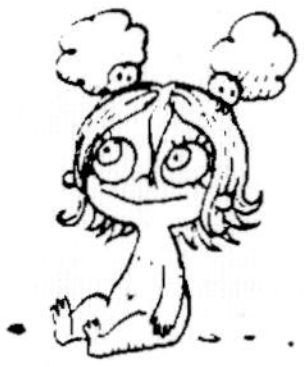

Gestation

Principal stages in the metamorphosis of the little mutant

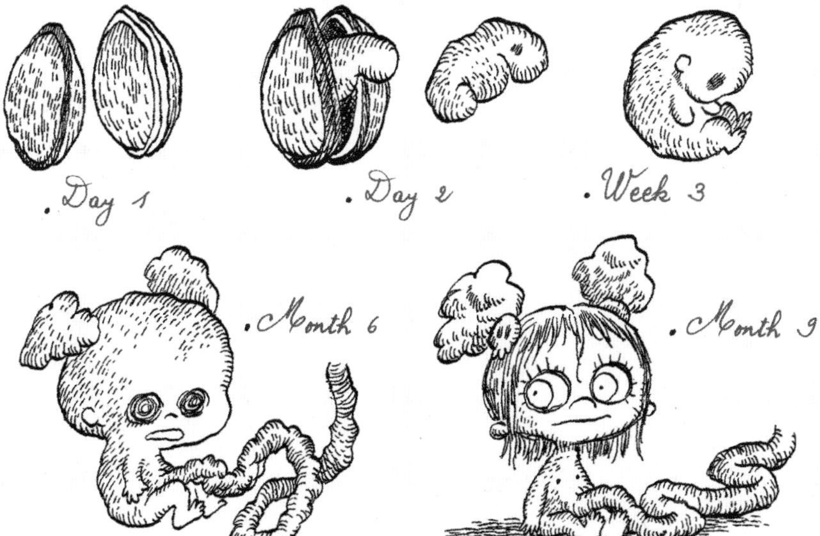

. Day 1
. Day 2
. Week 3
. Month 6
. Month 9

Despite many flaws, the kid sister can be a playmate perfect for brightening up long winter nights.

But don't ever let your guard down, and remember: the best defense is a good offense!

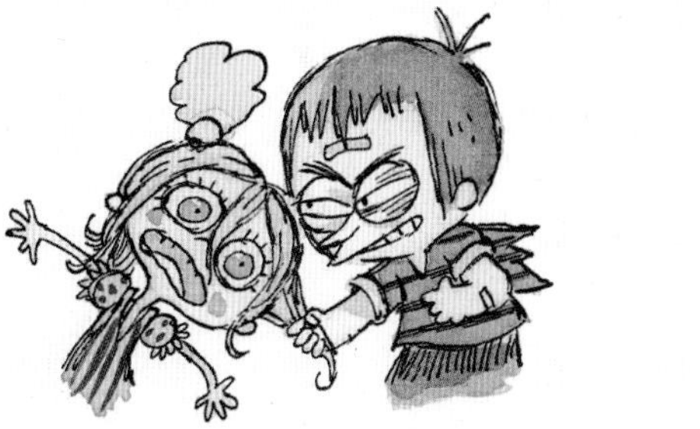

Clumsy, discreet, and affectionate way of showing your kid sister you love her, even though she's a girl.

Special Warning

It is strictly forbidden
to drink alcohol during pregnancy,
for this substance may transform your baby
into a two-headed hydrocephalic ghoul!

From the Curious and Bizarre Encyclopedia of Cryptozoology, by Billy Fog

Are you an only child? Is boredom your daily bread?
Do you require a harmless, kowtowing punching bag?
Stop pining away and try

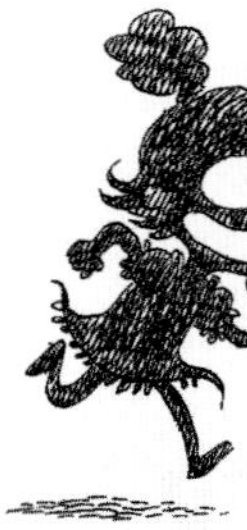

KID SISTER SEEDS

RESULTS GUARANTEED!

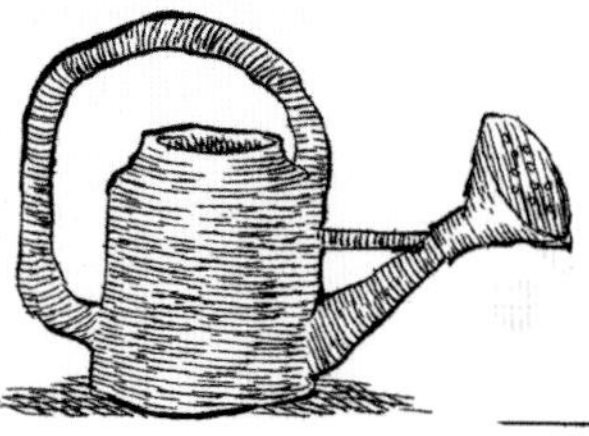

Your mother can swallow seeds too, but the gestation period is ***far too long*** (around 9 months).

Plant them in fertile soil, rich in mineral salts:
ALL IT TAKES IS 9 DAYS!

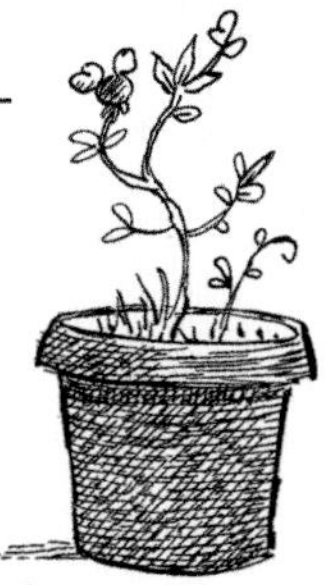

CLEVER TIP!

- *CAN'T MAKE HER STAND UP STRAIGHT?* -

USE A STAKE!

Your kid sister can lean on it to keep herself from growing up hunchbacked.

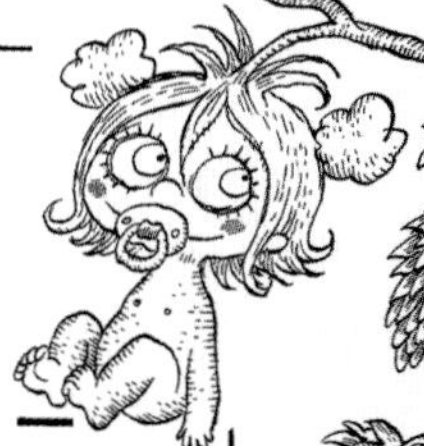

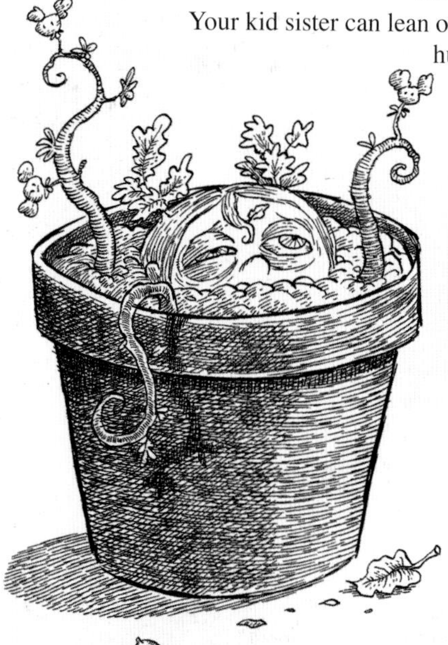

Special Offer!

PIGTAIL CLIPPERS

Buy 5 seed packets and get a pair of splendid cast iron garden shears for free! Use them to trim your kid sister's pigtails with precision, so her hair will grow back lush and luxuriant. Then you'll always be able to spot her: a bigger, easier target.

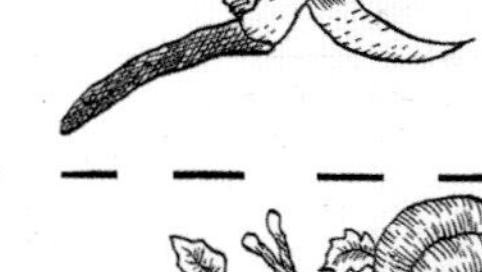

Satisfaction Guaranteed!

Should our product fail to satisfy, you will have one month to bring your kid sister back to a florist, or a vegetable stand, where you can exchange her for other seeds.

managed to give the "Bag Man" the slip, and brilliantly maneuvered the Machiavellian schemes of the Lady of the Well...

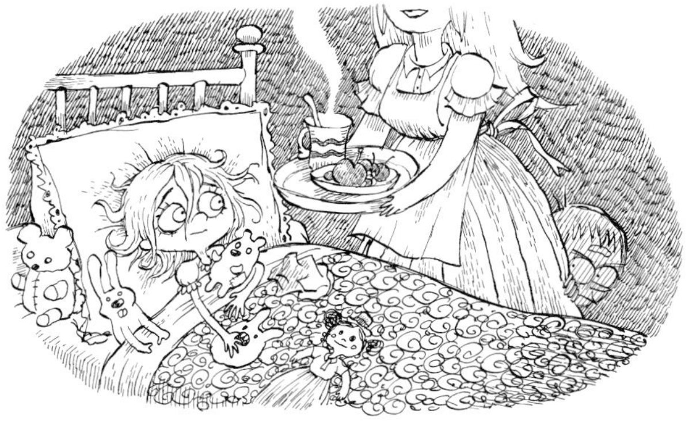

...successfully fought off the Ophiuchus....

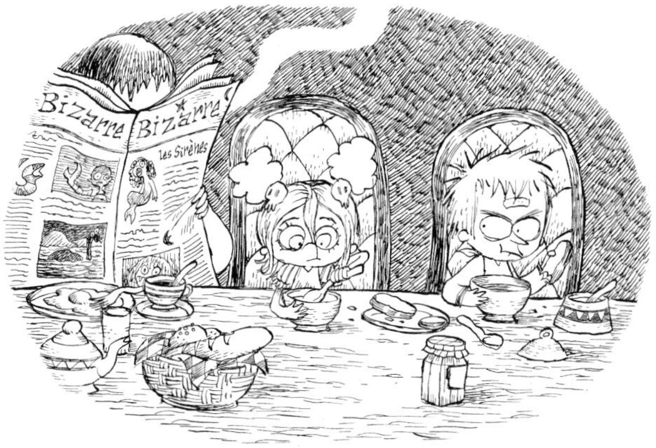
Bizarre
Bizarre

My only mistake had been to underestimate that most fearsome of creatures...

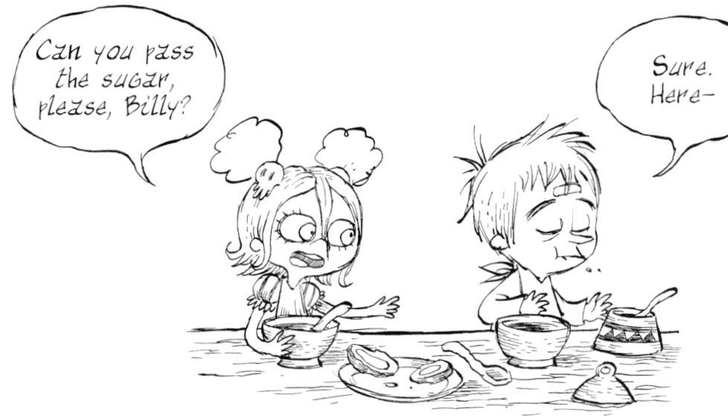
Can you pass the sugar, please, Billy?
Sure. Here-

My kid sister!

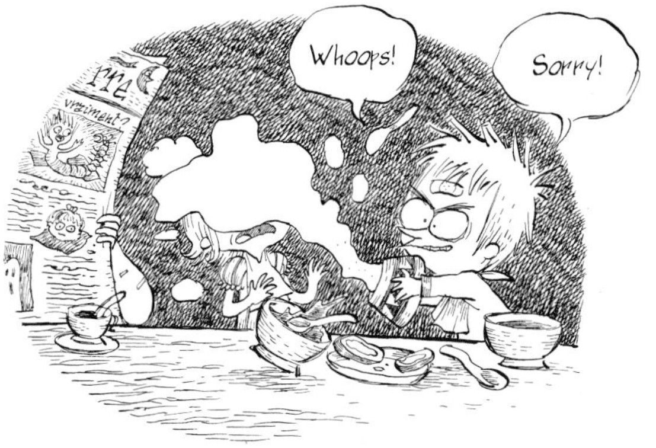
Whoops!
Sorry!

She would learn what fate awaited traitors.

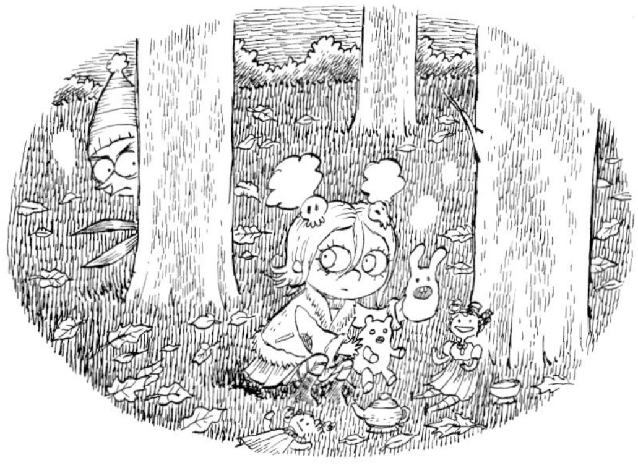

For if I had run aground so close to my goal, it was all her fault.

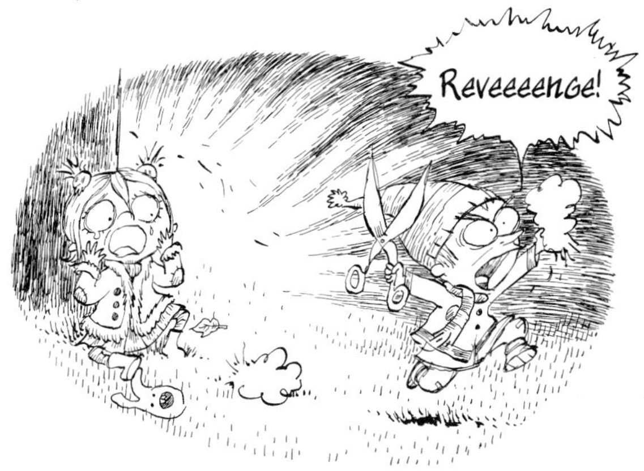
Reveeeenge!

But I wasn't the kind to let myself be defeated so easily.

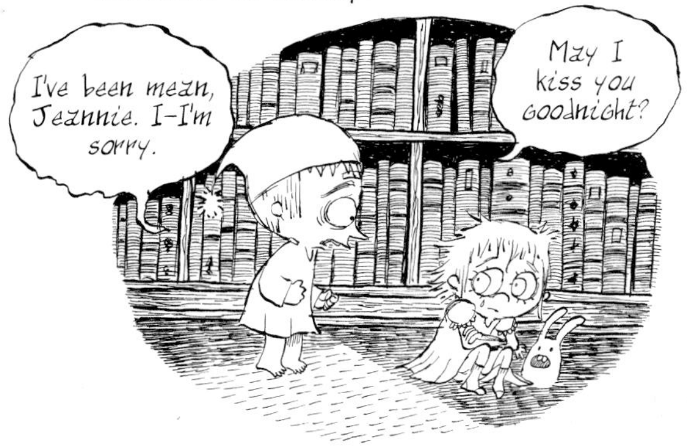
I've been mean, Jeannie. I-I'm sorry.
May I kiss you goodnight?

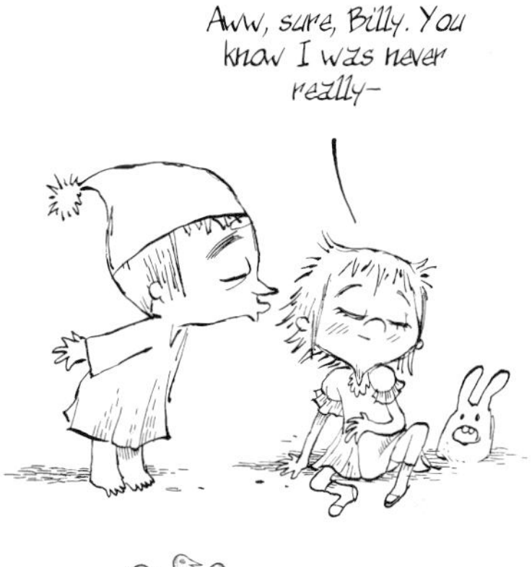
Aww, sure, Billy. You know I was never really-

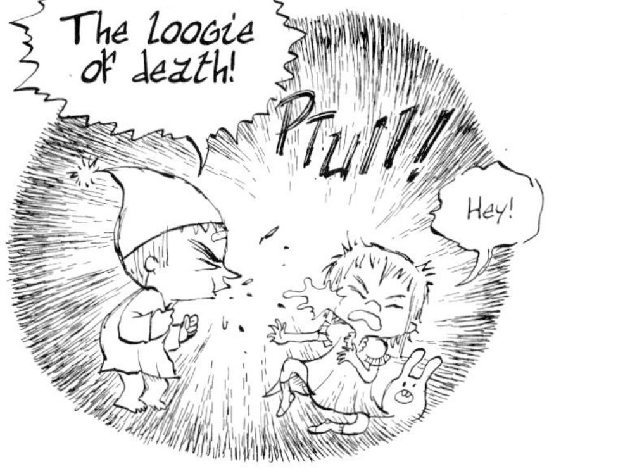
The loogie of death!
PTUI!!
Hey!

I was determined to develop a new escape plan, and go back to Lea's.

With her help, I'd free Tarzan from the clutches of darkness.

Then I'd capture death and put him out of commission...

...by locking him in a big, custom-made hermetically sealed jar.

I had to get out of here this very night.

I couldn't stand it here anymore.

This place was killing me.

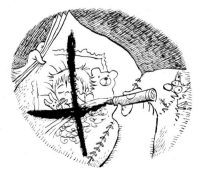

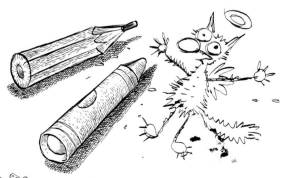

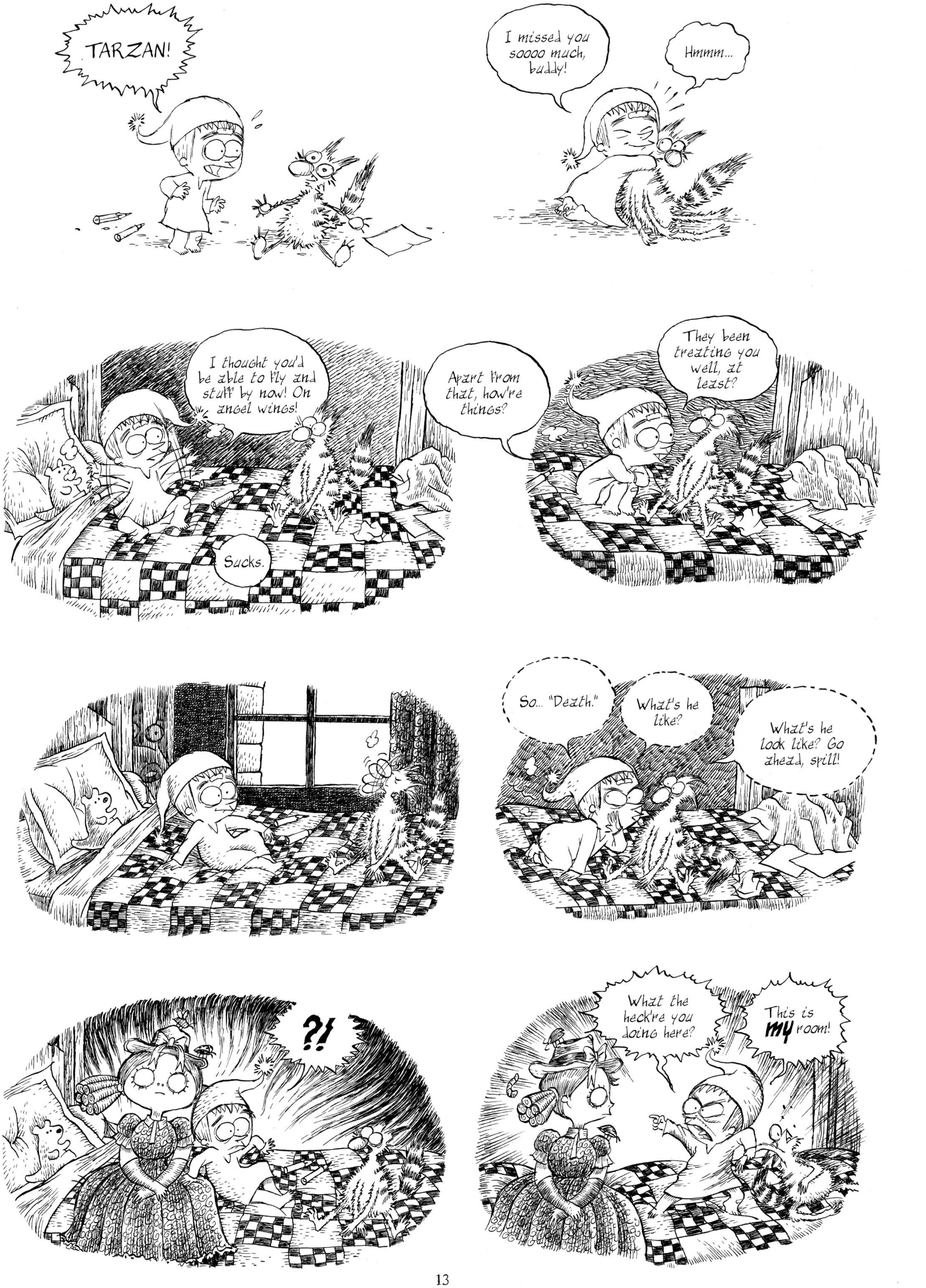
TARZAN!
I missed you soooo much, buddy!
Hmmm...
I thought you'd be able to fly and stuff by now! On angel wings!
Sucks.
Apart from that, how're things?
They been treating you well, at least?
So... "Death."
What's he like?
What's he look like? Go ahead, spill!
?!
What the heck're you doing here?
This is **my** room!

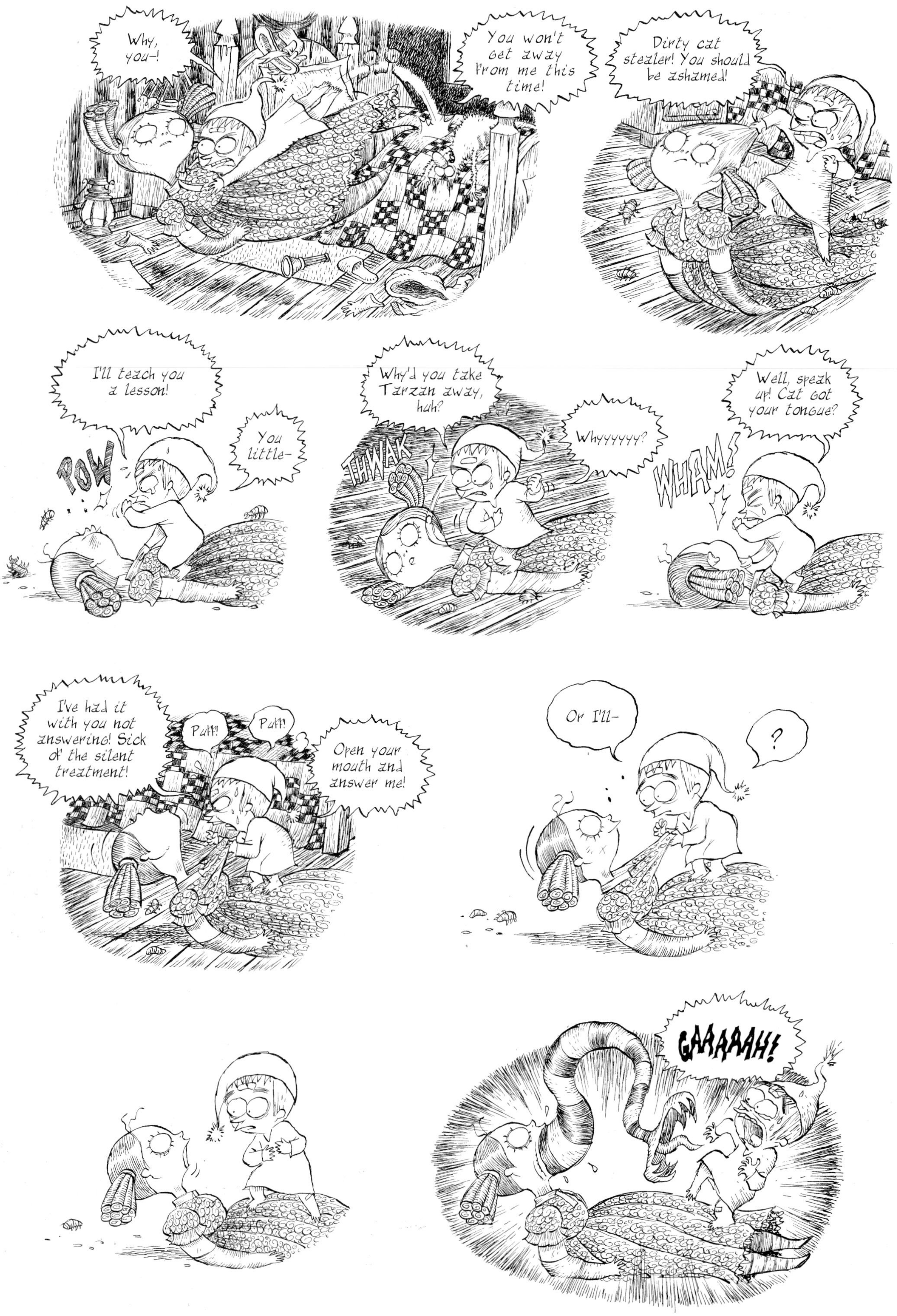
Why, you-!
You won't get away from me this time!
Dirty cat stealer! You should be ashamed!
I'll teach you a lesson!
POW
You little-
Why'd you take Tarzan away, huh?
THWAK
Whyyyyyy?
Well, speak up! Cat got your tongue?
WHAM!
I've had it with you not answering! Sick of the silent treatment!
Pull!
Pull!
Open your mouth and answer me!
Or I'll-
?
GARAAAH!

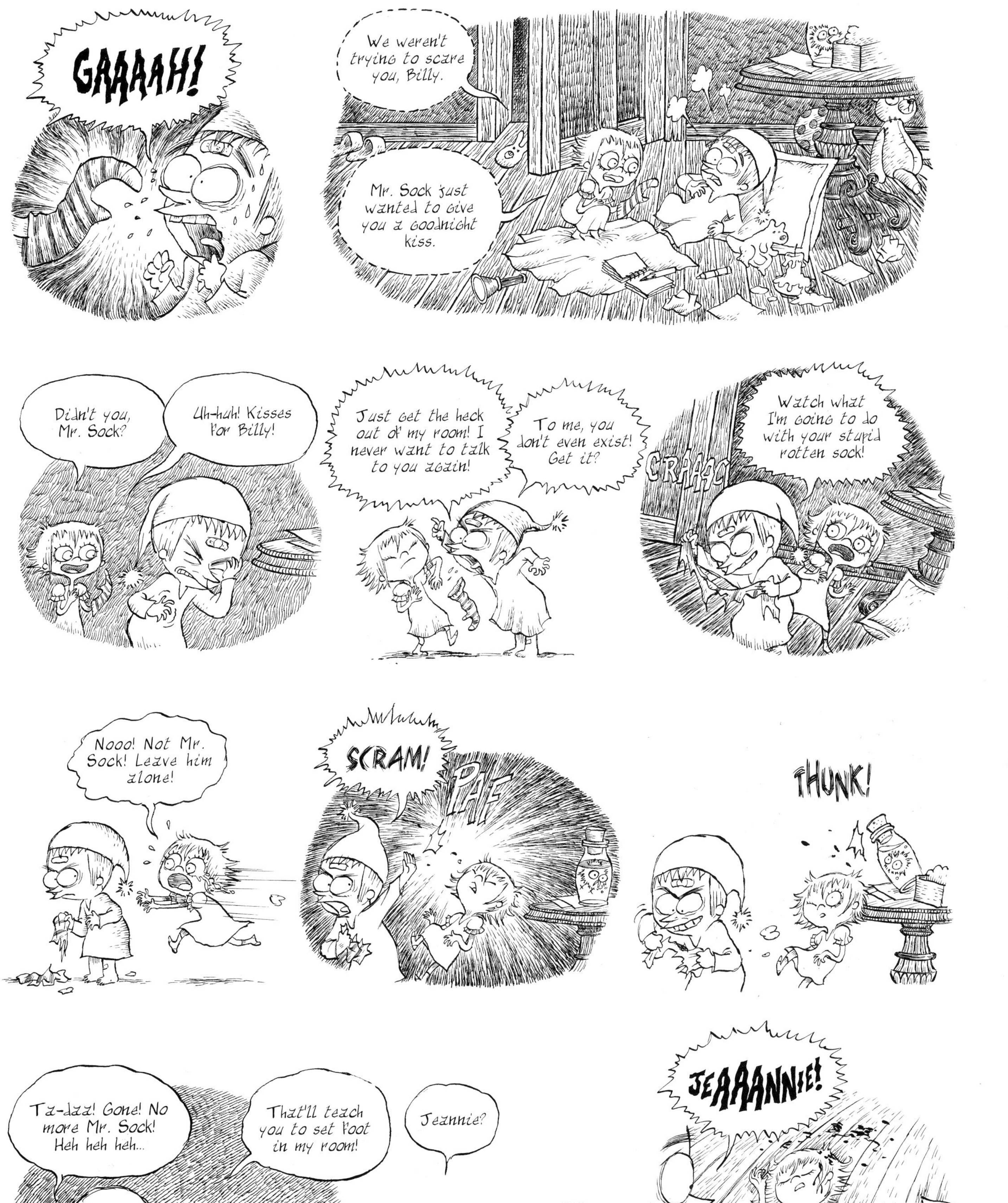

GRAAAH!
We weren't trying to scare you, Billy.
Mr. Sock just wanted to give you a goodnight kiss.
Didn't you, Mr. Sock?
Uh-huh! Kisses for Billy!
Just get the heck out of my room! I never want to talk to you again!
To me, you don't even exist! Get it?
CRAAAC
Watch what I'm going to do with your stupid rotten sock!
Nooo! Not Mr. Sock! Leave him alone!
SCRAM!
PAF
THUNK!
Ta-daa! Gone! No more Mr. Sock! Heh heh heh...
That'll teach you to set foot in my room!
Jeannie?
JEAAANNIE!

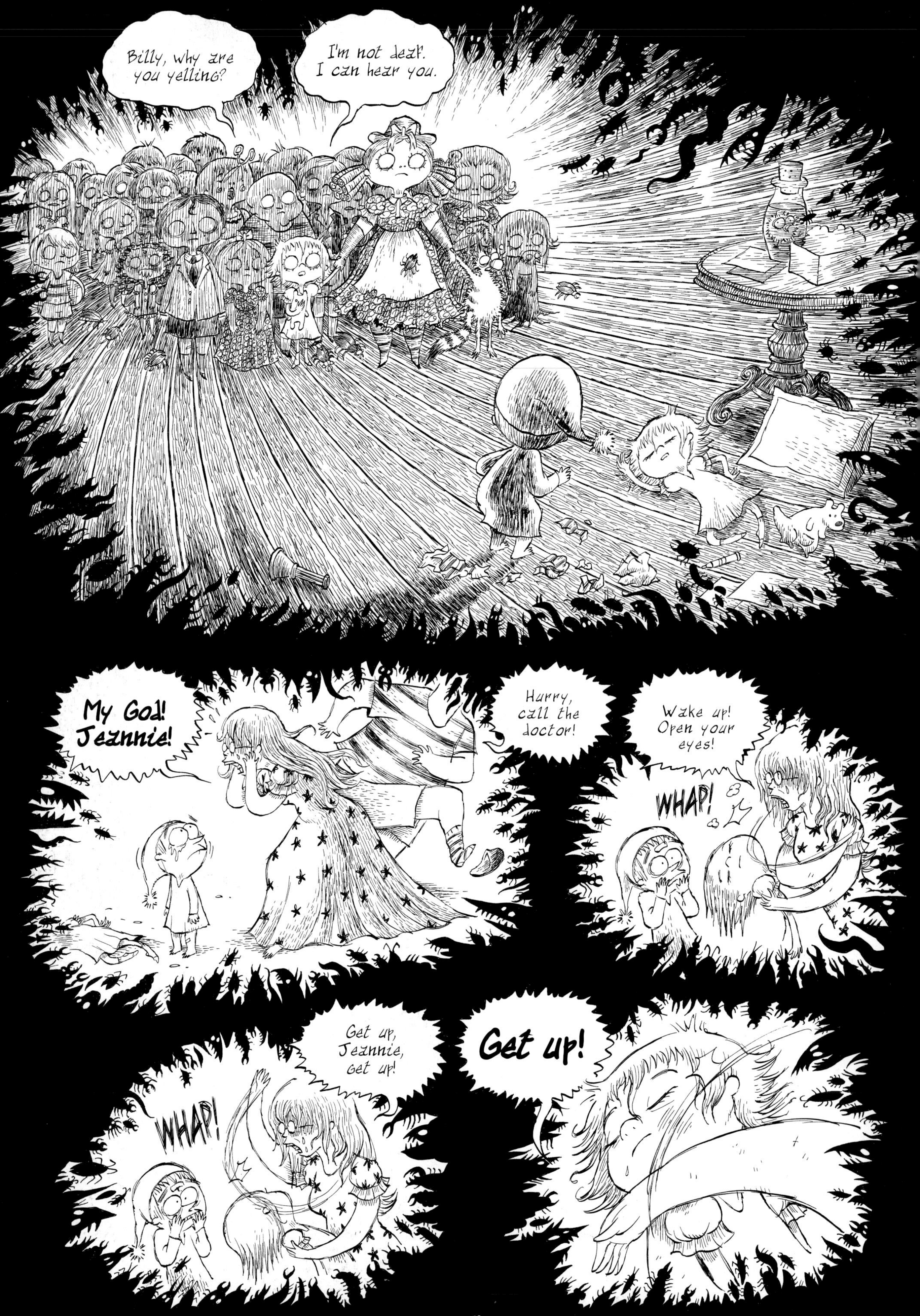
Billy, why are you yelling?
I'm not deaf! I can hear you.
My God! Jeannie!
Hurry, call the doctor!
Wake up! Open your eyes!
WHAP!
WHAP!
Get up, Jeannie, get up!
Get up!

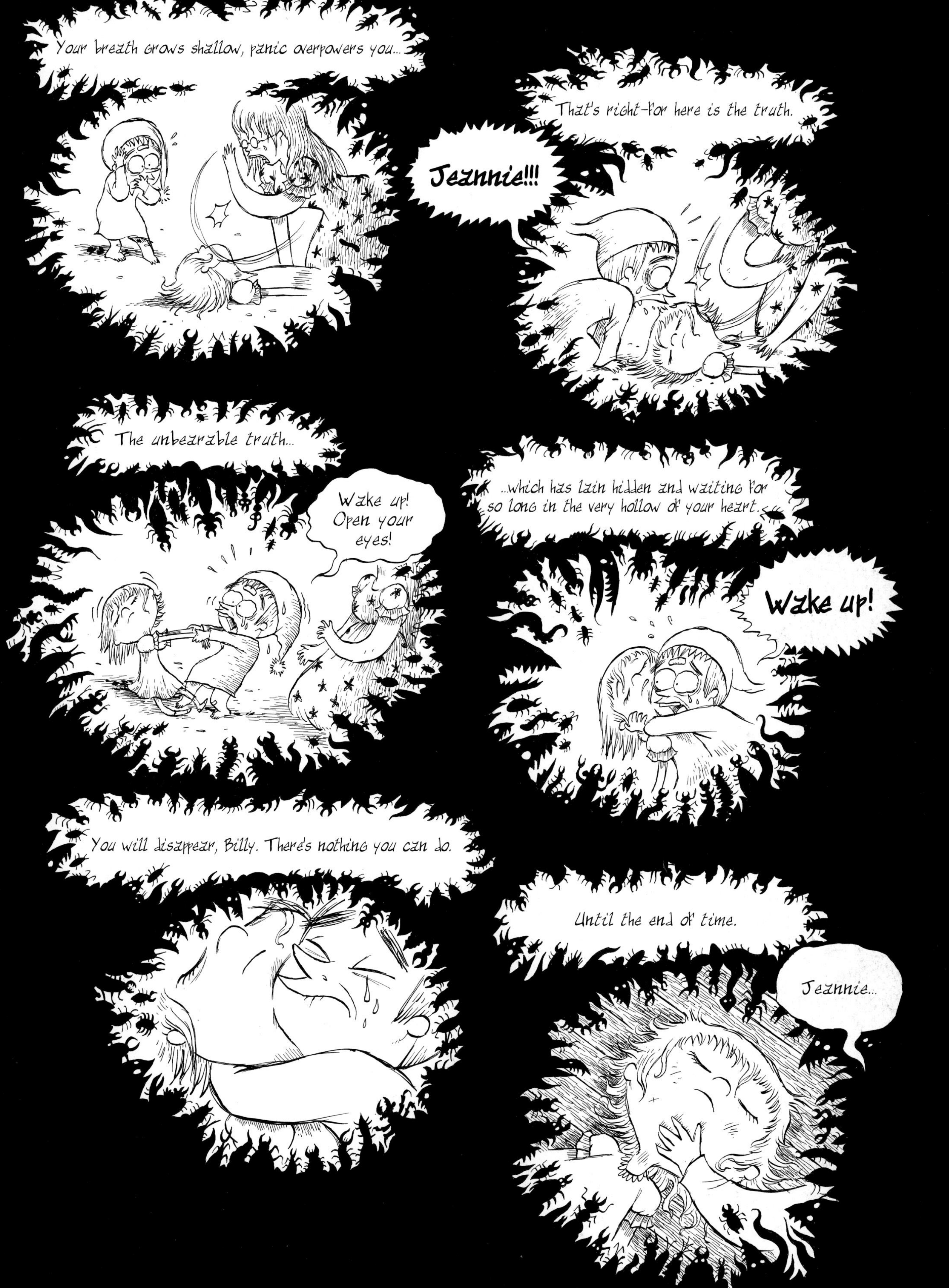
Your breath grows shallow, panic overpowers you...
That's right—for here is the truth.
Jeannie!!!
The unbearable truth...
Wake up! Open your eyes!
...which has lain hidden and waiting for so long in the very hollow of your heart.
Wake up!
You will disappear, Billy. There's nothing you can do.
Until the end of time.
Jeannie...

If it terrifies you when others disappear, Billy...

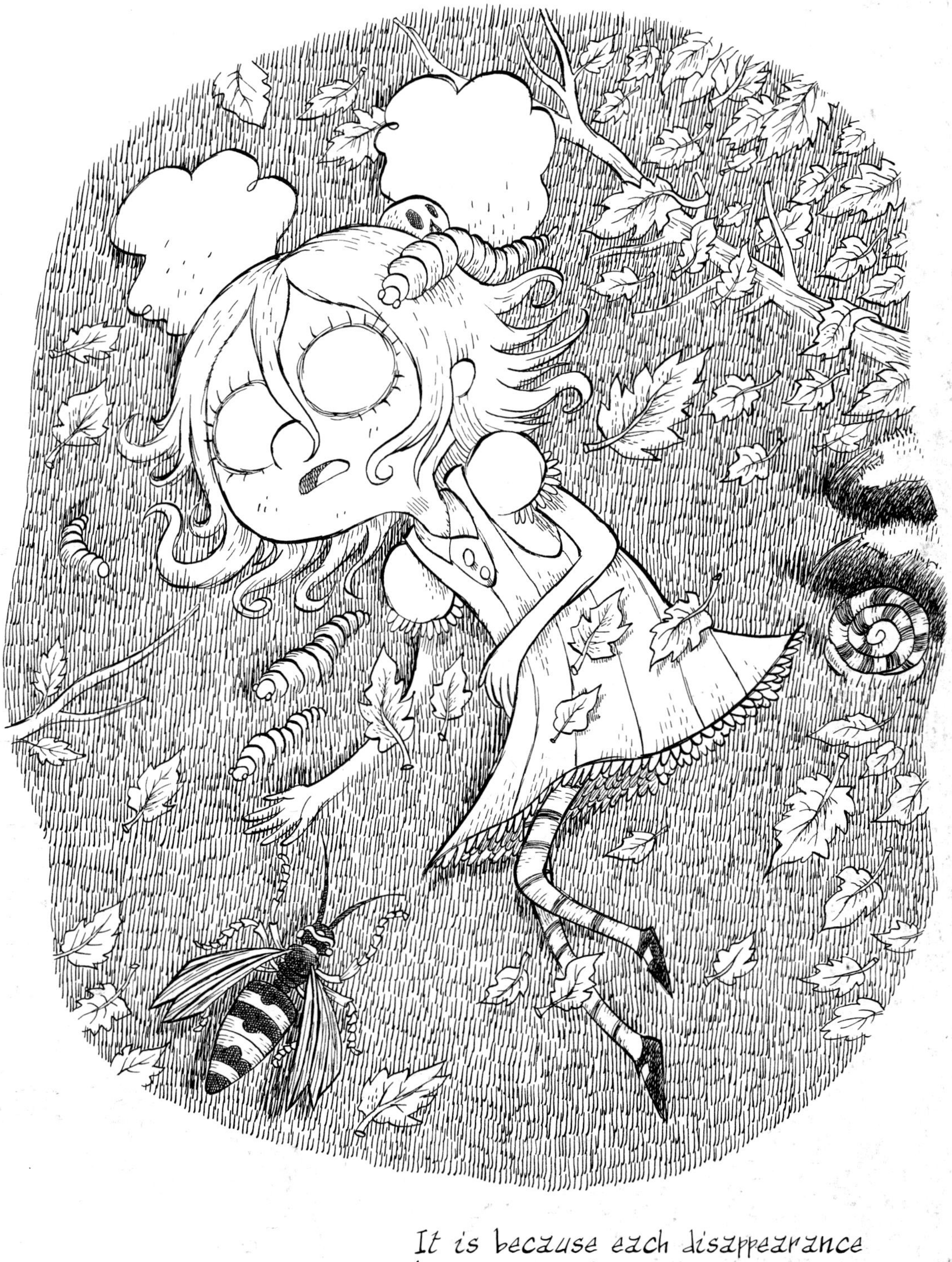

It is because each disappearance
brings you closer to your own.

The Little Girl Who Never Got Up Again

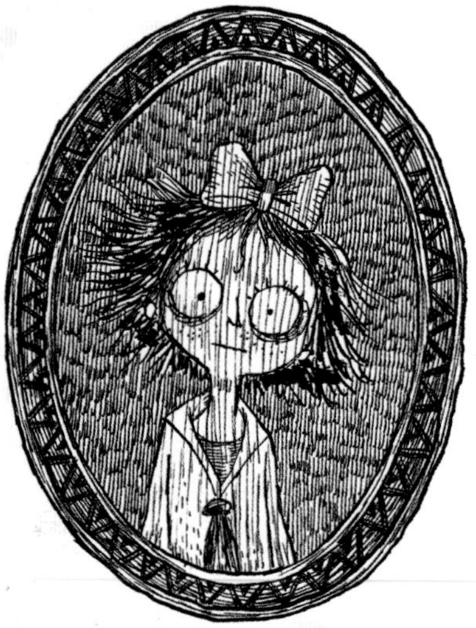

Katy opened her eyes from the deepest of slumber
To nosy, immodest sunbeams without number
Playing fleetly
In her little girl's room.

With her face in her pillow, she really felt merry,
Her gaze with whimsy and reverie was blurry,
Dreaming sweetly
In her little girl's room.

Why continue to rise? Life was only a chore.
In the Sandman's embrace she'd lie forevermore
Sleeping deeply
In her little girl's room.

Outside, how restless their contest for pleasure!
But the kingdom of dreams brimmed over with treasure
Gleaming discreetly
In her little girl's room.

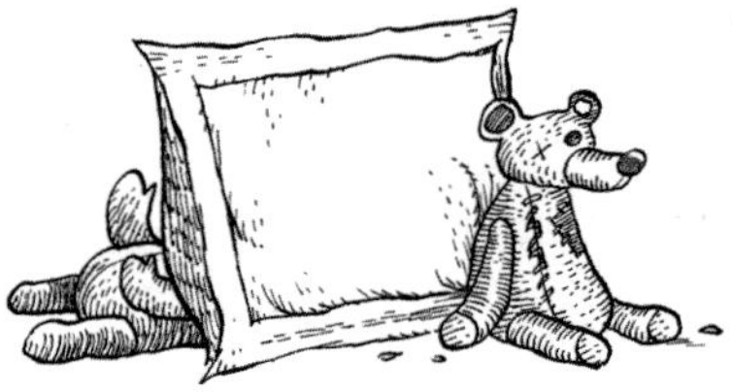

"I shall get up no longer. This sheet is my shroud.
Henceforth there will be no waking allowed."
Surrendering completely
In her little girl's room.

When they found her at last, the priest was depressed.
Her arms were already crossed over her chest.
Folded neatly
In her little girl's room.

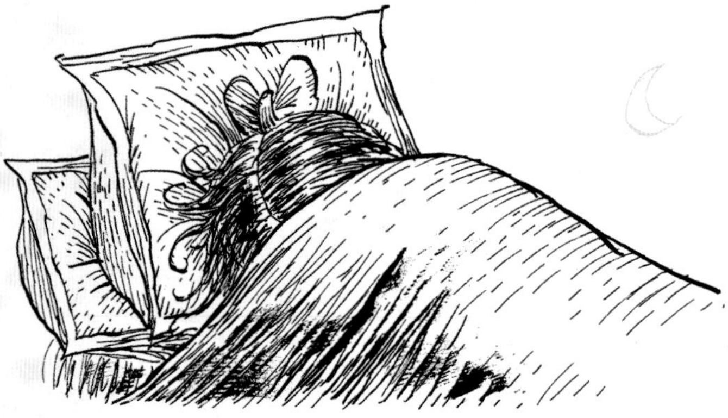

These many years later still can be heard
The slow peaceful breathing of a child, unstirred
Fled freely, dreamily
From her little girl's room.

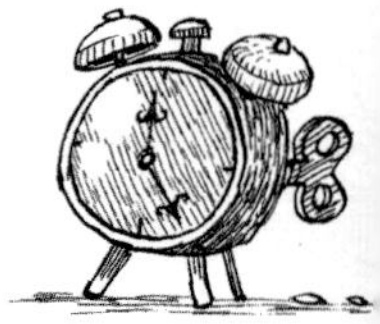

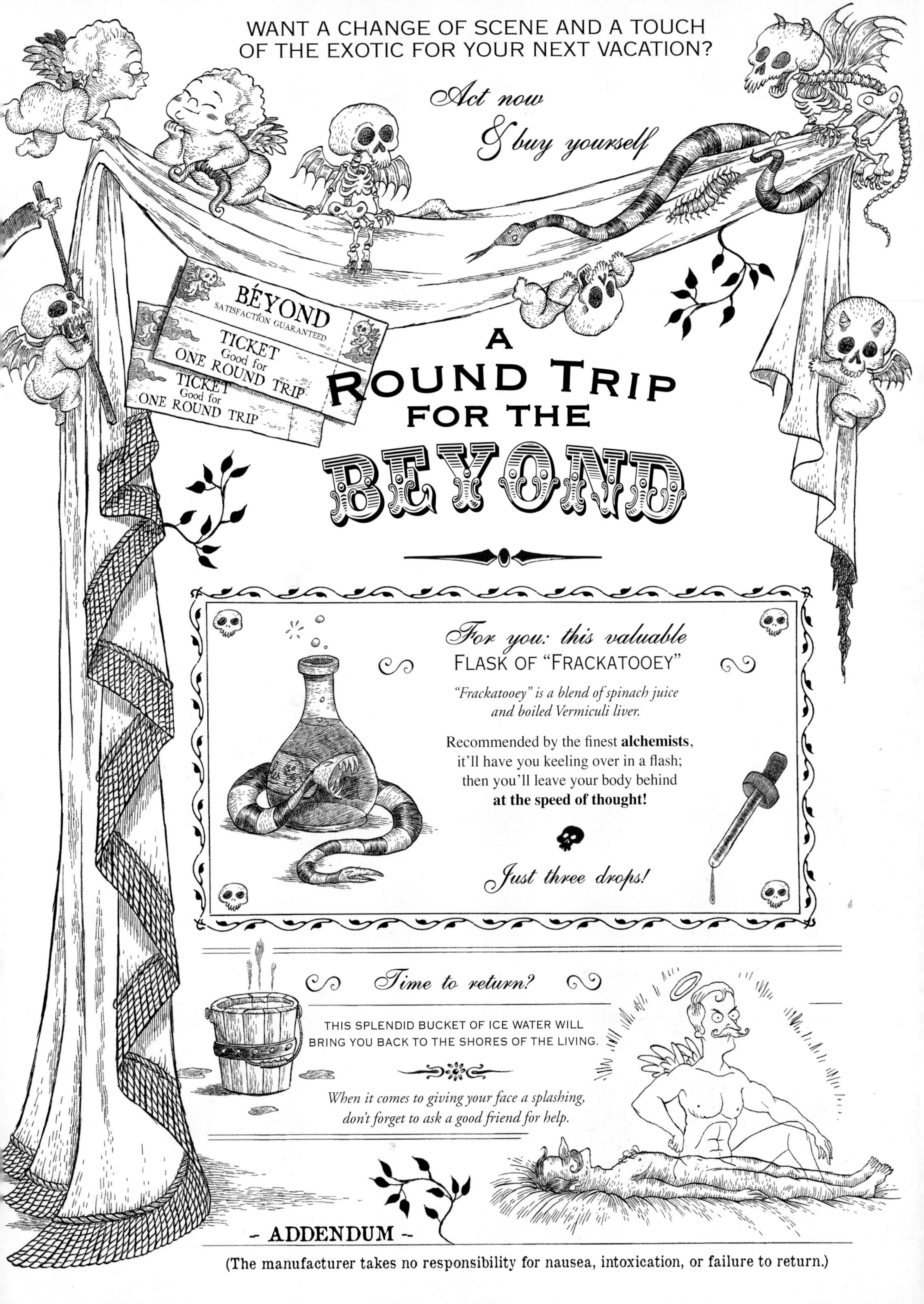
WANT A CHANGE OF SCENE AND A TOUCH OF THE EXOTIC FOR YOUR NEXT VACATION?
Act now & buy yourself
BÉYOND
SATISFACTION GUARANTEED
TICKET Good for ONE ROUND TRIP
TICKET Good for ONE ROUND TRIP
A ROUND TRIP FOR THE BEYOND
For you: this valuable
FLASK OF "FRACKATOOEY"
"Frackatooey" is a blend of spinach juice and boiled Vermiculi liver.
Recommended by the finest alchemists, it'll have you keeling over in a flash; then you'll leave your body behind at the speed of thought!
Just three drops!
Time to return?
THIS SPLENDID BUCKET OF ICE WATER WILL BRING YOU BACK TO THE SHORES OF THE LIVING.
When it comes to giving your face a splashing, don't forget to ask a good friend for help.
- ADDENDUM -
(The manufacturer takes no responsibility for nausea, intoxication, or failure to return.)

SPECIAL SECTION: PARAPSYCHOLOGY

"Life is slumber, death a waking-up, and between the two, man wanders like a ghost." - PROVERBIO ORIENTAL

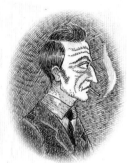

An exciting section written and researched by our mysterious Mr. **HARRY PRICE, the celebrated ghost hunter.**

WE all have material bodies; that much is undeniable. However, we also have **another** more subtle body, which is intangible:

THE ASTRAL BODY

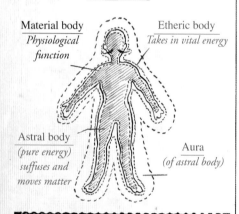

Material body
Physiological function
Etheric body
Takes in vital energy
Astral body
(pure energy) suffuses and moves matter
Aura
(of astral body)

ASTRAL PROJECTION can occur **consciously or unconsciously:** during sleep, while meditating, or as death draws near…

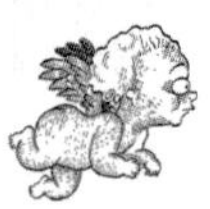

(We have all had the sensation, just before falling asleep, of missing a step and taken a sudden fall. This is, in fact, our astral body abruptly returning to us, as our conscious minds are not yet completely asleep.)

The etheric body vibrates at a much higher frequency, rendering it invisible to most people's eyes.

WHERE DOES THE ETHERIC BODY RESIDE?

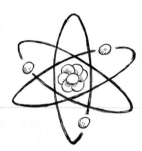

- ATOM -
(artist's rendering)

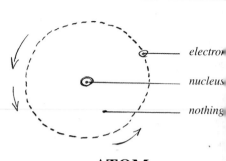

Scientists and spiritualists are divided. The ancients dubbed the etheric body "the soul" and situated it near the heart or brain. The Chinese claim this vital energy (chi) can be channeled to several points. In the abdomen, (three inches above the navel "Tan tien"); above the head, over the fontanelle (Sahasrara), and around the spinal column (Kundalini). The soul is hidden in the heart of matter…

electro
nucleus
nothing

- ATOM -
(cross-section)

Almost the entire mass of the atom is conce trated in its nucleus, orbited by one or m electrons. Its overall volume is comprised ***99% nothingness****. Which means that our m terial bodies are thus comprised of nothir ness. In this daytime, this nothingness is t seat of our astral bodies…*

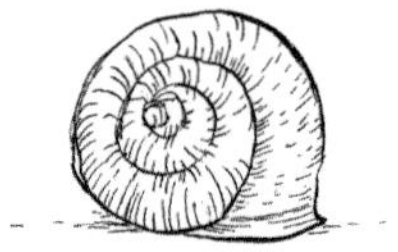

DO YOU JUST FEEL "OUT OF IT"?

Sometimes we feel woozy when we don't get enough sleep, or get woken up too early. It happens to all of us.

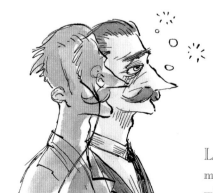

This feeling of being out of step, which may result in headaches or nausea, is due to the fact that your ASTRAL BODY is not entirely in sync with your material one.

Lie down and relax for fifteen minutes—no more—and everything will go back to normal.

ASTRAL TRAVEL

"The nature of all phenomena, of all appearance, is like the moon's reflection on the water." SIDDHARTA GAUTAMA

Nothing like a little night stroll on the astral plane to rest up, recharge your batteries, and get you raring to go!

*Once you are out, seeing your "inanimate" body may be an unpleasant experience. Fear will bring you back to your bed immediately, and **you'll have to start all over again.***

*With a bit of patience and practice, you won't ever pass up another chance at these nighttime flights over your neighborhood: **astral travel is healthy and invigorating.***

How to Proceed

There are a great many ways to go about it. Here is the simplest and most common:

a) - **Lie down alone** in a quiet, peaceful spot, eyes closed. Relax, breathing slowly and deeply.

b) - **Picture yourself**, focusing on every part of your body to relax every last muscle. Start with your feet, moving slowly up your legs, your back, your fingers, your hands—imagine all stress and tension evaporating from your body. Move up to the top of your neck. **You are completely relaxed and still.**
Your body is heavy, very heavy, a crushing weight you feel sinking deeper into your bed with every minute, every second.
An irrepressible desire to leave this cold, heavy armor slowly comes over you.

c) - **You are fully present.**
The hard part is not falling asleep, and remaining conscious in order to attain that state between sleep and waking: **the hypnagogic state**.)

d) - **You may hear** a kind of cracking sound, or a vibration, a muted but pleasant "vroom." **Don't be afraid:** *nothing will happen to you. Your astral body is merely detaching itself.*

e) - Still serene and cradled by deep breaths, picture a point six feet above your forehead, and imagine yourself floating above your head with your back against the ceiling, watching yourself sleep. You will notice a to-ing and fro-ing of your consciousness: now lying in your bed, now up on the ceiling watching you sleep.
*Keep this up for about fifteen minutes and you will find yourself actually projected up onto the ceiling, perhaps even **outside your house!***

THE SILVER CORD

THERE IS NO DANGER of floating off toward unknown skies, never to return, like an unmoored dirigible, during conscious projection.

The silver cord, a kind of astral umbilical cord, tethers securely your astral and material bodies via your navel. Just think about your body, and it will bring you safely back to shore at the speed of thought.

WARNING

Take care that astral projection becomes neither a caprice nor a flight from daily life. Disembodiment won't solve everything, and although very relaxing, will not settle our material problems.

NEXT WEEK: HARRY PRICE TELLS US ALL ABOUT INCREDIBLE CASES OF RESURRECTION!

Saturday, December 12th

Dear Billy,

I'm doing well, thanks. The trip around the world this year will be a tough one, but rest assured: my bushy beard protects me pretty well from the cold.

You asked me about death.
Answering a question like that isn't easy, my boy, not even for Santa Claus.

I am sorry about Tarzan, but sometimes things just happen, and we can't do anything about them. I know how terrible it is to lose a loved one forever; I know it's horrible to think that one day we too will disappear for who-knows-where. I won't tell you any made-up stories, because even if you are only 7, there's no point treating you like a fool.
From where I sit, Billy, atop my many years I've lived so long, known so many little children, had so many wonderful adventures that I've made up my own mind about life and death.

And so I'll let you make up your own, in your own way. Try to get an idea of what life is about, and you'll have an idea of what death is about too. One is a reflection of the other; they are twins, inseparable as a big brother and a little sister.

Life and death are each what you make of them. Watch out for fear! Don't listen to it. Get rid of it! It's the only thing that stands in your way. And don't forget to tell yourself there aren't really all that many reasons to worry, in the end.
As long as you keep thinking of him, Tarzan will be alive and well.
Take good care of your kid sister. She needs you more than you think.
Don't waste your time with being mean. Just watch the years go by in the blink of an eye Be good to your parents, and work hard at school.

I set aside a six-shooter for you, the one you like so much.

Santa Claus

Don't waste your time with being mean. Just watch—
the years go by in the blink of an eye...
Be good to your parents, and work hard at school."

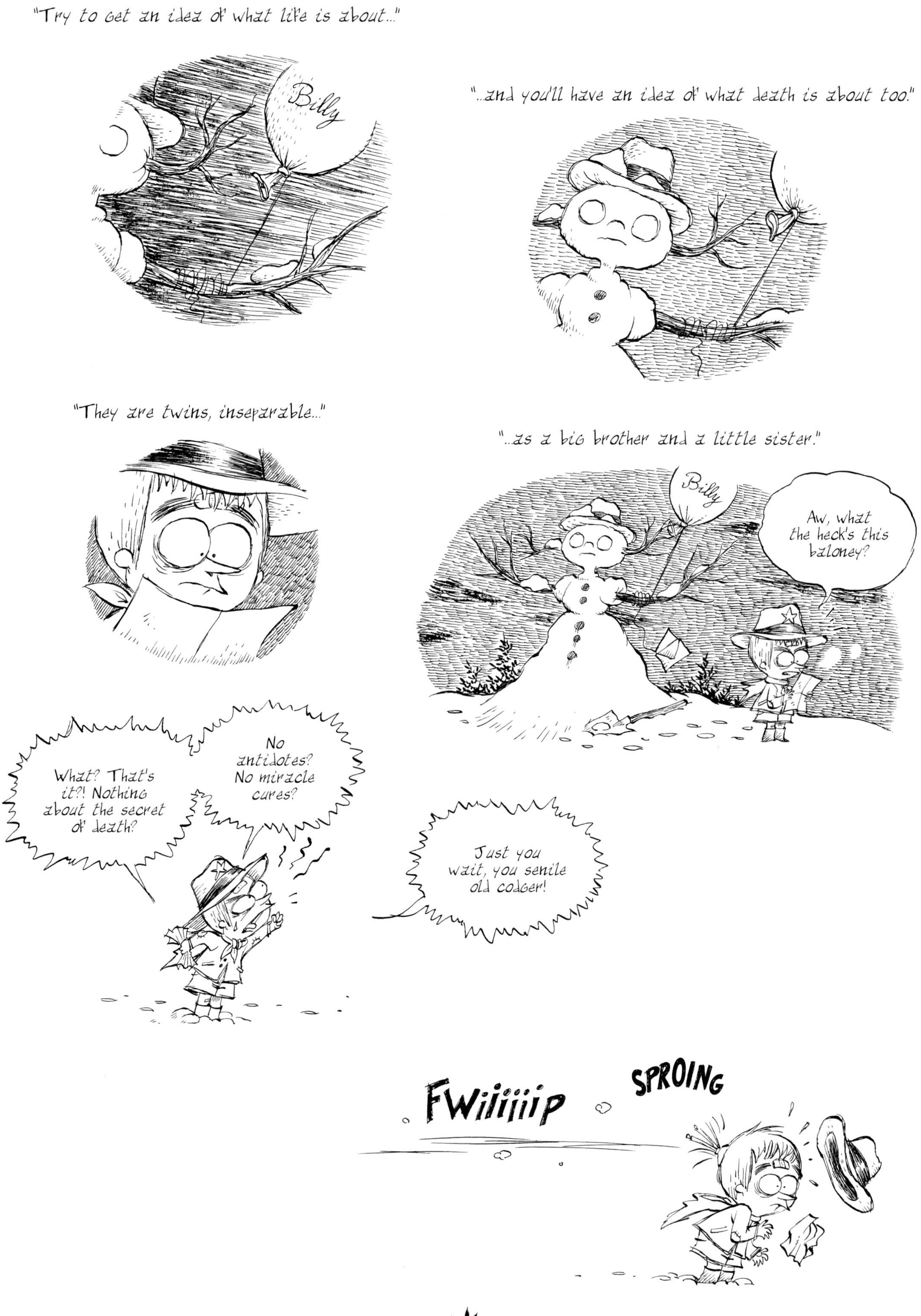
"Try to get an idea of what life is about..."
Billy
"...and you'll have an idea of what death is about too."
"They are twins, inseparable..."
"...as a big brother and a little sister."
Billy
Aw, what the heck's this baloney?
What? That's it?! Nothing about the secret of death?
No antidotes? No miracle cures?
Just you wait, you senile old codger!
FWiiiiiip
SPROING

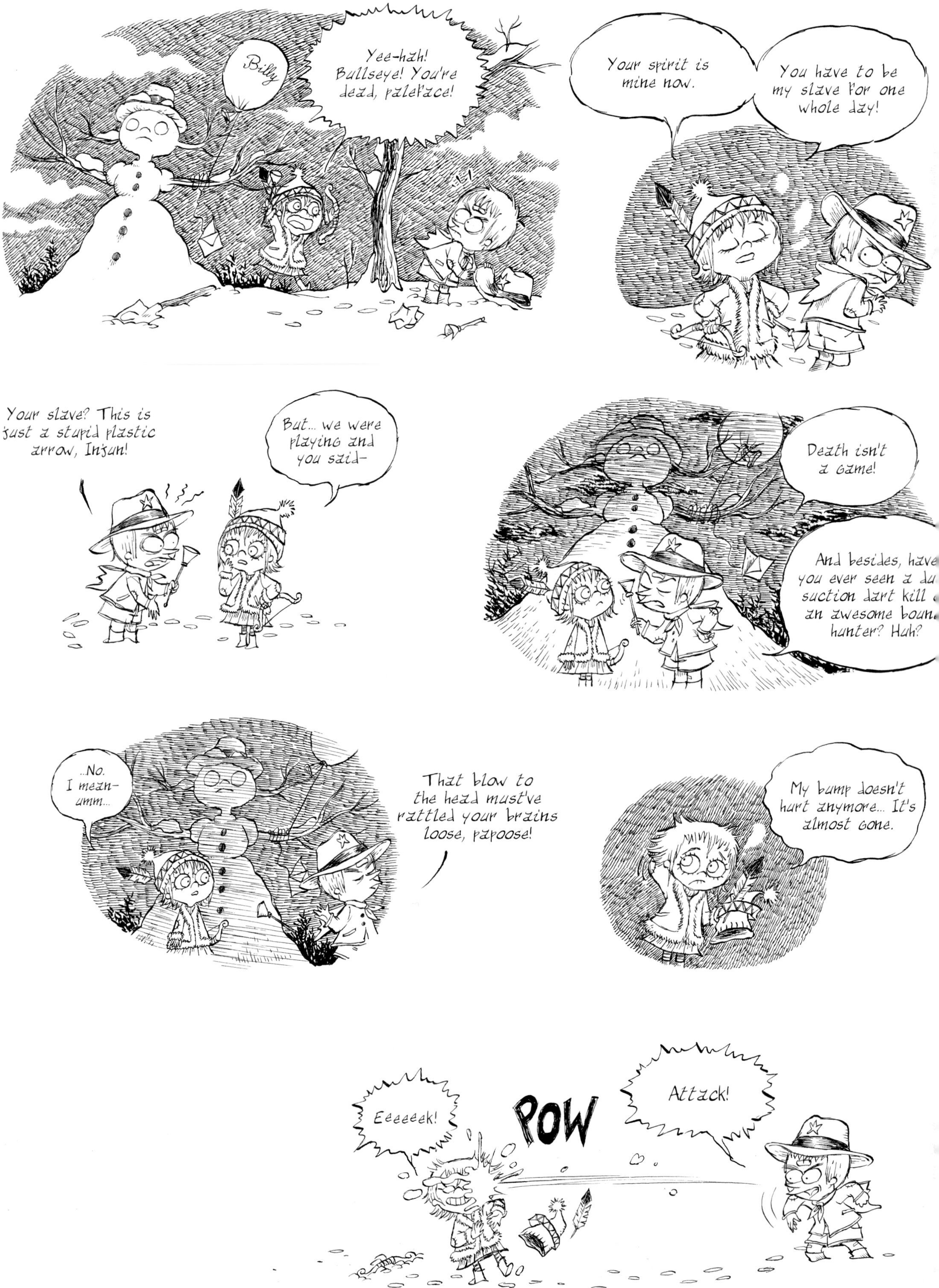
Billy
Yee-hah! Bullseye! You're dead, paleface!
Your spirit is mine now.
You have to be my slave for one whole day!
Your slave? This is just a stupid plastic arrow, Injun!
But... we were playing and you said-
Death isn't a game!
And besides, have you ever seen a du suction dart kill an awesome boun hunter? Huh?
...No. I mean-umm...
That blow to the head must've rattled your brains loose, papoose!
My bump doesn't hurt anymore... It's almost gone.
Eeeeeek!
POW
Attack!

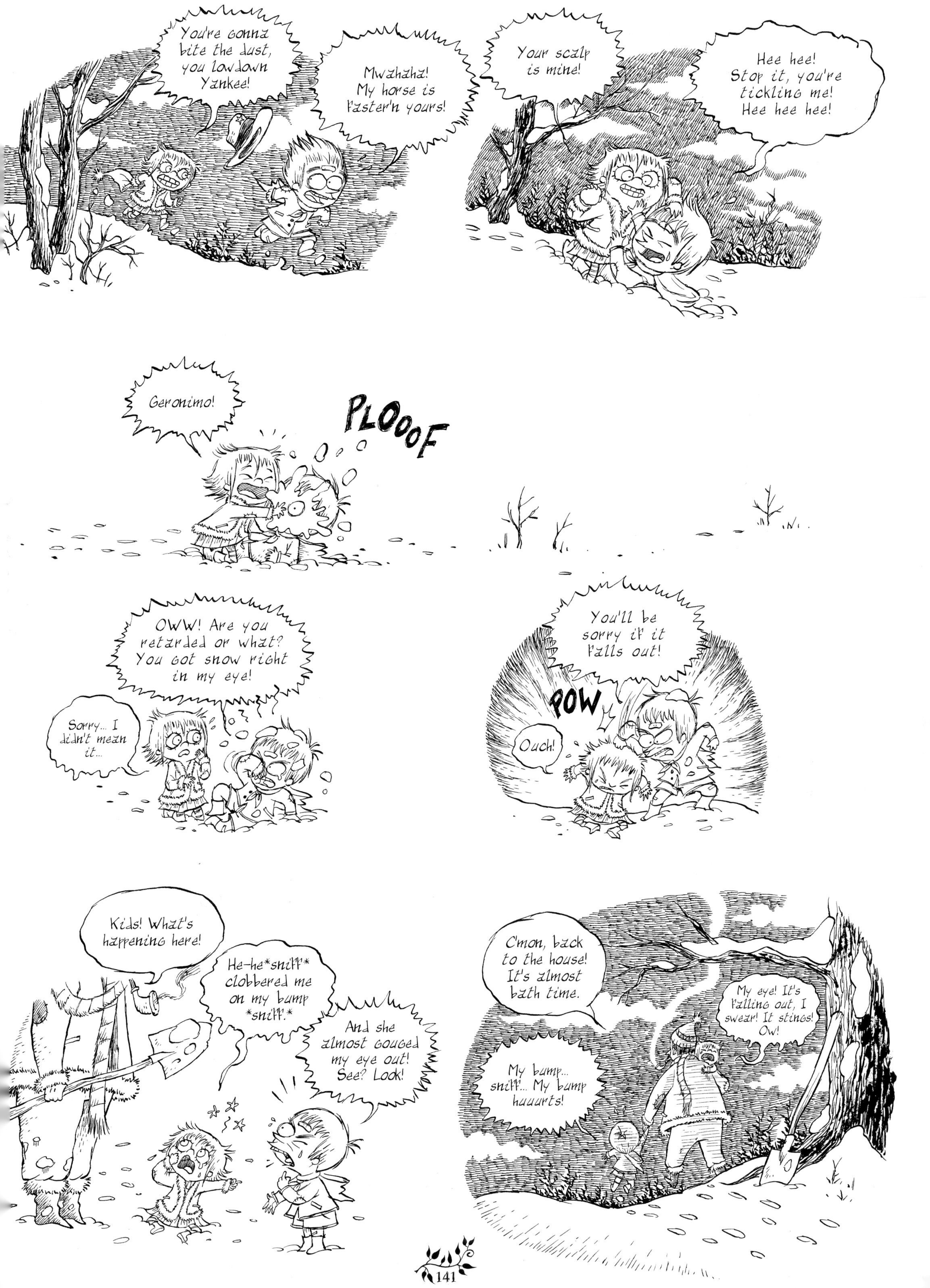

You're gonna bite the dust, you lowdown Yankee!
Mwahaha! My horse is faster'n yours!
Your scalp is mine!
Hee hee! Stop it, you're tickling me! Hee hee hee!
Geronimo!
PLOOOF
OWW! Are you retarded or what? You got snow right in my eye!
Sorry... I didn't mean it...
You'll be sorry if it falls out!
POW
Ouch!
Kids! What's happening here!
He-he*sniff* clobbered me on my bump *sniff*
And she almost gouged my eye out! See? Look!
C'mon, back to the house! It's almost bath time.
My eye! It's falling out, I swear! It stings! Ow!
My bump... sniff... My bump hauurts!

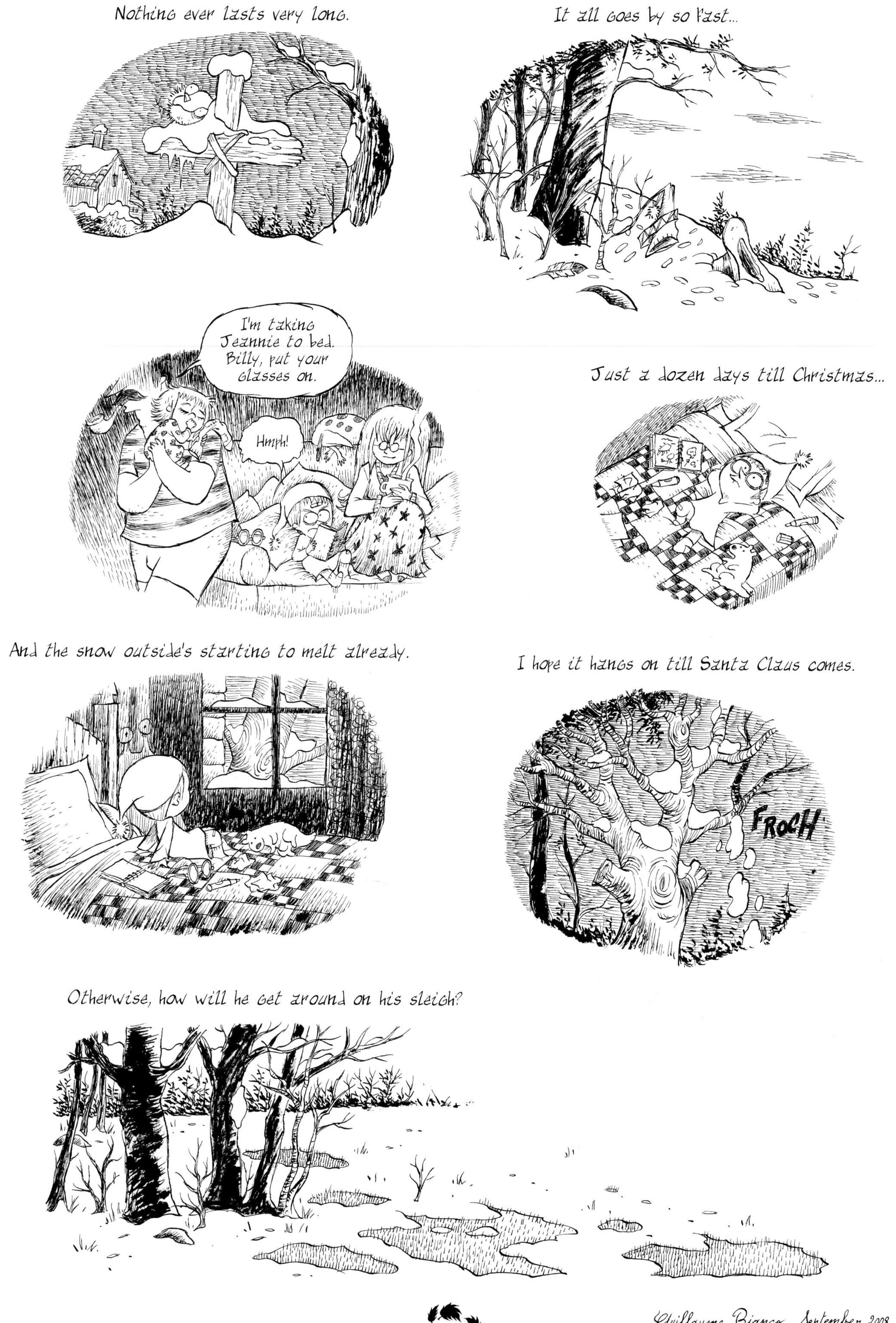
Nothing ever lasts very long.
It all goes by so fast...
I'm taking Jeannie to bed. Billy, put your glasses on.
Hmph!
Just a dozen days till Christmas...
And the snow outside's starting to melt already.
I hope it hangs on till Santa Claus comes.
FROCH
Otherwise, how will he get around on his sleigh?

Guillaume Bianco, September 2008

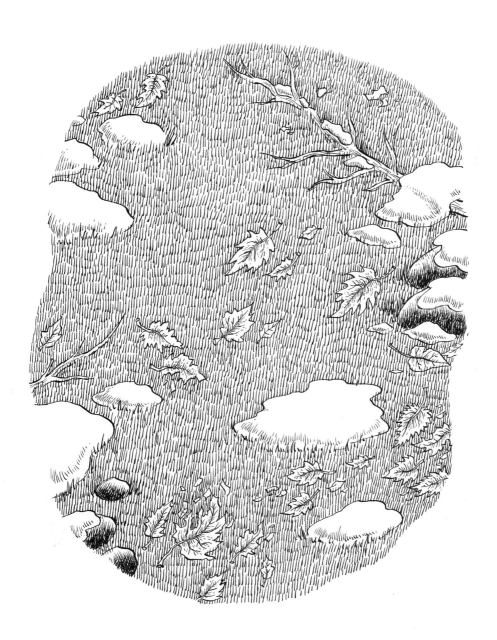

Thanks to Barbara, for waking up the little Billy slumbering in a corner of my mind…

Barbara Canepa and Clotilde Vu, *Directors,* COLLECTION MÉTAMORPHOSE
Paul Morrissey, *U.S. Editor*

Archaia Entertainment, LLC
PJ Bickett, *CEO*
Mark Smylie, *CCO*
Mike Kennedy, *Publisher*
Stephen Christy, *Editor-in-Chief*

Published by Archaia

Archaia Entertainment LLC
1680 Vine Street, Suite 1010
Los Angeles, California, 90028, USA
www.archaia.com

Originally published in France as part of COLLECTION MÉTAMORPHOSE (Editions Soleil).

BILLY FOG AND THE GIFT OF TROUBLE SIGHT.
November 2011. FIRST PRINTING

10 9 8 7 6 5 4 3 2 1
ISBN: 1-936393-39-5
ISBN-13: 978-1-936393-39-8